# JESSAMYN WEST

"She has a redeeming humor and a way with dialogue. Subjects seem to drift across the pages just as they happen to enter her pen—literary tonics."

*Christian Science Monitor*

"As diarists do, Miss West touches on many subjects. A disciple of Thoreau and true Quaker, she can appreciate the wonder and beauty of simple things, and express them in a style studded with sentences startling not only for their beauty, but for their illuminating insight."

*Library Journal*

# *To See the Dream*

"Anyone who has read *The Friendly Persuasion* will enjoy the account of the problems and excitement of its filming. Anyone who has seen the film will enjoy the backstage narrative of its creation. And anyone else will almost surely enjoy the play of thoughts and feelings in this vivacious book."

*Chicago Tribune*

"In TO SEE THE DREAM Jessamyn West proves again that in addition to her almost incredible technical proficiency, her writing is refreshingly and almost frighteningly perceptive. A remarkable segment from a remarkable life!"

*New York Times*

D0003944

## Avon Books by Jessamyn West

| | | |
|---|---|---|
| EXCEPT FOR ME AND THEE | 18671 | 1.25 |
| THE WITCH DIGGERS | 09530 | 1.25 |
| CRESS DELAHANTY | 06452 | .95 |
| A MATTER OF TIME | 06569 | .95 |
| LEAFY RIVERS | 08292 | .95 |
| SOUTH OF THE ANGELS | 10264 | 1.25 |

Where better paperbacks are sold, or directly from the publisher. Include 15¢ per copy for mailing; allow three weeks for delivery.

Avon Books, Mail Order Dept. 250 West 55th Street, New York, N. Y. 10019

# To See the Dream

# Jessamyn West

AVON
PUBLISHERS OF BARD, CAMELOT, DISCUS, EQUINOX AND FLARE BOOKS

AVON BOOKS
A division of
The Hearst Corporation
959 Eighth Avenue
New York, New York 10019

Copyright © 1956, 1957 by Jessamyn West.
Published by arrangement with
Harcourt Brace Jovanovich, Inc.

Library of Congress Catalog Card Number: 56-11961.

ISBN: 0-380-00008-3

All rights reserved, which includes the right
to reproduce this book or portions thereof in
any form whatsoever. For information address
Harcourt Brace Jovanovich, Inc., 757 Third Avenue,
New York, New York 10017.

First Avon Printing, May, 1974.

AVON TRADEMARK REG. U.S. PAT. OFF. AND
FOREIGN COUNTRIES, REGISTERED TRADEMARK—
MARCA REGISTRADA, HECHO EN CHICAGO, U.S.A.

Printed in the U.S.A.

*For Stu who got me into it and
Robert who helped me out of it*

# To See
## the Dream

# I

Sometimes I think I'm the luckiest woman in the world and tonight is one of those times. I like to write. I have pen, paper, and a room of my own in which to do my writing. Writing is so difficult that I often feel that writers, having had their hell on earth, will escape all punishment hereafter. At other times, tonight for instance, I fear there'll be no heaven for us. What joys can equal the writing of seven pages—which I did today—on "Terra Buena" or this room and the pen and ink with which to relive the day? People who keep journals have life twice. I know there is a feeling that journal-keepers are deficient in some way, poor sticks, bookkeepers of life rather than its spenders. I used to think that if it were known that I, like Pepys and Evelyn, like Emerson and Thoreau, was a journal-keeper it would increase my friends' regard for me. It doesn't. And I don't know that I would care for a live journal-keeper myself. I suppose journal keeping is a kind of talking to one's self—and that seems queer to everyone. But dead journal-keepers are my joy. If a writer of journals has life twice, the writer who reads journals has it three times. To my mind, no other kind of writing gives the reader so much the feel of what another person has experienced. Certainly not letters, where the writer, if he has any humanity or intelligence, changes color with his correspondents. But Mama hit the nail on the head when she asked me long ago when I was ill and she brought someone's journal home to me from the library, "What was wrong with him?" "What makes you think anything was wrong with him?" "I've noticed," she said, "that there is always something wrong with these people who keep notebooks and diaries." Katherine Mansfield, Gide, Gissing, Kafka, Dorothy Wordsworth, Virginia Woolf? Perhaps to want life twice, once experienced in action, once in words, is a sign in itself that something is wrong?

Somebody called from Hollywood today—I didn't get his name—about *The Friendly Persuasion*. I suppose I was careless about getting the name because there have been too many false alarms about that book and the movies. Frank Capra bought it ten years ago, a month or two after it came out, and since then I have read or been told by others that Bing Crosby or James Stewart or Spencer Tracy was going to be starred in it. At first I believed every one of these reports, accepted the congratulations of my friends, and waited impatiently for further news. There never was further news and I don't believe there ever will be. That book is not the kind that really interests Hollywood—interests it enough anyway to justify the work it would take to make a movie out of it.

Whoever I talked to was enthusiastic and loquacious. I stopped the telephone call out of regard for costs. If people are serious about making a movie, I don't want all the money spent on telephone calls before they get down to brass tacks. All this man wanted to know—in my mind's eye I see him as a cross between Charles Laughton and Groucho Marx; Laughton's bulk and Groucho's cigar —all he wanted to know was, would I be interested in talking about it? I said no. In the first place I don't want to take my mind off the new novel and its people, the Copes. In the second place I don't know anything about the movies. In the third place it's painful to go back to a piece of writing you've finished. The defects in it are now apparent; each sentence, almost, abrades your sensibilities.

The book which, while you worked on it, was alive becomes, when finished, dead. Or at least it has its life outside you. And rightly so. Mothers can't keep their babies forever in the womb. And a book, like a child, once the gestation period is over, cannot be reintroduced into the system. Not and stay alive. If you want a baby, have a new one. Don't baby the old one.

So I'm not going to talk to any Laughton-Marx about *Friendly Persuasion*—or even think about it. I will think about the new novel and the Copes instead. I have found that questions about your characters that you ask yourself before sleeping are often answered in the morning. I will ask myself some before I close my eyes.

Heavy rain tonight, the streams very loud and frogs croaking happily, like hoarse birds. I've been reading Simone Weil. She says that absolute attention is prayer, great attention is creativeness. Absolute attention, I suppose, makes you one with; and that was what Blake had in mind when he said the world could be seen in a grain of sand. I watch the raindrops on the windowpane—I don't doubt that worlds exist in each, but my attention isn't great enough to reveal them to me.

*The Friendly Persuasion* is both too complex and too simple for Hollywood. I don't know why they keep considering it for a movie. I certainly don't intend to.

*Thursday, Feb. 3*

Tonight my room is sweet with the combined scents of narcissus and kerosene—coal oil is what it was called when I was a child. I lit the two little glass lamps which belonged to Grandma and put them on the desk where I can see them from my bed. They are as pretty as flowers with their daffodil-colored flames, and the flames, veering in the draft, dance like Wordsworth's daffodils. But I lit them not to look at, but to smell. I wonder why the smell of a coal-oil lamp fills me with so much bliss? Is it because it makes me a child again and this California bedroom another Indiana sitting room? The smell of burning coal oil,

11

though less romantic than Proust's *madeleine*, slides me just as effectively into the past, puts the bright rag carpet on the floor, sets the logs to crackling in the fireplace, piles the snow against the windowpane, restores my parents to their bright and burnished twenties.

But I must blow out my little lamps and go to sleep. Tomorrow is a big day. Or what I, with my hermit blood, call a big day. Twelve of Max's colleagues, visiting school administrators in Napa for a conference, are coming out to the house for food and drink after their meeting. What to give them. Cheese fondue? I wish I could cure myself of the habit—or need—of making a crisis of each party by serving a dish I have never cooked before and really don't know how to cook. Why, I wonder, must I do this? Perhaps giving a party is like writing a story. Failure is better than repetition. But not for the visiting school men. Do they really want to be dipping pieces of bread into a pot of probably curdled cheese sauce? Poor school men. That is what I fear awaits them.

The Hollywood man called again. His name is Miller. He is now in San Francisco. He is a graduate of Stanford, a former writing student there under Wallace Stegner. This rather spoils my picture of him as a cross between C. Laughton and G. Marx. He is on his way to Palo Alto to visit old friends and wanted to know if he could stop in tomorrow to chat. He has read *The Friendly Persuasion* himself. I know how unusual this is thought to be in Hollywood. When I was there for thirty minutes, at the time Capra bought *The Friendly Persuasion,* someone in his office, bubbling with the wonder of it all, said to me, "You know Mr. Capra has *read* your book." "How," I asked, "could he buy it without reading it?" The secretary smiled at my ignorance. "A director," she said, "hasn't time to read books. He reads treatments. Or résumés of treatments. A good résumé can boil a book down to a single line." She made movie making sound like the housewife's rehabilitation of the dried apple which she by adding water makes juicy and palatable again. A director is handed a dehydrated novel which he, by an infusion of something or other, gives the shape and feel once more of approximately the real thing.

So, impressed by Mr. Miller's thoroughness as a reader, I asked him who he was.

"I am," he said with a pride that sixty miles of telephone wire did not disguise, "Mr. Wyler's assistant."

There was a silence in which Mr. Miller thought he had been disconnected. "Are you still there?" he asked.

I was still there. And still ignorant. "Who," I asked, "is Mr. Wyler?"

Now there was silence at the San Francisco end of the line. "I know," I explained, "I take it for granted that he is someone connected with the movies. In some way."

I could hear Mr. Miller swallowing in San Francisco. "Yes," he said. "Mr. Wyler is connected with the movies." He went on more slowly. "Did you ever see *Mrs. Miniver? The Best Years of Our Lives? Wuthering Heights? The Little Foxes? Roman Holiday.*"

I had seen them all.

"Mr. Wyler made them."

I have always despised people who read and enjoy but have no idea who wrote what they read. For instance, the person who says, "That wonderful story about the old man who catches a big fish, then loses it to the sharks."

"You mean Hemingway's *The Old Man and the Sea?*"

"I don't know who wrote it. What difference does it make who wrote it?"

I feel like saying to him, "What difference does it make that you know birds from bees, or flowers from persons, or land from water?"

How can you escape knowing who wrote what? You look the first time and after that, if the author is any good, his signature is in every line. Are there people who read the movies as I read books?

"I thought they were good pictures," I told Mr. Miller.

Mr. Miller, I knew, in the way one is able to pick up unspoken information from the telephone wire, considered this information coals carried very tardily to Newcastle. But he answered quietly, "They were very good pictures."

"And now," I asked, "Mr. Wyler is thinking of making a movie of *The Friendly Persuasion?*"

"Willy is *going* to make a movie of *The Friendly Persuasion.*"

I thought it unlikely. Mr. Miller may know Willy but I

know *The Friendly Persuasion* and its ten-year history of false starts in Hollywood. But there was no sense arguing the matter by long-distance. I said it would be very nice if Mr. Wyler did make a picture based on *The Friendly Persuasion*. Mr. Miller agreed and concluded, "It will be all right then if I stop by tomorrow to talk with you?" I said yes, but after four. I'm determined not to let anything get in the way of the novel-writing schedule.

Now I must really blow out the lamps. But I like having them here while I write the words Indiana, Maple Grove, back East, movie. Grandma is not Eliza in *The Friendly Persuasion*. She died when I was nine years old and I don't remember her well, but she was a doer, a person to tackle new things, and she would be energetically delighted with the prospect of a film. I can see how she would look—round, brisk, black hair sleekly coiled, stepping into my room, smiling at my news. I wonder what words she would use? She was Irish and Hoosier before she was Quaker, and she had picturesque ways of saying things: When she was warm she was "hot as a little red wagon"; when she cleaned, she "cleaned like fighting a fire." Disorder "made hell look like a lightning bug." When she died it was, to use her own words, "like the stopping of running water."

*Friday*

I shouldn't write one word here this morning. Journalizing, like reading, should be the sweet which comes after the meat and potatoes, not before. But this morning I'm having the sweet first. This is the most beautiful, beautiful morning of wind. Of all the phenomena of weather, wind is to me—I started to say "the most moving" but there is a pun in that and I'm too serious about the wind to permit any levity in speaking of it. I have no idea why this should be so; why, if I hear a strong wind coming up, my heart swells with a prophet's pleasure on hearing God's voice speak out of the whirlwind. In fact, I am such a wind lover, the voice of the whirlwind itself is enough to transport me. (Pun, again, alas!) When I was a child, I often went out to our barn for the pleasure of hearing the wind blow through its cracks. I would sit there on a sack of rolled barley and listen to that ancient, everlasting, and universal voice. Someone commenting upon the inordinate joy Thoreau took in the sound of the wind blowing through telegraph wires put it down to his lack of opportunity to hear music. Poor Thoreau, the gist of this comment was, having to substitute the sound of wind whistling through telegraph wires for Mozart and Beethoven. That writer may have understood music, but he didn't know a thing about the wind—or Thoreau. The wind is no substitute for music, any more than the sea is a substitute for Debussy's *La Mer*.

If I had not lived as a child in a place where the wind blew perhaps I would not have learned to love it so. Or to love it so much, anyway. For I am afraid that one of our limitations as human beings is our inability as we grow up to increase our lovingness by increasing the number of things to which we respond. So I may be a wind-lover by the chance of living in Yorba Linda as a child, where every afternoon one could hear and feel the wind that came inland off the sea, and experience on less frequent and more exciting occasions the glory of being buffeted by the great dusty Santa Ana which roared in off the desert through the San Gorogino Pass, scaring orange groves and filling the airy bungalows with layers of sand. I have always loved the names of the great winds of the world and have collected and cherished them as other women collect cups or lusterware. Monsoon, williwaw, mistral, simoom, chinook . . . Recently, reading Guy Murchie's *The Song of the Sky*, I had the most—maternal, I think, is the word—pleasure in finding the Santa Ana, the much loved wind of my girlhood, listed among the great winds of the world. I smiled with all the fondness of a mother who sees by the papers that her daughter has been elected home-coming queen. Local wind makes good! My Santa Ana listed and defined. For the Santa Ana, I discovered, is a "down wind," very treacherous, a wind that has caused more air accidents than any other. I never knew in my girlhood that the Santa Ana was a "down wind," a wind falling off mountain heights into valleys; but I did know, when the

15

green-gray dust cloud, which presaged its coming, rose like a pillar sixty miles away, anticipations of great joy. Ranchers and housewives hated the Santa Ana. But its coming was a lark for children—or it made children larks. We fashioned sails, kitelike of paper, or shiplike of cloth, and abandoned ourselves to its power; and if we were not lofted like birds we were at least winged and wind-propelled.

This Napa wind is nothing like as strong or exciting as a Santa Ana. In the first place it has a dull name. It is called a "north wind," a sure sign that no one has loved it or feared it. Perhaps, if I live here long enough and love this wind enough, I can get it renamed. It comes after rain: the air clears and in February seems to take into solution some of the greenness of the grassy earth. In the night after such a clearing I dream of the ocean. I hear the beat of heavy surf along a shallow beach; I hear crested waves draining back without violence to deep water. But sometime in the night I waken and recognize the surf sound for what it is and smile and think, Wind Tomorrow! For the first audible sign of the coming wind is this ocean imitation in a long double row of ancient eucalyptus trees a quarter of a mile from here.

The single most beautiful tree I have ever seen in my life is a eucalyptus on the road between here and St. Helena. Most beautiful because in addition to the grandeur of its size and the perfection of its shape (a real tree-shaped tree if ever I saw one) it is subtly colored, in shades that range from the bone white of its massive trunk through all possible variations of greens and grays and blues. And here and there is a flame-colored leaf burning like a candle in the depths of the green-gray Gothic nave. I haven't much Druid blood in my veins, but if I were to worship trees I know the one I'd kneel to.

Poems, in spite of the fact that only God can make a tree, have given me more pleasure than trees. I think, though I pray I may never have to make the decision, that if I were required to choose whether the trees of the world or the poetry of the world should disappear, I would say, "Good-by trees." A poet, after all, can bring

16

trees into being in his poems. But no tree has ever written a poem.

I might love trees more if we didn't have so many about our house—big-limbed, thick-leaved valley oaks which dispute the sun and the stars with me. Unlike Eastern people who, I understand, greet the first swelling buds of spring with pleasure, I sometimes shake my fist at the big oaks when I see them preparing to open once again their dense green umbrellas. I think sun is better than shade, stars better than leaves, and blue skies better than green canopies. Try to tell an oak that, though! It will laugh a green leaf right in your face.

Indidivual trees, however, I do revere. I know an acacia which carries more that is glittering than the Mother Lode —and does it in a better place. Slanting over a stream so all of its mirrored gold is multiplied by two—and even when it parts with its load of blossoms, it gilds the stream beneath once again. Eucalyptus—acacia. These are not natives of California but came to us from Australia and New Zealand—and I never see nor smell acacia without remembering what the tree is called there—mimosa—and that mimosa was Katherine Mansfield's favorite scent. It is easy to understand why. Katherine Mansfield, ill for so long, hated the cold and suffered from it—and loved the sun and warmth; and if there is any scent under heaven which is heavy with warmth and colored by sunshine it is the mimosa. It is best to smell it *in* sunshine, as all good things are even better when the circumstances are toward. But I don't know any other scent, unless it is that of red roses, that will so lighten gray skies and warm icy airs.

There is a madroña which I can see at this minute standing on the bank of one of the two streams that circle the hill on which this house is built. It, like the eucalyptus, sheds its old bark each year to reveal trunk and limbs as satiny-smooth and cinnamon-shining as those of the Indians who gave Napa its name. In fact its contours and colors are so human that, in long days of rain, I am concerned for its drenching and wish I could ask it in to dry. This is the truth, and it proves, I hope, that I am no undiscriminating tree hater. I only hate *some* trees, as even dog lovers admit to feeling some dogs pestiferous. If I traveled around the country as Oliver Wendell Holmes, Senior, did, in a horse-pulled gig, I would be a tree lover of his kind. He loved individual trees and knew the vital statistics of the notable ones in his neighborhood in the same way today's connoisseurs know the vital statistics of movie stars—and he learned those statistics in the same way: through measurement.

So, a tree is to measure, as a hole is to dig. And it is also, like the cracks in the barn, to make a wind sound like God's trumpet—or his oboe or his flute. Or all of them together in a full-dress orchestration. John Muir could tell by sound alone through what kind of tree a wind was blowing. I can't do that, but I think I could never mistake, in whatever part of the world I should hear it, the sound of the wind in a tall eucalyptus.

These enormous oaks, which appear in calm weather rigid and unmovable as rocks, are switching about now like buggy whips. I don't know what sounds they make. Occasionally there is a lull in the eucalyptus roar and then I think I hear the unmusical horse-fiddle scrapings of the oaks. But if no treat for the ears, the oaks are now a sight for the eyes. Dr. Johnson did not appreciate an act simply because it was rare or difficult—women preaching, dogs walking on their hind legs. But part of my pleasure in the present sinuosity of these oaks is accounted for by the difficulty. How do they do it? How *can* they do it? Pepys—and my mother—were of a different breed from Johnson. Pepys said he was always like a child with curiosity to see any new thing. And Mama too. I am halfway between Dr. Johnson on one hand and Mama and Pepys on the other. I will not go very *far* to see a new thing, but if it appears outside my windows I won't scorn it because it's unusual. And I will admit that the sight of oak limbs flexible as kittens' tails is more interesting to me than willows similarly supple. And if a willow wants my attention, let it become sturdy. Thus do we conspire to see nothing truly, but only objects out of character.

This is the time of the year when I hate the oaks least. Now, except for a few live oaks, they are leafless. At evening they crosshatch, but do not shut out the sunset. Its light blazes through the interstices green and gold and apricot. In the morning through these openings I watch the spur of a faraway hill change from blue to purple to rose. It is my alarm clock by color. Rose means: get up. Perhaps, like the rest of the contrary world, I would not value these revelations if I had them scot-free, season in and season out with no need to outwit leaves to win them. No pleasure without defiance. I hope this is not true of me; the fact that I hope probably proves it is.

I admire people who live in the hour, especially housewives who don't rehearse all day long the dinner parties they are to give in the evening. My trouble rises out of an attempt to have my cake and eat it too: give the dinner party, but don't waste—that's what I call it—the whole day on it. I can keep myself here in my room, away from the hurly-burly of cheese grating and silver polishing but I cannot keep my mind off the things to be done—nor off wondering whether or not Mrs. Curry has done them. I decided that with the educators *and* Mr. Miller, I had better have someone besides Fred to help me. Any eighteen-year-old schoolboy is naturally of the wrong age and sex to be the perfect right hand to the hostess. Fred has for me the further disadvantage that his ambitions are exactly the same as mine: to remain sufficiently fresh and untired when guests arrive to be, if not the life of the party, at least a lively part of it. And since he cares less than I do about the silver and the cheese he is more likely to achieve his ambition. So I asked Mrs. Curry to come in this afternoon to help. She is the best cook and one of the handsomest women I ever saw. She is (I understand that Negroes prefer to be called "colored") colored. This is a strange preference to my mind. By the same nomenclature we are either colorless or uncolored. It would be a less trivial and more significant way of designating peoples if some more pertinent label than that of color could be hit upon. "Colored" means "black," I suppose, and Mrs. Curry isn't that either. She's a peanut-butter shade and just as smooth and glossy.

The first time I saw her I didn't catch her name. She had come out, as she says, to interview me. I had been making a curry for supper and I don't believe in halfway curries. The house was as Indian as that condiment can make it. The modern open kitchen, which its designers praise because it permits the cook to share the conversation, also permits the guests to share the smells. My apologies about the smell of curry kept sending Mrs. Curry into gales of laughter. I couldn't help feeling that in some obscure way I was being witty and I kept rephrasing my apologies in an attempt to justify the laughter. Justified or not I continued to get it. When Mrs. Curry left she once again told me her name: Curry. "No wonder," she said, "the house smelled of curry. I can't very well smell like anything else."

So we got off to a good start from the beginning. Today she asked me a question. She had her fifteen-year-old son with her, a boy six feet tall but thin, with a little boy's face and big round eyes which do two things simultaneously—watch the world and watch his mother to be sure that his response to what he sees meets her approval. This is not just any child's regard for his mother's opinion. It is the regard of a Negro boy for his mother's warning that his very life may hang upon the way he carries himself before white people. His great round eyes begin to shine with pleasure, then, remembering that he has forgotten all about whites and blacks and that blacks must always be careful to please whites, he dims the shine, takes a quick look at his mother to see if she has noticed his lapse, and retreats into the prison of his blackness. It is a pity. I see it and don't know what to say. Teach him here to be spontaneous and he may learn a spontaneity the rest of the world won't permit. Best thing's just to let his mother handle it.

I had told Mrs. Curry who was going to be here: the school men and Mr. Miller from Hollywood. A few minutes ago she knocked on my door.

"I don't like to disturb you," she said, "but this is awfully important to Bert."

I knew I wasn't going to do any more work today so I told her to come in. She leaned against the door thinking how to put it.

"Is there some work Bert can do while Mr. Miller is here? Something he can do in the house? Where Mr. Miller is?"

Bert was a good boy but no more interested in work usually than the average fifteen-year-old. I suppose I showed my surprise.

"It has been the ambition of Bert's life," Mrs. Curry said, "to meet someone from Hollywood."

I couldn't think what Bert could busy himself with while Mr. Miller and I visited. He couldn't stand like an old retainer polishing the silver, or sit in the corner shelling peas. "He's welcome just to come in, sit down, and listen," I said.

Mrs. Curry shook her head. "Bert's too backward for that. He's got to have a reason." And she had thought of the reason. "He could bring in wood. Little loads. He could make it take three, four trips to fill the basket." The basket stood by the fireplace. "And with stirring up the fire and putting on new wood he could spend quite a bit of time in the front room with you and Mr. Miller. I've already had him carry the wood out so there'll be a need."

I knew something about Mr. Wyler now. But I didn't know much about Mr. Miller. I wasn't sure Bert would think him *worth* a lot of wood carrying. "This man," I told Mrs. Curry, "is not a star or anything like that. He's just the assistant to a director, and for all I know a director may have dozens of assistants."

"That is perfect," Mrs. Curry said. "Just perfect. Bert don't care about meeting stars. He wants to *be* a star. He wants to be a cowboy star. That is the sole ambition he has ever had."

The only thing I could think of to say was, "Does Bert ride?"

"He don't *yet*. But he knows a man who owns a horse. And sometimes he curries it." Usually Mrs. Curry would have noticed this play on words, but she was way beyond puns for the present. "And now he meets a director. Oh, it will be a big day for Bert."

She hurried out to tell him what had been arranged.

Cuthbert—that is Bert's name—wanting to be a cowboy movie star makes me very sad, an utterly impossible ambition, I judge.

Mrs. Curry, too, has an ambition which I also fear is hopeless. She wants to write. No, anyone can write. Everyone can write. The sometimes hopeless ambition is to be read. What Mrs. Curry writes is of great interest to me. I read her every word with pleasure. Her latest novel, not yet finished—I read it as she produces it—is called "The Devil Spoke to Me"—a good title. It begins this way.

The wind was howling through the cottonwood trees just as though a ghost was standing nearby.
The blue skies were clear as a crystal ball except for a few scattered clouds in the extreme northwest portion of the sky. The moon was at its peak, full of bloom and seems to be making a light for those pretty cloud shaped angels to fly home by.

Well, I could copy "The Devil Spoke to Me" forever. As a matter of fact I can copy anything I like forever. If all of Thoreau's writings were to vanish from the earth there is still enough of him copied into my journals to preserve his essence for future readers. There are people who don't understand this and I don't understand it completely myself—the best analogy, I think, is that of a pianist wanting to *play* the music he reads.

Mrs. Curry's characters are all "uncolored," though not in any literary sense "colorless." They have red hair, flaxen hair, and "chestnut colored eyes." I do not know whether this is because she thinks most readers would not care to read about colored people or whether she writes of what she'd like to—flaxen-haired—chestnut-eyed.

What a household we are! All of us putting the core of our living outside the circumference of our lives. All writers do that, in a way—but Mrs. Curry more than most with her unpublishable novel of unbelievable whites; Cuthbert wanting to be a movie cowboy; Fred determined to be an immediate adult. Only Max, the three horses, Private Eye the cat, and Spec the German Short Hair, appear to be living existentially, experiencing what they are rather than spending their days lost in a dream of being—non-Max, nonequine, nonfeline, noncanine. And even Max confesses to me now and then a lost dream of being a singer, and a dream, still not abandoned, of being a rancher.

Each week I have seven Sundays, the usual one of twenty-four hours and six shorter Sundays each day of about two hours. Every day the two hours before dark are sabbath to me, hours with a Sunday-shine, holy hours.

Oh they are often full of scuttle and bustle, hurry and flurry. But I am sorry if this is so, and if I can manage it, I see that it is not so. I am not sure whether I prefer to spend these hours inside or out. An orderly and tranquil room facing west, a room with white walls, if possible, is a wonderful place to watch the shadows lengthen until finally the room is awash with darkness. And when I say "watch," I mean it. Not reading, or writing, or peeling potatoes, or mending socks. Sitting perfectly still, observant and listening, until one's own blood seems to ebb with the light and one is empty of everything but the quiet and the dark.

I went outside, though, this evening. With Mrs. Curry in the kitchen I have riches of time to spend. I went out partly because of the wind; to feel it as well as see it. The big oaks were still aswirl, supple as grasses in water, lively as Van Gogh's cypresses. This is the hour of the buzzards, the most beautiful, to me, of all birds in flight. They come out from their roosting places in the eucalyptus trees just before dusk and fill the sky with their lovely, effortless soaring. They fly as other birds sing. They soar more beautifully than leopards prowl. (I know this from watching Disney's films.) Other birds at dusk hustle by, bound for home or hunting for food. Crows, cawing all the way, are commuters making the second half of their daily round trip. Swallows are picking up their suppers. Only the buzzards hold this hour holy and leave their homes for a communal service in the sky. No buzzard would think of eating at dusk. Instead, he praises God with his wings, mounts, in this wind, to speck-size, and slides down some shaft of stillness to buzzard-size again in no time. I don't know how many buzzards live in the eucalyptus trees. A hundred at least. Perhaps twice that many. They have traffic problems sometimes and need a director to say, "Half of you go up toward St. Helena and fly there."

Six cranes, herons they are, share the eucalyptus trees with the buzzards. The buzzards, who are a quiet people, must hate having their silence ruined by these screamers. If the sounds of a squeaking gate and a crying chick could be homogenized and amplified, the heron's cry would be the result. Herons enjoy screaming the way buzzards enjoy flying. Ever since —and probably before—Sarah Orne

23

Jewett wrote her story "The Heron's Nest," people have had romantic notions about herons. I don't know why. They make nests the size of washtubs—they have to, of course, if they're going to get into them; they make them out of what looks from the ground to be kindling wood. Then they place these great cumbersome things (if anything ever *looked* like a mare's nest they do) at the top of a very spindly tree where everyone, except possibly a heron, worries all season long for fear it will fall. In this nest they produce young who begin to scream with adult proficiency the minute they get their beaks outside the egg shell. What they yell for is food, and this, father and mother heron, yelling themselves and humpbacked from fish carrying, provide them ceaselessly—provide them until the herons in the nest appear to be larger and *are* certainly better fed than the herons outside. Never do the herons fly for pleasure as the buzzards do. They are simply, as far as I can see, air-borne fishmongers. Yes, I will admit that a heron plodding homeward tonight, gray against the wind-washed glass-green sky and settling without seeming pause into his airy tub, was impressive. But not lovable, as the buzzards are. So I praise God from whom all buzzards fly. Lee Vernon and I are always happy to meet because we can carry on our discussion of gulls versus buzzards. Lee says it's an argument. Since he, in addition to being a Presbyterian minister, is surely one of the ten best men on earth, he is possibly right about this. Though he is wrong about sea gulls. They are far too abrupt, angry, and noisy for beauty. They, like the herons, are utilitarian fliers. If I were required to name the two most beautiful sights in the natural world I should name the soaring of buzzards and the movement of grass in the wind. Until I wrote them down I had not thought that the two had anything in common. Besides the wind, which is a home for buzzards and the breath of life for grass, they, as much as any objects in nature, symbolize for me the persistence of life. Buzzards who defy death by living on it; grass which races across graves and battlefields and is only temporarily dismayed by cities. In grass and buzzards are found: the wind, silence, joy in movement, persistence, solitude, everlastingness, resurrection. I think nature, with buzzards at death and grass for rebirth, manages "passing on" better than man with morticians and casket blankets of carnations. And if one were free to choose in such matters (and in California one is not) my choice on that occasion would be buzzards for my cleansing, grass for my flowering.

When I was first married I spent almost as much time in the evenings outside our house as in it. Our first house was a whitewashed many-windowed cottage. It stood on a hilltop; it was embowered with honeysuckle, roses, and geraniums. It looked out across a valley toward the Pacific twenty miles away. To the north there were, first, foothills, then big mountains. To the east were, first, medium-sized mountains, then great mountains. This cottage, which consisted of a living room and kitchen in one building and a bedroom, which was another building a hundred feet distant, was furnished with lots of chintz, several books, a wicker settee, a braided rug, an airtight heater, and a fumed-oak table. I loved it and thought it the most beautiful room, cottage, location, and time in the world. I still do. I loved it so much that every so often each evening I had to put down my book and run outside to gaze in upon this treasure. This room, too, was lighted with coal-oil lamps. My life then seemed like a story and one of my reasons, I think, for running outside lay in the belief that by looking at the room from there I might check on the truth of that story. A thing that was the same outside and in had to be true, didn't it? If I ran fast enough I might even see myself in the rocking chair by the lamp with the white china shade. But run as I would, by the time I got outside the rocking chair was always empty.

This evening (evening is what I call day after four o'clock) I walked, Private Eye by my side, about the house, looking in. I no longer expect to see myself in two places at once—I have come to live more in my skin than I did, but I still like to look into my own (or, for that matter, anyone else's) house. Nowadays I indulge in a new fantasy, perhaps a truer one than that of my girlhood. Instead of hunting the "real me" who is back in the house, I try to find the stranger who paces the windy lane with me outside. I looked into the house with a stranger's eyes.

25

I see Mrs. Curry grating cheese, Fred sitting on his bed practicing "Goober Peas" on his guitar. Bert has already lit the fire. There are too many daffodils in too many vases. What is going on in this place, I wonder? The annual Daffodil Tea of the Women's Club? Something in there waits for some event. What is it?

Five-year-old Dolores, who lives on the other side of the stream in a house hidden from us by the trees, comes to pace with me. She does not like Private Eye, who will not let her pick him up, fold him like a handkerchief, and carry him over her arm.

She addresses him first. "You old crock-eyed lizard." Private Eye gives her his hard tomcat stare but does not answer. Four or five cars, one passing another, go along the road at the bottom of the hill. "It's the evening traffic jam," Dolores tells me, "beads on a string."

I have an inclination to play Boswell to Dolores' Dr. Johnson, to follow her with a notebook in hand taking down her words. Why not? She's about as wise as old Dr. Sam and a lot funnier. No one could possibly look less like the Doctor, or less like her own name for that matter. A Dolores should be a Spanish or Mexican girl, all spitfire black with dark corkscrew curls and spindly legs. Not a spindle or a corkscrew; nor has any fire ever, to my knowledge, been spat by this Dolores. This Dolores is a naiad. All her colors are sea colors, all her moods sea-cool and sea-open. There is a legend that children fathered by mermen or born of mermaids, though they walk the earth on two legs, finless and scaleless, still give away their origin by the color of their hair: greenish like seaweed or the tips of waves. Dolores' hair *is* greenish, very heavy, straight, and soft. Her skin is olive, like rocks under water; her brows and lashes are dark and her eyes are the true sea color—gray. Her teeth protrude a little, keeping her human in spite of all this unearthly beauty.

I never used to think of children as people. I thought of them as a little inhuman race, like chipmunks, or guppys. If one likes chipmunks, considers them lovable, one likes all chipmunks. I never heard a chipmunk lover express reservations about any one particular chipmunk—or a guppy fancier say, "See that guppy there in the corner

26

of the tank? I am not drawn to him." Since I liked children, I thought that I should love all children indiscriminately and could not understand why I was occasionally repelled by a perfectly good little specimen of a species I admired. "I like children," I would tell myself dismayed, "and here is a child, doing nothing wrong, not yelling, or snuffling, or maltreating a cat, and, except as duty, I wouldn't touch him with a ten-foot pole. Why? What's wrong with me? Don't I really love children?"

I am a slow learner. This, in a way, is a handicap; on the other hand it insures me an interesting life right down to the grave; and dying itself, since I live in this hand-to-mouth fashion, will probably bring revelations. A brighter person would have discovered earlier that children aren't chipmunks. They are people. Since children are a kind of helpless people, one owes them the same consideration one owes the handicapped of any age; however, one doesn't, because of this, rob them of their status as human beings and give them guppy love.

The test of one's love for a child (perhaps for an adult, too, though with the adult this is not so easily *put* to a test) is this: Do you want to hug the child? Do you feel in your arms an impulse to embrace? If not, the child in front of you may be honored, respected, helped. But you do not love him. Unless, of course, you are a grownup who takes no pleasure in touch. Such a grownup lives in a world so foreign to me I cannot even speculate on *his* response to a child. Wanting to hug is a test of loving; but wanting is not the license for the act. Hugging is a co-operative venture, and reciprocal trade treaties have to be signed by the eyes before the child is lifted or the hair ruffled or the cheek pressed. Some children don't like to be touched, especially by middle-aged grownups, persons so large, and to the child, surely, often so big-toothed, bristly, and unpleasantly scented.

Dolores' brother Stephen, who is seven, I honor, respect, and like, but we two keep our distance. I'd as soon think of embracing a grasshopper; and Stevie, I'm sure, would be as capable as a grasshopper of spitting tobacco juice on anyone who laid an uninvited hand upon him.

I saw Dolores and Stevie for the first time one summer afternoon. They came walking onto the terrace in back of

27

the house where I sat reading and writing. Stevie, though the day was warm, had a blanket around his neck which trailed behind him along the ground.

"Why," I asked, after we had introduced ourselves, "are you wearing that blanket?"

Stevie, for reasons I did not yet understand, appeared to consider the question irrelevant, or perhaps impertinent. Dolores answered for him. "He is wearing it because he is a king." I understood then the function of the blanket but I couldn't help joking a little. "Do king's always wear blankets?" "Of course not," Dolores told me. "Sometimes they wear sheets."

This evening Dolores took my hand and walked with me on my Peeping Tom tour around my own house. Eucalyptus leaves came sailing in at us like blunt arrows. The wind parted Private Eye's fur to show that cats belong to the colorless race. The buzzards in the sharp wind were executing violent scissoring patterns calculated, it appeared, to cut holes in the glass-green sky.

We gazed into the living room where Cuthbert was busy discouraging the fire. Because Dolores' opinions interest me, I said, "Cuthbert wants to be a cowboy in the movies."

Dolores, who is a great follower of TV Westerns said, "He can't."

"Why can't he?"

"Because he's black."

"Why can't a boy who is black take care of cows? That's what a cowboy does. Being black wouldn't keep Cuthbert from being a good cowboy."

"It wouldn't look right."

"Cows don't care about the looks of people who take care of them."

"Cows don't go to the movies," said Dolores.

Millar (he spells his name with an a instead of an e) came on Friday. This is Wednesday. He didn't look like any of our ideas of the assistant to a movie producer. If the assistant looks like this, God knows what the assisted will look like: Toscanini maybe, or Shelley. I don't mean by this that Millar looked anything like a poet or musician. People's looks baffle me. *Are* people their faces? Fred thinks so. He was trying to tell me about one of his teachers. He suddenly abandoned his analysis of character and said, "Well, you know how he looks. That's the way he *is*." The way this teacher looks is like a crumpet, fairly worn, fairly sweet, but crumbling slightly at the edges. Is that the way he *is*?

Well, there are no crumbs on Millar and all his edges are seemingly intact.

Mr. Millar's car shook Cuthbert's faith before he'd had a chance to judge him by his face. He stopped his car at the bridge at the bottom of the driveway to check the name on the mailbox; this told us who he was though it didn't tell him who we are, since our name isn't on the mailbox. He came on anyway, and as he drove slowly up the hill, a pace his car, not the hill, required, I was sorry for Cuthbert. A De Mille chariot would have surprised him less. This vehicle had wheels, it moved, we heard its engine; it was an automobile, but beyond this neither Cuthbert nor Fred, who is an expert on these matters, cared to go. I could feel myself losing face with my household. This movie making, which had seemed unlikely for ten years, was not becoming more believable.

Mr. Millar offset the age of his car. He looked like a college boy to me, a very tall one in slacks and a pull-over blue sweater. He wears his hair shorter than a crew cut but longer than a tonsure. It's black and looks something like the fur of unborn lamb. It's evidently very curly, and since he is about six feet seven or so, if he would only let it grow and comb it into a pompadour he could compete with any Bushman. He has very large, somewhat heavily lashed hazel eyes. He is nearsighted, and his eyes have the characteristic swimming, melting appearance of the nearsighted. A peculiarity is that while the eyes of most nearsighted persons appear larger behind their spectacles, Millar's seem to grow bigger when he takes his off. His mouth is large; the lips are full, firmly molded, and curling. I once read that such mouths betoken cruelty and the idea has stuck with me. I've been trying to remember the nose and can't. This is evidently a face dominated by the eyes and mouth. He has a high, not red but apricot, color on the cheekbones above the heavy beard shadow, and the whole impression of the face is one on energy and intensity. I don't think it a handsome face, but it is a very strong and positive one—a face and a figure which could triumph over the trappings of most offices, political or priestly.

Men can be very attractive *and* ugly. But they can't, as far as I'm concerned, be attractive and meagerly featured.

I would like to make a pact with myself to write my first impressions of faces—second impressions are no good. In the matter of what you feel about appearances—face, room, or landscape—the snap judgment is everything. After that you are tempering your true impression with kind or practical or snobbish considerations. That face you hated on first sight, afterward learning to control the initial recoil because the man was kind or learned or merely pitiful: Beware, beware! That way lie the lost years, the unhappy marriages, the impossible partnerships. The room out of which you'd like to walk, do not be reconciled to it. Endure it, if need be, but don't forget that when you first saw it you hated it.

I adapt so quickly and dangerously that, after the first seeing, a face scarcely exists for me. It becomes corroded —sometimes enhanced—by what I feel the person to be, or perhaps even more by what I feel him not to be. Women, I think, are less likely to forgive sins of omission than sins of commission. Question a bitter woman, a woman who really hates some man, and the root of her hatred will be found to lie not in what the man did but in what he didn't do. So, the paradox of all the women you read about, and sometimes know, who not only put up with, but protest love for, drunken or abusive husbands, and the women who walk out on the apparently blameless husbands, the good providers and docile fathers. Where your treasure is, there your heart is also. But can your treasure be nothing?

Anyway, treasures aside, Mr. Millar and I presented each other with our faces, and no doubt while I was saying to myself, "College boy, nice," he was saying—I know not what.

I said, "College boy, nice," because the easiest, and, under certain conditions, the pleasantest person in the world for a middle-aged woman to talk with is a young man of twenty-five. The certain conditions are these: that they have some interests in common and that the young man be able to accept a woman who is of the same generation as his mother as a human being. The young man may have the same trouble with the middle-aged that the grownup has with the child. The grownup thinks he loves *all* children, because he doesn't really consider them persons; the young hate *all* middle-aged people for the same reason. I myself as a young person preferred snakes and houseflies to the middle-aged. They, at lease, were alive, and the middle-aged, I supposed, were empty shells, still visible but devoid of all significant life. However, if the young man is able to accept the middle-aged woman as human being having, beneath her weathered shell, a heart and brain still functioning, she at least will have a delightful time—that is, if beneath his fresh and unweathered shell a heart and brain also function. She will have all the pleasures of talking with a man (and the twenty-five-year-old is nothing if not male) with none of the responsibilities and burdens she cannot resist assuming with men of her own age: burdens, that is, of charming and attracting him as a female. The middle-aged woman can't, no matter how attractive she is, appear in this light to the twenty-five-year-old. Knowing this she doesn't have to try. Her failure here is not as an individual, but as a member of a class. The middle-aged woman with the young man doesn't have to worry about whether he considers her hairdo chic, her figure good, or her perfume appealing. Such things, as far as he is concerned, would be gilding the kitchen range or the Frigidaire.

Free of such worries, the middle-aged woman, if she is accepted by this stripling as alive and human, can be with him perhaps *more* alive and more human than with any other person in the world. With him she escapes the doldrums of like herding with like, of people of the same age ceaselessly offering each other duplicates of what each already possesses.

Of course when I write of the "burden" of "appearing" charming, attractive, etc., I speak for myself, a plain woman. Perhaps for the woman who is naturally beautiful, charming, attractive, there are no burdens, only opportunities. And such a woman might not care for the company of a twenty-five-year-old. His lack of response would be a personal failure. On the other hand, his response might constitute a complication with which she would prefer not to be bothered.

I don't know. And praise God, since this is not a novel, I don't have to figure out what such a woman feels with a twenty-five-year-old. This is my story, not hers. That is the danger and delight of journalizing. I don't have to make the effort to be any other woman. Just "me—me," that old easy opera.

I don't mean to belittle journalizing. Fiction writing is in some ways easier. There you can invent. But the whole point of keeping a journal is that you don't invent, can't invent, that you try to get at the truth in spite of the facts.

This whole subject of the middle-aged woman and the young man reminds me of Hemingway. Danger, said he, is the test of a man. Reading this, I wondered what (to be as simple about it as Mr. Hemingway) was the test of a woman. Men, I decided; men are women's test. They *are* danger to women. If a man is to be judged by the way he responds to danger, a woman should be judged by the way she responds to men. Does she lose her head at the mere sight of one? Run away, hide behind something real or imagined? Shoot to kill before the poor fellow is properly in the field? Or does she face him unafraid, this Jacob's angel with his unexpected blessings and his ladder, which she, wingless, must ascend if she expects to find a heaven? Was my pleasure in Millar, the bespectacled student, in part at least, a reaction to a nondangerous encounter? Perhaps.

Anyway, I was pleased. I asked Mr. Millar to sit down. I asked him if he would like a drink. I do this as quickly as possible with people for whom I am the Quaker author of *The Friendly Persuasion* and nothing else. I do it on the theory that a few sharp shocks are less painful than a number of smaller ones. My appearance has been their first disappointment. They have expected someone older, sweeter, frailer, someone more spiritual in appearance. No one can be sure of how his own appearance strikes others. Sometimes I think I look a good deal like former President Hoover—a man recently more appreciated than formerly, though still not highly regarded on the score of personal comeliness. At other times the face I see in the mirror looks to me like that of a pleasant, hearty barmaid in an Irish pub—certainly not a role Hoover could play with any conviction. So I am of two, and frequently more, but always contradictory, minds on this subject; but whatever the truth is here, I do know that my appearance disappoints readers of *The Friendly Persuasion*.

I first discovered this at an autographing party in New York at the time the book was published. A young man, who for some time had been standing, book in hand, in front of me, hoping, it appeared, to preserve one final illusion, asked, "You don't drive a car, do you?"

"Since I was twelve," I told him honestly, and he departed, not bothering to have me autograph, with the hand that had grasped a steering wheel, the book he evidently liked.

At another time, a Japanese man surprised me by suddenly asking if he might see my palm. Whether he was interested in discovering there signs of contact with a steering wheel, I knew not. Mutely I extended my hand, palm up, and mutely he examined it. He, however, was pleased with every line he saw. He grew more and more cheerful. He returned my hand with a little bow, like a gift, and with the gift he made a little presentation speech. "Much, much better," he said. Better than what? I thought. "Very much better than I expected. Yes, indeed. Much, much more delicate. Much, much more spiritual. Thank you. Thank you so much."

I was pleased that I possessed a palm that, if not absolutely delicate and spiritual, was at least more so than anyone would have imagined. But there is no way of fronting the world, palms up, to demonstrate this fact. So if Mr. Millar was disappointed in me as a Quaker and the author of a Quaker book I thought I'd better let him know the worst at once. There was liquor in the house.

Liquor in the house! That phrase alone probably shows my upbringing and background. The southern Indiana backwoods and the Quaker rectitude—or narrowness—depending upon your viewpoint. There, anyway, and among those people, alcohol's only purpose was drunkenness. My father demanded of the doctor, when he suggested a daily glass of beer as a stimulant for my tubercular lack of appetite, a regular medical prescription as for strychnine or opium. He had no intention of letting the proprietor of the liquor store think he was buying beer for pleasurable purposes. And Max's mother is not only a Quaker but a crusading member of the W.C.T.U. When she visits us, all bottles are locked away to spare her sensibilities and our spirits.

If liquor in the house shocked Millar, he didn't show it. He asked for Scotch. I gave it to him, and he drank a large glass thirstily. I had the feeling that he *was* thirsty and would have preferred beer—or water. He had driven all the way from Los Angeles since morning.

Cuthbert began at once to bring in wood. Between trips he stood stirring the fire like a pudding. He stood, back to the fireplace, and stirred over one shoulder. Millar, sweatered and full of whisky, began to sweat. I opened a window. This reduced the heat but didn't explain the stares.

"Is there something wrong with me?" Millar asked when we were momentarily alone.

I explained to him Cuthbert's ambition and the part he played in it as the assistant to a producer. Mr. Millar looked sad. "Of course," I told him, "I know that a colored boy can never be a movie cowboy."

Millar's sadness hadn't been for the colored boy wanting to be a cowboy star, but for any boy wanting to be a star. A colored boy might just have a chance, he said. A funny colored cowboy might be just the foil, just the shading in dark a big white cowboy needs, just the object to save us viewers from snow blindness, staring at all that sugared snowdrift of serious blondness and unrelieved virtue.

"Maybe he doesn't want to be funny," I said. "Maybe he wants to be a tragic hero."

"He had better want to be funny," Millar said.

Cuthbert was again muddling the fire, looking at us with eyes as big and liquid as Millar's, but so much more tentative, so much more ready to extinguish themselves, to retreat into a black hiddenness.

"Cuthbert," asked Millar, "would you like to make people laugh?"

"Yes, sir," said Cuthbert, far from abashed, and surprising me with his aplomb. "I *can* make people laugh."

"How?"

"Telling funny stories. Singing. Dancing funny."

"I thought you wanted to be a cowboy?"

"Yes, sir."

"Cowboys don't have much chance to dance and tell funny stories. They've got to stay on their horses and shoot bad men."

"I have to be a cowboy, sir."

"Why don't you sit down now, Cuthbert?" I asked. If he felt easy enough to talk, he ought to feel easy enough to stop stirring up the fire.

Cuthbert sat down, and Fred joined us. Fred likes to get things just right. If he thinks you are ignorant he'll explain things to you. If he thinks he's ignorant (this is a rarer situation) he'll ask questions.

"Are you an employee of William Wyler's?" he asked Mr. Millar.

Mr. Millar said he was.

"Is Mr. Wyler an employee of Paramount's?"

"Let us say he is associated with Paramount."

"Is . . ."

"Paramount is a joint-stock company."

Both boys decided to listen for a while.

I told Mr. Millar I no longer took seriously anybody's talk of making a movie of *The Friendly Persuasion.*

"You can take this seriously. Willy has never started a picture he didn't finish. And you are surely interested in having a good movie made of your book?"

"It's none of my concern. My business is writing. I try to write good books. It's the movie-makers' business to make good movies. If they don't, it's their tragedy, not mine."

"Wouldn't it hurt you to see a poor picture made and called *The Friendly Persuasion?*"

"They probably wouldn't call it *The Friendly Peruasion* anyway."

Mr. Millar laughed. "All right—they probably wouldn't. But that wasn't my question. Would you like to see a stupid movie based on your book?"

"I don't like stupid movies—based on anybody's books

—or dreamed-up originals for the occasion. Other than that I don't give a whit."

Millar said, "You're joking."

"I'm not joking. I am sorry for every word I write which could or ought to be better. But when I sell you a book, it's yours. The responsibility is yours. Film it badly and I'll never shed a tear."

"People will judge you by the movie."

"They oughtn't to. I didn't make it."

"What if you had a hand in the making?"

"What do you mean, hand?"

"Oh—I don't know. Were around. Could talk to us about it."

"If I had responsibility, then I'd feel responsible if things I could control were done wrong. But I don't know anything about the movies. I might personally be able to ruin any movie I had anything to do with—with the very best intentions."

Mr. Millar smiled at me the way he had at Fred. "Willy's not a man to let his movies get ruined easily."

I asked Mr. Millar to share the fondue with the administrators; but one or the other, or the combination, did not appeal to him. He said he had a date in Palo Alto for dinner.

"Perhaps you'd like to come down to Hollywood and talk to Willy?"

I told him I couldn't. "Next week I go to Stanford for three days to teach. Then I have only one week at home before I go to the University of Washington for a week of teaching. Those are the only interruptions I'm going to permit myself until the novel's done."

"I'll be at Stanford until Sunday. I could bring a friend of mine along, pick you up and drive you back there if you like."

I thought that would be fine. In the doorway, leaving, he said, "In your story of Jess, a Quaker who doesn't believe in fighting, you never confront him with the need of fighting. He never has to make up his mind—fight or let my house be burned—fight or watch my wife be attacked. Why?"

"What makes you think it's either-or? The history of

36

war has been fight *and* watch my house be burned, fight *and* watch my wife be attacked."

Millar said, "I'm not talking about Quaker doctrine. I'm talking about story writing. Why did you in *The Friendly Persuasion* avoid what seems to most people to be the fundamental thing about Quakers?"

"You mean it's as if I wrote about an alcoholic who by chance always lived where there wasn't any alcohol?"

Millar nodded, though rather reluctantly, as if the comparison didn't seem just.

"Maybe people are more interesting to me when they aren't so concentrated about partial issues."

"War and alcohol?" Millar asked, as if he himself didn't consider them so partial. "Shakespeare didn't think so."

"Nor Carrie Nation, either. We all have our limitations. Maybe mine is wanting to avoid conflict. In stories and out."

"The best writing has to do with conflict."

"I agree with you."

"But you didn't give Jess any conflict."

"Yes, I did. Every day of his life was a conflict."

"What conflict?"

"Did you ever read Thoreau?"

"I didn't ask you if you'd ever seen a movie."

"Every day of Jess's life, like Thoreau's, was a fight to keep himself alive to the wonder of being alive."

"That wouldn't be a conflict very easy to show in Vista-Vision."

"That's what I've always thought. And that, thank God, is your problem not mine. See you Sunday."

I thought Mr. Millar had gone, but he came back to the still-opened door.

"What would Jess have done if either he had to kill or watch his son killed?"

"I don't know."

Millar looked appalled. He thought, I could see, that a writer knew all about his characters offhand. "Jess himself wouldn't know until he was in the midst of that happening. Jess didn't live by rules imposed from outside. He lived from the inside out. I can't know more about Jess than he knows about himself. I'd have to put myself in his shoes

37

before I'd know. And maybe they wouldn't fit well enough for me ever to know that."

"What do you think?"

"I really don't know."

Millar stood there, trying, I could see, to put *himself* in Jess's shoes. "Me either," he said.

Inside, after Millar had gone, Fred's and Cuthbert's reactions were typical of the two boys. I said, "I didn't expect a college boy."

Fred answered. "College boy! Why he's in his thirties. He's old enough to be my father."

This is an old and admitted weakness of Fred's and we both laughed at this reappearance of it.

"O.K.," Fred said, "maybe he's not old enough to be my father. But I hate to see young people so successful."

"Why, Fred?" asked Cuthbert.

"It reflects on me," Fred said, and explained. "Eighteen and not a thing to show for it yet."

"We seen a director," Cuthbert said.

"Assistant to a director," Fred reminded him.

The fire, now that Cuthbert didn't have to account for his presence by stoking it, had died down to a pleasant heap of rosy coals. I felt tired. The boys felt excited. Mrs. Curry brought me a saucer of fondue and a hunk of French bread. "Try it," she said, "before the men get here." To the boys she said, "Get on out to the kitchen and I'll give you some."

Fred, not moving, said, "I'm looking forward to meeting Dr. Albright. He's a charming chap. Got a real head on him."

"Dr. Albright is not present at the minute," Mrs. Curry told Fred, and waited for him to rise. He rose. Fred buffaloes a good many people, but not Mrs. Curry.

On the way to the kitchen Cuthbert said, "I've got a rope in the car. I can do tricks with it. Would you like to see some of them, Fred?"

Fred has no stomach for trivia of this sort, and I waited to hear what he would say. "Sure, Cuthbert," he said, and Cuthbert bounded out the door for his rope.

*Thursday*

Headache, headache, headache! When I hear someone say, "I can't remember when I had a headache," I feel almost as if I were talking to a man from Mars. To be human is to have headaches. I am ashamed of my headaches. Migraine is something, everyone is agreed, that the migraine sufferer elects. He aches because he chooses to ache. Organically there is no explanation. It is as if you took a car which refused to run to the garage and the mechanics said, "Everything is in perfect order." Then you step on the starter, the motor hums. You take it for a trial run. It couldn't be smoother. Nevertheless, it occasionally stops dead. Balks. Spooky, crazy car. Spooky, crazy human beings who have migraine.

I went once, just to be sure that there was no organic cause, to the Stanford Lane Hospital, stayed three days, had pins stuck in my scalp, X rays taken, etc. Nothing. After the organic explanations were ruled out, the doctors tried to get at it inorganically.

"Does your head ever ache when you are away from your husband?"

"Yes."

"More than when with him?"

"No."

"Does he smoke?"

"No."

"Does it ache when you are going to have guests?"

"Sometimes."

"Does it ache when you are alone?"

"Sometimes."

If my headache is protest, it is protest against situations more fundamental than any of these. As far as I know I never use it as a weapon. None of my friends or family say, "We must be careful or Jessamyn will have a migraine." Since they accept, as I do, its total unpredictability it is useless to take precautions of any kind. When I have a headache, which is ordinarily at least two days out of every week, no one need be quiet, or fetch pills or smelling salts. A hurricane could blow up or an atom bomb be dropped and I, lost in the eye of my own storm, bombarded by my own radioactive fall-out, would not care. On the other hand, if I do not ask for much during these times I don't give much either.

Is this the explanation? Am I too uncourageous to retreat from—not just persons—but the world itself, except under the disguise of illness? Is migraine the thrifty man's drink, the stay-at-home's travel, the careful man's epilepsy, the timid man's love affair? It takes you out of yourself. Where it takes you is another matter—a real hell sometimes. But after a little of that, a night, or a night and a day, how happy you are to come home to nonpain. Nonpain, appears, after one of those bouts, to be the paradise you've been seeking. Who would be such a fool as to want anything more? You walk outside teasing your acheless head like a babe newborn to delights which once you took for granted.

We migraine lovers (I accept the psychiatrist's opinion that unless we loved our headaches we wouldn't have them) may have our headaches not as a protest against anything but as a real good in themselves. Except for last night's headache (my headaches like those of most migraine sufferers come on as I sleep) I wouldn't be reclining here, reconciled to death, happy to be alive, with my world still only a little larger than the circumference of my own skull. As the pain lets up, my world extends an inch, a foot, a yard beyond my brow. And in so small a world I see things I never saw before. I don't ever remember seeing a shoe before, seeing it, that is, as other then something created whole, the offspring of another shoe, an object as integral as an egg. As the pain retreated and the world outside the skull came into focus I saw one of my red loafers beside the bed. It was as pretty as a daisy to me, but much stranger. I picked it up and turned it over and about in my hand, filled with a kind of cheerful marveling content. What a wonderful intricate, unbelievable thing. So marvelously foot-shaped, more difficult to make than a cathedral—which can be any shape whatsoever. And so useful. Only in a world shrunk by migraine, delicately balanced between pain

40

and resurrection, are shoes and like objects really visible. The label on a bottle is as surrealist as Dali, and a spoon in a glass of clear water is as full of suggestions as a painting by Utrillo—and something like it. Only in a spoon-sized, shoe-sized world can one see spoons and shoes. The minute the world gets larger they disappear as objects in themselves. I wouldn't care to be a permanent resident in such a Lilliput, strange and delightful as it is. But never to have entered? Never to have seen a shoe? Is migraine worth it? No, it takes too much time.

Simone Weil tried by electing personal suffering, by starving in England when her countrymen starved in France, by working in a factory since most of her fellow human beings were condemned to such work, to share the lives of others. Does the migraine suffer unconsciously elect his headache for the same reason? To become one with the pain of the world? Is he more compassionate because of his own pain? Or rather does his pain enclose him in a private world and exclude concern for everything beyond the portals of his own pounding head? Does pain teach us that pain is endurable and thus lessen our sympathy for other sufferers? Do we sympathize most with what we must wholly imagine? Is death the pain we have never experienced and has it as a result an enormity only the imagination can give? Though some acts—those of the Germans in their concentration camps—have a magnitude of horror beyond what any mind seems capable of imagining. One is appalled at what they did; but behind the revulsion for the deed is the stunned realization that before the deeds were performed by machines and hands, minds had imagined them.

In novels, all female suffers of migraine are horrible creatures. They use their headaches as weapons to gain special attention. They are frustrated creatures unable to look their real needs in the face. They are listless and pallid, liable to puke and prone to whine. Their husbands are reduced to the status of pill-bearers and their children must always tiptoe and whisper, "Mama has a headache." The reader knows full well that mama, behind the closed door and in the gloom of the shadowy room, is deeply enjoying herself—the wheel of domestic life is revolving furi-

41

ously about her, the malingering hub, while she is happily out of it all.

Fiction reveals truths that reality obscures—so the headachey female of the novel may be a truer picture than I, still aching a little, can ever paint. The history of battles is seldom well written by their participants, and the person needed, perhaps, to give the definitive word on the headache is a hearty male novelist who never in his life had a pain above the neck.

Since I do not enjoy being identified with these tiresome sickly and sickening headachers of fiction, I try to think of some nontiresome, nonfictional migrainous females. Offhand I think of Jane Welsh Carlyle, George Eliot, and Virginia Woolf. No one, I think, would call these ladies tiresome, though I do not doubt that they may very well have been trying on occasion. They were all married, all childless. Mother Nature may also know best on occasion. There is no evidence that their husbands, if pill-bearers, were unhappy in the role. Carlyle, certainly, was enough to give any sane woman a headache, and the majority of the pills borne in that household moved from Jane to Thomas rather than vice versa. George Eliot, headaches and all, snared (the word is perhaps not exact) a husband of forty when she was sixty, a feat most of us would not attempt though in perfect health. Virginia Woolf, if one is to judge by her diary and by the accounts of Stephen Spender and others who knew her, was in spite of—or perhaps because of—her headaches, a rare companion.

There is perhaps a touch of desperation in the relationships and communications of the migrainous. They have been so often prevented by pain from being what they consider "themselves" with others that they, when free of pain, try to crowd into that golden hour enough meaning and joy and intensity to make up for all the golden hours of which they have been in the past, and will be in the future, robbed. This desperation, this intensity may make the migrainous person almost as unbearable in health as in sickness, and friends, hit with the full blast of their determination to live it up while they can, may long for the quietude which suffering and a handful of Optalidon might bestow upon all their noisy health. Too ill when

42

they'll ill, too well when they're well, the perfect time to call upon the migrainous is right now—at this minute when subdued by recent pain I emerge somewhat reticently and shyly into well-being. *Then* we are at our best and anything will charm us. Too weary and too fearful (any undue excitement may send the head to pounding again) to talk as fast as usual, we are at this minute fine listeners —and your slightest observation will, like the shoe, appear to us full of meaning we would never have been able, in any other state, to apprehend.

I have read that those who suffer from epilepsy are able to anticipate an attack because it is preceded by a state of exultation. I have noticed something of the same kind with migraine and think that migraine may be, instead of a protest, or an effort to share the pain of the world or a ruse to dominate one's husband, something as simple as the cliff off which one jumps into oblivion—of a kind— when the joy becomes too great to bear.

By joy I don't mean anything as measurable and one-dimensional as being left a million unexpected dollars by an aunt or winning a Prix de Rome or coming home with a perfect permanent. I mean that totally unexplainable tide of grace—and alas excitement—which takes its beginning in some perhaps ordinarily insignificant sensuous thing—the light on a string of orange-colored wooden beads hanging across the back of a maple chair . . . the wind flattening the short grass which alternates in waves of silver and blue-green . . . the sweet smell of snow falling on a high dry mesa land where no snow was expected. Beginning sometimes with these known stimuli, beginning sometimes with nothing that can be remembered, but alike in a swelling tide of joy with which one cannot cope. One prays, at such times. I do not mean on knee bones or with foreknown words, but one prays constantly. Every word of one's unceasing interior conversation becomes directed upward. Upward? Well at least outward. This joy, which, whatever its source, is characterized by the need to share and to communicate, demands prayer. Migraine may possibly be defined as defective prayer, as a poor way of saying something that must be said. Were the channels of outgo less clogged, one might never experience a twinge.

Migraine may be the smoke of imperfect psychic combustion, an emotional smog.

However, I know where last night's headache started. In yesterday's sabbath, the two hours before sundown, with a good day's work behind me and the air sweet with blossoming acacia and narcissus. I decided not to ride, as usual, but to walk. Since I discovered horseback riding so late in life, late at least for a horseback rider, I have become more scornful of walking than any born-in-the-saddle cowpoke. I have already walked for twice as many years as I'll be able to ride, so why, I have reasoned, waste more time on that act, already overperformed? And except for such acts as must be performed out of the saddle, shopping, getting books from the library, I elect nowadays to do my traveling on horseback. And even though one thinks, because it is so much more leisurely than riding in a car, that no sight whatsoever will be missed, still on a horse at a lope some sights which might have been examined on foot are missed. Riding Dandy down the road the other day I caught a glimpse, out of the corner of my eye, of a strange sight: in the prune orchard, surrounded by bare-limbed trees, was one tree in full bloom, a fountain of stained cream prune blossoms. I decided to make a pilgrimage to this tree, to have a closer look at this foolish virgin who when spring came was going to be without means of celebrating that advent.

The blossoming tree was deep in the orchard on the other side of the arroyo which splits the ranch, and I set out toward it guiding myself by its creamy candle. Walking thus with my eyes far ahead of my feet I saw suddenly that where the arroyo should have been there was now a stretch of gray-green, autumn-colored water mirroring on its surface in the clouded way of old gunmetal-colored mirror, clouds themselves, moving like falling blossoms amidst the also mirrored limbs of the prune trees which surrounded the water. I could not believe my eyes. Blossoms in a nonflowering season. Water in a waterless land. I was walking into the sun and, in order to see more clearly, I inclined my head, and went toward the unbelievable lake planning to test its wetness with other senses than those of sight. So, walking slowly, peering closely, mistrusting my eyes, I saw around another bend of

44

the lake a vision more unbelievable than water: lilies, dozens, hundreds of lilies. Not water lilies, but Easter lilies standing, it appeared six feet high, a mass of them blinding me with their sun-reflecting silvery sheen.

They stopped me in my tracks. They were unbelievable —and yet I saw them. Water in a place where no water had been and lilies in a season when there should be no lilies. This is not the country of mirages. I accepted both, not as miraculous or illusory but as proof of how much one loses on horseback, moving fast along known pathways. Seeing these lilies I thought of Thoreau, who reported it his custom, and that of the other young men of Concord, to pick water lilies in the hot summer weather, and wear them inside their shirts. These lilies growing above the water would have been better for that practice, I thought. A big wet water lily, however sweet smelling (and it was for scent, not coolness, the boys wore them), must have felt like a big wet flabby frog next the skin. To say nothing of appearances! There is scarcely any place. I will not follow Thoreau—but I draw the line at water lilies inside the shirt. I would have given anything, almost (oh, cautious Jessamyn), to have watched Thoreau watch this wonder of lilies in the field.

Then, as I stood marveling, another marvel came to join the first. Or rather, since it had been there all the time, *I* went to join the second marvel: music, the concerted singing of many birds. At home, we have many birds: jays, woodpeckers, cranes, buzzards, owls, hummingbirds, robins, towhees, grosbeaks, but soloists all, every man Jack of them. There is a constant hubbub of noise from this crew, but such of them as can sing, rather than scream or yell or bellow, do so alone. And even the screamers have no cheerleader. What I was hearing was song, from a large body of singers who were by training or instinct able to harmonize, producing a melody as beautiful to my ears as the lilies were to my eyes. I couldn't (the sun was still in my eyes) see these singers and I didn't care to. The song was enough. Some birds, musicians though they are, do their piping through mighty tinny instruments—shrill little fifes and twangy little French harps. These were round and sweet and sullen notes, untouched by any metal. (How omnipresent is the hell of universal advertising!

There is a reminiscent flavor of cigarettes and garters in one's response even to transcendent experiences.) But I will not rewrite to purge the prose. The taint is deeper than words. The notes of these birds, to be as plain about it as possible, were flutelike.

Standing there, facing my threefold miracle—water and lilies and song—I, who had unhorsed myself for the practical purpose of coming close to one little off-season bloomer, began to experience that familiar sense of joy and wonder with which, finally, only migraine can cope. It was a miracle, and even had it been the routine five o'clock experience of every late winter afternoon, still a wonder. Water where no water had been, lilies, silvery bright, and birds, now that I saw them, clustering like dark frost-bitten blossoms on the bare wood of the prune trees that bordered the pond. For a moment, listening to their sweet, low, sad, and joyous melody I believed all the tales of travelers who have, by chance, blundered through a gate or down steps into a place out of this world—and a time out of this time. The lilies, the birds, and the water. And when there was a momentary pause in the song—whose theme was death in life and parting foreseen at the very moment when the clasping is warmest—from away off in the manzanita thickets doves, with their built-in assent to change and sorrow, answered most beautifully, "Yes, yes, it is all true."

I took another step, the sun directly in my eyes, to see the birds better. A person really knowledgeable about birds would have been able to identify them by their song. But I am not knowledgeable. An owl hoots, a buzzard soars, a crow caws. This is about the extent of my birdlore. At my approach the birds moved, and I caught, in spite of the sun, the flash of red as they spread their wings. Redwinged blackbirds! Of course; though at home, only a half-mile away, I had never in twenty years once caught sight of one. For birds, a half-mile makes another world; and why, if sunlight and water are your home, fool around with the shadows of dark oaks and the dryness of hillsides? No answer if you're a bird.

I took another step, putting my head on my shoulder, in an effort to see without being blinded by the sun in my eyes, and I succeeded. Succeeded so well that without semi-blindness my lilies became cattails, completely raveled out and, by some chance of calm weather, still retaining in lily-sized clumps all the floss of their silvery seed-bearing silk. I lifted my head and with the dazzle back in my eyes they were once again lilies. I wagged my head: shoulder, cattails—upright, lilies. I moved on and saw that this miraculous body of water was a small reservoir created by putting a dam across the arroyo. So all was lost? Lilies and choir and lake? Nothing left but ordinary doves and ordinary red-winged blackbirds singing at the sunset? Ordinary cattails growing at the edge of ordinary irrigation water?

No, all was not gone. Irony was left, itself a miracle: the miracle of the two-in-one, the Janus-faced, the double-leader, the kiss-that-kills, the blow-that-saves. A taste for irony has kept more hearts from breaking than a sense of humor—for it takes irony to appreciate the joke which is on oneself. A sense of humor shows one the jolly fun in the banana peel beneath another's feet. Only irony, as your own feet go out from under you, will show you how side-splitting this event can really be.

So I wasn't disappointed. My glory took another dimension. I laughed at my bargain, summer in winter, flowering in decay, beauty in use. The birds were real, the song was real; a reservoir is actually a do-it-yourself lake. And the cattails, without benefit of irony, or the illusion of lilies, were radiant in their silvery disembowelment. The lone tree, which I had not yet reached, but which had led me like a beacon, appeared, after the revelations I had just witnessed, of lesser stature than the events it heralded. It was a mild little thing, but sweet. And something sweet to smell, after all the glut I'd had of seeing and hearing, was just what I needed.

The glory which heralds migraine can't always be accounted for. I know where last night's headache started and what it was: the cliff over which I threw myself (baby with the bath) when the glory became too great. What might its other uses be? And why *uses*? Must everything be utilized, harnessed? Even glory? Throw it away, if the pressure becomes too great, and forget utilitarianism. If migraine is imperfect prayer, it is also imperfect poetry and imperfect loving. If it can't be expressed in prayer or poetry or love, accept the ache. Suffering is also one of the ways of knowing you're alive.

Alone with Private Eye, five February Gold daffodils, and Mozart on my tomato-can bedroom radio. The day has reached that point of waning when the limbs of the oak trees are still a darker green-gray than the green-gray sky.

I went to town at four to buy groceries. Bought also, at a winter sale, a sun top for twenty-nine cents. A saleslady told me that she could chart the course of a love affair by what a woman was buying. "First she buys lingerie, night-gowns, brassières, fancy girdles, and panties. After that phase has passed she buys dresses for dinner and the theater. Finally street dresses. That marks the end. She's looking for someone else."

Max and Fred are both at public meetings; Max at a superintendent's council meeting, Fred at a conclave of student-body officers. Fred has become a junior statesman, and the school's gain is my loss. The two-and-a-half hours' work he is supposed to do here every day has begun to shrink. When I spoke to him about it the other night he said, "I was absent for constitutional reasons." He meant the constitution of Napa Junior College, but I felt as frustrated as a judge with a witness who invokes the Fifth Amendment. I was very loath, in the face of this holy word, to mention scrubbing, but I brought myself to it.

I wonder if the world is as full of square pegs in round holes as it is thought to be? In this household, while the fit may not be a hundred per cent perfect, rotundity has found openings more or less round and the squares (me) stay home filling, if not brightening, corners. Reading books, writing words, fondling cats, lighting fires, I am amazed at a world so richly furnished with objects that permit me to do what I like most to do. My head may ache, but oh! my soul is free.

I have been given Anne Morrow Lindbergh's *Gift from the Sea,* which everyone is reading and praising. This is a sermon, beautifully written, with sentences as stately in their effortless movement as swans; but it is not a sermon which speaks to my condition. The text of Mrs. Lindbergh's sermon is: "Do not let yourself be dissipated by too much activity." I need another text. "Don't let yourself be separated from others by too much solitude." Mrs. Lindbergh's boon is my bane.

Anyone with a real taste for solitude who indulges that taste encounters the dangers of any other drug-taker. The habit grows. You become an addict. Opium is a sugar pill compared with this dream-maker. Absorbed in the visions of solitude, human beings are only interruptions. What voice can equal the voices of solitude? What sights equal the movement of a single day's tide of light across the floor boards of one room? What drama be as continuously absorbing as the interior one? I understand hermits, but not people who can't understand hermits. Hermits I understand all too well and their dangerous addiction to a state of complete separation: a state where the only world is the world reported to them by their senses, undiluted by any outside comment. In that state, the sky, a rim of hills, the passing clouds that dapple the hills are beautiful in themselves; but they are doubly beautiful, and in a dangerous way, because these sounding boards and mirrors give you back endlessly yourself.

The most murderous hatred in the world is that of the solitary for the person who deprives him of his drug. The true solitary hates the intruder not because of anything he does but simply because he exists. Those who have never tasted the drug cannot understand the frightful pains of deprivation, the ache of withdrawal from elements that have become an extension of the self into a world of the nonself, the world of the neighbors, their dogs, their children. The objects that require you to substitute doing for being.

No, Mrs. Lindbergh's sermon will not do for me. I need someone to preach me the gospel of relatedness, and the gift I need from the sea is not a handful of shells with their reminders of various forms of separated living, but the whole encompassing, touching sea itself, with its memories of common beginnings. Someone said that, had Mrs. Lindbergh taken her two-week vacation at "Camp Happy" in the Catskills, rather than by the sea, and had she not happened upon the extended simile of the shells, by which she gives form to her observations, her remarks would not have had much point. But she did go to the

49

sea and she did use the simile of the shells and her meanings are expanded by these facts.

Nevertheless, her advice is not for me—and my going, as I have promised, to Stanford, the University of Washington, and Mills College in the next few weeks is as much my effort to correct the solitary predilections of my nature as her seashore visit was an effort to offset the continual gregariousness demanded of her. The opposite cure for the opposite disease. And I have learned to know myself well enough in this small matter, at least, to know that I must commit myself, sign contracts, make promises, or I'll never arrive at the cures. I must say yes quickly over the phone, making going my bounden duty, otherwise I can't pull myself out of the blissful inertia of solitude. It is a weakness to be able to reach my pleasures only through promises made to others; but if I possess this weakness it is surely wisdom to recognize it. If I have to have my pills turned wrong side out—sugar on the inside, bitter on the outside, before I can swallow them, disguise my pleasures as duties, then hurrah for being smart enough to know it.

*Friday*

I adore being the only one awake in the house, a thief grabbing morning delights of gold before anyone else can touch them. Headache of the past two nights and yesterday gone, so that I awaken crying, "Joy, joy." But quietly. I'm not sure of myself yet. I move carefully, handle myself like a newly laid egg, precious and breakable. And I don't want to break. I want to save myself for hatching. I want to hatch a beautiful bird of a book, a good novel.

There was frost in the night, and when I first opened my eyes the season was pure winter, grass-white, trees black and naked, no sun. Now the sun has come over the wall of hills behind us, the frost has melted, the grass has a sheen of golden light; in two hours we have passed from winter to spring.

If *The Friendly Persuasion* were made into a movie it would have to center around the Civil War story. In the book forty years pass. That's too much time to show in an hour-and-a-half movie. Nothing, then, because of the speed required, can be properly dramatized, and I begin, when I see such movies, to be more interested in the make-up man's art in building double chins and baggy eyes onto young faces, than in the story itself.

How would a movie deal with a Quaker family like the Birdwells? It isn't just that the Birdwells were "good" people. The movies like to portray good people now and then, but movie "good" people are ordinarily either pompous, complacent, and platitudinous or else mighty quirky folk. Somebody did a movie script of the book ten years ago in which Quakers were made out to be a bunch of adult Boy Scouts of both sexes, their days devoted to good turns of every nature. They were busy from dawn to dusk saving runaway slaves, teaching them to read, rolling bandages, and turning the other cheek. In an effort, I suppose, to present Quaker pacifism in a good light, soldiers were made out to be hundred per cent ruffians who would rather taunt a Quaker any day than fight the enemy. I don't know whether this presentation was the result of standing outside Quakerism and seeing them in the way non-Catholics tend to see nuns and priests as persons good, but scarcely human, or was the result of standing inside movie tradition from where only two shades are to be seen in the world: black and white.

This is the one thing that this movie must avoid. The Birdwells are not Quakers who happen to be people. There isn't a complacent or platitudinous bone in Jess Birdwell. He lived his goodness on his pulses. He risked it every day. He was really a Quaker existentialist. He exposed himself to life. Nothing, not even morality, had hardened in him. He was alive in all of his senses. He loved the earth, its inhabitants, its furnishings, himself, and God. He really made, this Hoosier Quaker, a stab at what we call nowadays the "good life." And he was willing to risk the respect of his neighbors, the understanding of his fellow members in the Society of Friends, and the love of his wife to do so. And none of this in the big bombastic movie style, nor the dull pompous movie style, nor the little quirky "papa is a card" movie style. Makes my blood boil with excitement to think about it, so I'll stop. Curse Millar anyway. Why do I answer phones?

*Evening*

I've been reading a child's life of George Fox since I stopped work. An odd thing, to be propelled in that direction by Hollywood! Fox had so piercing a gaze that the minister at Firbank Chapel felt, when Fox fixed his eyes on him, that "he could be killed with a crab apple." Gazes and phrases have softened since Fox's day, alas.

Brinton, in his book *Friends for 300 Years,* says Quakers aren't Protestants; says that in many ways Quakers are nearer Catholics. There are mystics in both the Society of Friends and the Holy Roman Church; though the mystic in the Church of Rome is always in danger of breaking through the ritualistic machinery of his church into heresy. A Catholic saint is apparently a man on the verge of becoming a good Quaker. (This is my observation, not Brinton's—and probably not that of any Catholic, either.)

Kierkegaard, neither Friend nor Catholic, says that the mystic is a person who hasn't the patience to wait for God's revelations. By that definition a Quaker is an impatient Protestant—or a Protestant a slow-motion Quaker.

A wonderful thing happened when I went riding this evening. I saved a bird's life. I had stopped to look across the valley, and saw a movement, or heard a sound, I don't know which, at Dandy's feet. I looked down and saw a small bird. It stirred in a peculiar way, and when I dismounted I found that both its feet were caught in wiry strands of grass so that it was miserably staked to the earth. It was not exhausted but it was resigned. It looked at me, with that depth of confidence which animals sometimes have in distress, a look which often seems to exceed in power of communication the looks humans exchange. I have often thought, after long talk with a human, that not once was there any speaking with the eyes; without which two tape recorders had as well reeled off their words. But this bird gave me with a glance his whole being and condition. It took me some time to get him free. Afterward he sat for a while in my palm, not huddling but upright. We looked into each other's eyes once more, then he took off, leisurely, into his proper element.

Since so small a good deed gives me so much pleasure I ought to make plans whereby I might perform some larger ones. That's just the trouble! I want to be an angel unawares. A good deed planned seems as phony as a handmade halo. I like to save small birds, so why not join the "Ladies Small Bird Saving Circle"? But such a circle is no place for a square peg like me.

Riding and exulting are all one to me, and I don't forgive myself the inertia that prevented my discovering this earlier. If I were to join a circle of any kind it would be a circle that required its members to try something new at least once a month. The new thing could be very inconsequential: steak for breakfast, frog hunting, attending the church of the four Square Gospel, walking on stilts, memorizing a stanza of poetry, reading aloud, staying up outdoors all night, making up a dance and dancing it, speaking to a stranger, chinning yourself, milking a goat, reading the Bible, working as a waitress: anything not ordinarily done. And nothing to be done for discipline but only on the chance of discovering something you love. Much can be intuited, but not all. Some things have to be tried. I could not have intuited riding a horse and I hate to admit I owe so much to the chance of once having mounted one.

I don't mind riding with others but I don't like to talk or hear talk when I ride—exclamations. "Look!" "How beautiful!" "I'll race you." Nothing more. Talk while riding is just as out of place as talk while dancing or listening to music. And for the same reasons. It breaks the rhythm, the communion.

This doesn't apply to the man who does a daylong job in the saddle, but it does to "pleasure riders."

In a movie of *The Friendly Persuasion*, Gard's and Mattie's love story would have to be told more fully.

We always feel that we can absolutely and easily abstain

53

from what we are inevitably approaching. Me and this movie, for instance.

Only a fool would refuse to enter a fool's paradise—when that's the only paradise he'll ever have a chance to enter.

A woman with an achievement on her hands and no man to hand it to is a worse case than a woman with a bastard—that, at least, was begotten in a giving.

Liberate one small bird and feel like Lincoln all evening! So much enhanced by one small good deed, so little cast down by many big bad ones, I ought to be a happy woman. And I wouldn't say I wasn't. No. I wouldn't. Not tonight anyway.

*Sunday—Stanford*

I ought to be exhausted after such a day. By "ought to be" I mean I often am after such a day. One of the truest things Mrs. Lindbergh says is that pretense tires. When we're young we scarcely ever pretend. We don't know what to pretend then. We learn as we grow older what's expected of us, and with our ebbing strength assay more and more difficult roles. Today I pretended nothing and so, though I talked and felt much, I am not, since I moved always in the direction of my inclinations, any more than happily weary.

Yesterday Millar phoned Napa asking if we had television—he hadn't noticed—because he would like very much to see James Agee's "Lincoln," which was to be shown in a condensed version on Omnibus. We do have, and I also had hoped to see it again. I watched all of it last year. And shed tears. Not because I'm a Lincoln idolater; I'm not, nor any great movie fan either. I am a James Agee fan though, and the script he had written, together with the acting of Royal Dano, provided me with more truth and beauty than I could absorb without a simultaneous displacement of tears. Agee showed Lincoln's complexity: a man able to love—and not love at the same time; to be ambitious—and to hate ambition. Agee gave simple actions, visually lovely in themselves, horizons of meaning way beyond the eye's seeing. A scene of foot washing at nightfall—the tired workers, sitting on the doorstep as it grows darker, all of the fatigue of hoe and ax and scythe plainly showing in their bodies, making an effort toward cleanliness before bedtime, half relishing, half resenting the chore, speaking few words, listening to the sundown chirp of birds leaving the small clearing for the dark encircling forest, sighing as they cleaned themselves, but contentedly, for the day's work was over and there was rest and sleep to come. There was more of pioneering and man's worth and man's weariness in that slight scene than in many pictures which fill a wide screen for a hundred and fifteen minutes. And that meaning didn't get there by chance. It was put there, by James Agee.

The friend Millar brought to Napa was Hannah Greene, a girl I know, a teaching fellow at Stanford who was in a class of mine here a year or so ago. We watched "Lincoln" and heard Agee himself, a dark and somewhat tired-appearing man, speak of the film. We wept as the train bearing Lincoln's body home to Springfield moved across the spring country, its slow bell tolling at the crossings, its whistle leaving a white plume against the newly leafed trees.

Should a Negro woman, Millar wondered, have been chosen to put the nosegay in Lincoln's hand? Did that push the sentiment too hard? There was no question but that Negro women *did* bring flowers to Lincoln; no question but that to see this woman do so reminded us of the whole meaning of Lincoln's relationship with the Negro. Here, though, was that hairline of honesty one must walk in writing: Does the scene illuminate the meanings of the story—or is it thrown in craftily, for purposes of moving the reader? Do you (the writer) cheat the reader in this way? Seduce him, prostitute yourself? Coldly, yourself, build up the scene which will melt the reader? Or viewer? He may never know he was seduced. Weeping, he may never understand that though his tears are genuine the scene is bogus. And if he doesn't know, and if to be stirred is all he asks, why should you refuse to give the reader what he wants?

There is no reason why you should refuse if writing is the same to you as the manufacture of can openers or nutmeg graters. Then, you give the consumer what he wants, a good mechical gadget, useful, and the more impersonal the more marketable. But in nonmechanical writing you must first of all please yourself. And such writing, it is true, may be far less effective than the craftman's skillfully made mechanism.

There is no test for such scenes as the one we were discussing but the writer's own intuitions. If it moves him and seems pertinent and useful to him in developing his story the episode must be included. He must take a chance. The writer must be willing, above everything else, to take chances, to risk making a fool of himself—or even to risk revealing the fact that he *is* a fool. Oh, it's a risky affair, writing, and can never be played close to the chest, hiding everything which may give you away. That's what writing is—giving yourself away. That's the difference between real writing and writing which is concocted; the latter betrays the reader without giving away the writer.

Of course everything in writing depends upon who you are. You may give yourself away all right, and no one may want the gift. What if the self you give away, when you write, is stupid, complacent, dull, selfish, pretentious, mean? That's part of the risk. And truly stupid, dull, selfish is better than falsely wise, bright, and generous. We can love an honest rogue, but what is more offensive than a false saint?

I always feel that what moves me will move others. And I would guess that the success of books like *The Sheik* was due to no calculated effort on the author's part to excite readers, but to the writer's own excitement and bewitchment as she wrote of this desert lover so dear to her own imagination.

Millar, Hannah, and I talked about all this for two hours after the Lincoln picture was finished. Hannah writes and teaches students of writing. Millar has an unpublished novel. I have come late to writing and, except when I'm here at Stanford or places like Stanford, I can't speak of writing. Writing, in a small town, is still thought to be a strange and rather embarrassing activity. I would as soon think of beginning a conversation at a local dinner party by saying "I'm in the midst of a new love affair" than by saying "I'm in the midst of a new short story." The two announcements would be equally effective in killing further talk—until I left, anyway.

So Hannah, Millar, and I pounded the table and talked.

Millar said: "That train whistle! That beautiful heart-breaking train whistle! I wish Thomas Wolfe could've heard that."

Hannah said: "If there had to be a national sound, as there are national birds and national colors, it should be the sound of a train whistle."

Millar said: "A train whistle echoing across a prairie, at sunset. And one boy beside a soddy, listening and looking."

Hannah said: "Would it sound different, across a prairie?"

Millar said: "Very different. Didn't that train whistle from a train moving across a land of farms in spring and carrying the dead Lincoln have a different sound from any other you've ever heard?"

Hannah said: "It did, it did."

Miller said: "Why does a train whistle mean so much to Americans?"

I said: "It stitches us together. And it separated us. We got on a westbound train with all our household goods. We said good-by to the folks back East and to the old homestead and the known climate and the familiar ways. And the train whistled as we pulled out of the depot, and mother's face—we were never to see it again—was wet with tears. And the train whistled as we crossed the thousands and thousands of miles, the big rivers, the everlasting deserts, the sky-touching mountains. And it whistled when it pulled into another depot, a depot surrounded by geraniums head-tall; and we got out and looked up at a blank cloudless sky through the fronds of palm trees that moved together with a dry homesick sound. And we stood there, strangers in a strange land, and the train moved away slowly. And we listened to it whistling in the distance, out of sight. And the sound was the same sound we had heard as we kissed mother good-by; and the sound was the same sound we had heard as we lay in our beds back East and longed fiercely to escape from the worn-out farm and the worn-out ways and the mean prejudices and the piddling virtues to something bigger and better. Oh, it's the sound that separated us and it's the sound that stitches us together. And we can't hear it without crying for what's lost, without marveling at what lies in between, and without rejoicing at having escaped, and without yearning for what lies ahead. It's the strongest, most moving sound for an American there is."

Millar said: "Tom Wolfe was the first to recognize it."

Hannah said: "If the distances weren't so great it wouldn't be the same. I suppose only the Russians can feel about a train whistle as we do."

Millar said: "Tsk, tsk. Don't go comparing us with the Russians."

I said: "They've got still another dimension to their train whistling—Siberia. They must cry even harder when they hear it . . . than we do."

Millar said: "Tom Wolfe's *Look Homeward, Angel* must be made into a movie someday."

I said: "That would be a hard book to put on the screen."

Millar said: "Willy could do it. He must do it."

I said: *"The Friendly Persuasion* doesn't seem to me an easy book to film."

Millar said: "It will not be easy. But ws can lick the book."

He said this in quotes, but I was startled to have those Quaker stories spoken of as a tiger to be tamed. Then I talked for an hour without stopping about how I thought it should be done. When I finished, Millar said, "It's a great pity that you are too deep in your novel to give any thought to the film."

"Yes," I said, "it is. But those Quakers are past history with me. I can't understand writing a book about fishing or hoboes or the South Seas and then becoming a fish or a hobo or a South Seas writer for the rest of your life. I have no intention of becoming the sweet singer of Quakerdom, the good gray novelist."

Millar said, "That's fine," and had another glass of beer.

I said, "I refuse to spend my days thinking about something that I finished with ten years ago."

Millar said, "If you have finished with them, that would certainly be folly."

"Completely finished," I assured him. "Though I wish you luck in your project."

"Thank you," said Millar. "I will tell Willy you wish him luck."

By this time it was about four. Except for beer, peanuts, and the like, none of us had had anything to eat since a midmorning breakfast. "Now," I said. "I will cook us something to eat." But Millar had a much better idea. "I will buy us something to eat on the way to Palo Alto."

I can't cook and talk. I can't even walk and talk. I can't anything and anything. So, since I was still full of talk, I had hated to substitute potatoes and lettuce leaves and knives and forks for words. My bags were already packed for Palo Alto, so we were on our way in a few minutes, still talking.

There are two barriers that often prevent communication between the young and their elders. The first is middle-aged forgetfulness of the fact that they themselves are no longer young. The second is youthful ignorance of the fact that the middle aged are still alive. It is so easy for a middle-aged person, in the presence of youth, to be deluded about his own age. The young faces are so exactly like the one he saw in his own mirror—only day before yesterday, it seems.

The young, on the other hand, look into visages dull-eyed, long-toothed, wattle-necked, and chop-fallen, something they have never been and which they cannot imagine ever being. The young (to judge by myself when young) look at the middle-aged and despise them for permitting this to happen to them. If it occurs to a young person, looking at us, that this is the direction in which he himself travels, how can he forgive, let alone bear the sight of, us, who constantly bring him the bad news of our own faces, bitter signposts pointing to his own destination?

These signposts are most easily disregarded, though never entirely forgotten, when young and old do the same work. The young farmer talks happily to the old farmer, the young printer to the old printer, the young horse trainer to the old horse trainer, because they live outside appearances.

So Millar and Hannah and I talked together like word farmers interested in planting and harvesting a crop of good writing. We stopped outside San Francisco at a place that serves roast beef and fresh horse-radish and salads made of vegetables that, though detached from the soil, have not yet died. We had a bottle of Napa Valley wine. Millar and Hannah had experienced a life common to their generation and of which I knew nothing except by hearsay. Millar had been a soldier in Europe; Hannah had worked for a year in a displaced-persons camp. It is a wonder to me that such persons are willing to make the effort to communicate something of that world to us outsiders. It is not difficult, somebody said, to communicate another age or life to others, it is impossible. It probably is, but I caught glimpses.

Millar, because he and Hannah were going to be late to a party, left the table to make a phone call. Turning to see where he went, I saw at the table next to ours two Napa people, owners of a shop where I often buy paper and ink. When Millar left the phone booth, I rose to meet him and to introduce him to my townspeople. I don't know how to move leisurely. I had on high heels. I was heated with conversation. I traversed the distance between their table and ours on the backside of my natural-silk dress, splendid for scooting, and pulled up with dazzling dexterity on my knees in a position remindful of the late Al Jolson, and there presented not Mammy but "Mr. Millar, Mr. Wyler's assistant" to the Napanese. Mr. Millar, who had missed seeing the means by which I achieved this attitude of prayer and song, was astounded. My townspeople, who had seen all, including the bottle on the table, were aghast. Mr. Millar hauled me to my feet, where I explained. "I am unaccustomed to high heels." This, I could see, was not what anyone felt I was unaccustomed to. I tottered back, assisted by Mr. Millar, to our table, giving proof at every step, I thought, of the truth of my explanation. But on further thought, perhaps not.

"I often tell myself," I told Hannah and Mr. Millar, "that I should like to live like a poet. But when I do what poets have often done I think it would be better to wish only to write like a poet."

"Dylan Thomas," said Hannah, "never took a better prat fall."

Mr. Millar, to whom things were now explained, said,

"I never get inside a telephone booth without regretting it."

*Monday*
5:00 P.M.

No one can be taught to be a writer. But it is possible to learn to write better. This can be done by reading, writing, and living. In just what order I'm not sure. I do too much reading. I was amazed, envious, and awed to read Gladys Schmitt's statement that she permitted herself only half an hour of reading a day. I wish I had that discipline!

What environments are best for learning to write better? Is a university campus, on which other writers live and to which other writers come, a good environment? Will it hurt a young writer to talk to other and older writers? I don't know. I don't come over here to help young writers. How could I, when I'm not sure that I and others like me *are* a help? I don't come over to make money. The way for a novelist and short-story writer to make money is by writing novels and short stories. I come over here to help myself. I come over here because I do not want to become a confirmed solitary, to forget the modes of human speech, or to live outside the currents of my own times. I come over here because I love books, I love writing, and like all lovers, I enjoy speaking of my beloved. I come over here because it is comfortable to have my writing taken for granted. I come over here for some of the same reasons that bring veterans of foreign wars, plumbers, and typesetters to conventions. All conversations in which anything must be explained are stymied before they start. I come over here because I like the people here—Stegner and Scowcroft, who head the writing school, and their wives.

I have found that writers do less conversational skirmishing around in the outskirts of the platitudinous, the careful, and the conventional than most people. They are quicker to say what they feel (and God knows why anything else should ever be said) than most people. Stegner,

61

walking with me today across the grass of the campus, said, after some silence, "I remember when I saw the first lawns, the first grass planted in regularly shaped plots—not for the crop, not for any use except to look pretty. I came down from Saskatchewan, and I saw these rectangles and squares of mowed grass. I'll never forget the feeling . . . the amazement, though I can't remember exactly what its content was. It was of strangeness, I suppose, mostly. That people lived like this. That while I'd been living in Saskatchewan, this had been going on. And that Saskatchewan would seem as strange to them."

This is what one person can give another if he is willing to speak from the inside out: Stegner gave me in fifty words a boy's life twenty-five years ago in the pioneer-world of Saskatchewan. I shall never see lawns again without thinking of it.

*Tuesday*

Hannah brought me some coffee from the student eating place, so I don't have to get up, dress, and go out to get some. I have to make a speech tonight, and the thought of it woke me up half a dozen times in the night. And I woke up for good and all, or for bad and all, at five and went over it again. The idea of speechmaking nauseates me. Why do I do it? As far as I can see, there are only three reasons for speechmaking. 1. To make money: a job like wood chopping or window washing. But I don't need the money. 2. To grind an ax. To persuade people to be vegetarians or Socialists or to vote the party ticket or to join the army. I don't have an ax to grind. 3. To entertain people. To put on an act. To be a Mark Twain or a Chauncey Depew. To "perform," to do a "turn" as jugglers or monocylists do. Well, I can't do this either. In addition to my own feelings of nausea, remembering that I must make a speech, I have no memory of having ever heard, to my pleasure or profit, a speech made by anyone else. If they're good, they go too fast for me; if they're not good, they don't go fast enough.

62

Look at the women who have made speeches: Carry Nation, Emma Willard, Emmeline Pankhurst, and Mrs. Percy B. Pennybacker. Good women, all. Look at the women who haven't made speeches: Emily Brontë, Jane Austen, Emily Dickinson, Duse, Pavlova, and Maude Adams. I am certainly not on the side of the angels! Carry, Emma, Emmeline, and Mrs. Percy B., here I come. And they, with their causes, had justification for speaking. What's my justification? What, even, is the stumbling block that sends me tripping onto a platform?

I say yes reluctantly to invitations to speak. I despise the process of writing a speech. I have the megrims and the mulligrubs for twenty-four hours before speaking. I hate myself, and particularly I hate Max, if he's around, for permitting me to get into such a predicament. He knows how I feel about speaking; he knows how weak my character is in the matter of being unable to say no; he puts his foot down about plenty of things. Why didn't he put his foot down about this? I feel like calling him this minute to tell him how much I blame him for this misery. True, if he put his foot down about an invitation to speak I had accepted, phoned Stegner, for instance, to say, "I'm sorry but I have forbidden Jessamyn to make any more speeches," I would undoubtedly make things quite uncomfortable for him for a while. But must he always be thinking of his own comfort?

Why do I do it? Because it's difficult? Because unconsciously I remember something? Remember that once in a while midway in a speech something strange happens? I have been lumbering and sweating along, when suddenly, out of the audience in front of me comes something to which no name can be given but which has the power of conveying the impression that my isolation as a human being is forever finished. Only one person speaks—me—but at that moment of nuptial union (and I drank half a cup of coffee before deciding that those two words were the right ones) at that moment my voice seems to be theirs, or rather my voice seems to be an instrument for expressing them. And if this happens to me, delivering a prepared speech on an unexciting literary topic, what, what must be the glories and temptations, the sweet evil powers of oratory for the born orator? The man who *has* an ax to grind; who is able to make of his body, his voice, and his eyes and his hands instruments for the communication and arousing of emotion. The preacher and the politican may be less men who use speechmaking to forward religious and political causes than men so in love with the sensations of this mystical mass union that they have found professions in which they can regularly experience these sensations. For the real orator, the old-fashioned uninhibited ranter, the union between audience and himself may be a substitute for sexual union or an incitement to sexual union.

Speechmaking, which is prolonged talk, is as excessive in its way as is solitude, which is prolonged silence. Did Blake say, "Excesses are the path to wisdom"? One more speech or so and I should be wise.

And yet, when it is all over, how good is the peace and quiet, the feeling of convalescence after illness, and the reassuring conviction that enough antibodies have now been built up to save you for a long time from another such attack. Speechmaking is something like "natural birth," I suppose. Painful to endure, but oh, the glorious sense of achievement afterward. Question: How many female speechmakers are childless?

*Stanford*
*Friday, 4:00* P.M.

Waiting for Max. Sitting on one wicker chair, feet on the other, areaway window by my side. I can't sit in a room with my back to the window—any more than I can sit (with any pleasure) in a restaurant with my back to the people. Now I see students, not going anywhere, but sitting, walking, talking; posture, pace, and intonation saying "Friday." For anyone who has done considerable going to school, or teaching, Friday afternoons feel like prison gates opening. Monday is light-years away. The students go past my window with everlastingness in their gait and forever in their voices. They drawl, twine fingers, don't bother to laugh—as they have been doing all week. Time for that tomorrow. Polyps and corals in time. Boys and girls lean against the railing. There is time to touch the bark of a tree, to watch a fat cat who is pretending to himself that he could catch a towhee if he wanted to.

My week's work is finished, should have been better. Should have found one word to say which would have lowered one rail of the fence that keeps someone from breaking through into clearer? purer? truer? expression. Can't take down my own fence rails. Blind leading the blind.

Max will be late. Temperamentally he is the artist in this family. I wish God had not set a little tin alarm clock ticking some place at the back of my skull. I know the time of day. I can look at the clock on the hour, every hour. If Max says, "We should be on our way at six in the morning," I am awake with a start at five. He sleeps on. I am far too suggestible, particularly to the wrong suggestions. I would like to live like Max and Napoleon and Caesar, sleeping as I breathe—when I need a breath. Max loses himself in a job; I do not. I know the position of the sun in the sky, and have a tropism, no less demanding than Blake's sunflower, that compels me to follow it. Max leads a far more natural life than I: he can rise at any hour, sleep at any hour, eat at any hour—or not sleep and not eat for hours. I wish I had this gift, but it is not one to be had by mere imitation. I can, by an act of will, imitate him. But my imitation does not result in a reasonable facsimile. It results in an unreasonable invalid.

And yet . . . and yet. Mama, whom I resemble, am like in these matters, though I'm a pale copy, has had two strokes—which, except for some impairment of memory, have not troubled her much. One of the things she forgot was that she couldn't sleep well, that noises troubled her, that her sleeping times must be regular. Having forgotten all of this she sleeps as she breathes now, naturally and when she needs it. Is habitualness a learned weakness?

I wish I could forget, as I wish I could unlearn, the need to "straighten" the house before writing. One flower hanging lopsided from a jar will interrupt the best sentence I ever wrote. Rebecca West said somewhere that there is a slut in all the best writers, and I believe it. But there's no use trying to imitate sluttishness, either. If at birth your bad fairy put a curse of housekeeping blood in your veins

65

there is no escape except to work it out. You can't be free of it till the beds are made and the flowers picked and the fire laid. After *that*, you can pick up the pen. I envy men who write, who *can* write, without having their pen hands yearning toward a plow handle. Men were farmers and women were housekeepers for centuries together. But men moved easily away from hog trough and sheep barn and upland meadow. Why is the breakaway so much harder for women? Are women a thousand times more habitual than men? The "power of the first" is strong for persons of both sexes. Is it a thousand times stronger for women? Are they committed with bonds of which men know nothing to the first man in their lives? Does this "power of the first" explain the guilt I feel if I write before shaking the tablecloth or stacking the magazines? Women tidied up before they ever wrote, and at heart, or at diaphram or cerebellum . . . wherever these things center, are still housekeepers.

We drove at dusk yesterday through hills along a winding road to the Stegners' for a party.

I call a party any occasion when twelve people or more meet after dark to eat and drink. I don't often go to parties. Perhaps that is why I like them. I like the counterpoint of voices and ideas, of movement and laughter. I like the eddying of a party in a house as large as the Stegners', where one can idle in a backwater or fight for footing where the current is the strongest. I like our meeting now and then to honor each other with our best food and our prettiest dresses. I like the putting out of mind for an evening and for the sake of others our resentments and sorrows (insofar as this is possible). I like the religious sound of a party. Religious? Religious. A party, like a meeting for worship, is not operating on the level of reason. It, too, is transcendental. It transcends logic. It slides willingly and consciously (if it is a good party) toward a celebration of the fact of being alive. The celebrants at a party share bread and wine and reach toward a communal touching, for a moment, of an existence that is not limited by the individual ego. The sound of a party is a sound of amity, of human beings who have become for a moment, and for nonaggressive reasons, something outside themselves.

After supper, when people were talking by threes and fours instead of dozens, Mary Stegner came walking through the rooms calling, "Jessamyn, Jessamyn, a long-distance call."

"Long-distance?" I asked. We don't expect bad news by telegraph any more, but by long-distance.

Either to reassure me or to dramatize this moment, with an audience attentive to the drama, she said, "Long-distance. Hollywood calling Miss Jessamyn West." The audience already knew that I had been brought to Stanford by Hollywood and it was prepared and even eager for further developments. Though if one were to receive a call from Hollywood this was not the perfect audience to listen in on the conversation. This was, by any present-day standards, a collection of eggheads, and, while most of them did not hate the movies, none of them felt, either, that the best writing of this decade was coming out of Hollywood.

I went into Mary's room, sat on the bed, and spoke into the phone.

"Miss West?"

"This is she."

"One moment for Hollywood, please."

Hollywood was Mr. Millar, as I had supposed it would be. He had returned to Hollywood, driving all night, after he had delivered me here on Sunday.

"Jezzamyn?" Mr. Millar makes z's of the s's in my name, giving it a sound of bees preparing to swarm, which I like.

"Mr. Millar?" I would like to get away from calling Mr. Millar, Mr. Millar. I don't know why it is difficult for me to call people by their first names. Old-fashioned, rural, stand-offish? It is no Quaker custom. Even Quaker children called adult strangers by their names. "Good morning, John Woolman," without any nonsense of "Mistering." Sometimes I think it is the residue of a false coquettishness, picked up from the reading of hundreds of romantic novels when I was a child. In those books females did not break down into masculine first names until a tenderly significant moment came along, at which time they raised

67

their shamefast eyes and said with wonderful, brave, adorable, hesitation, "Mr. Woolman . . . John." And it meant something, in those novels I read when I was nine, when a woman said for the first time a man's first name. It was about the equal in excitement of—I don't know *what* in a modern novel. In the realm of the meetings of the sexes perhaps nothing nowadays equals it. As Henri Michaux says, "After two or three rapes, a few flagellations and acts against nature, say what you may the astonishment wears off and you fall asleep over your book." Perhaps no one nowadays appreciates sex as did the maiden ladies who wrote the novels of my childhood. However, the time is past both personally and fictionally for me to try to revive the excitement of the postponed first name. Mr. Millar is never going to be aware of the moment or its tenderness when I lift my eyes the twelve inches they will have to travel to reach his, and say, "Stuart." And I myself may become too lost in talk of the kind we had Sunday to remember to memorialize the moment.

Stuart said: "Willy would like you to come down for a week and talk about *The Friendly Persuasion* with him. He'll pay your expenses and salary."

From this proposal I retreated as quickly as possible. Not for egghead reasons, but for my own less sensible ones. I can quickly and impulsively go after something. But I cannot quickly and impulsively say yes in answer to an invitation. I must first say no if it is possible, and by this maneuver, if that is the word for it, put the offer (of whatever it is) almost beyond my reach. Then when I have rid myself of the menace of something moving toward me, when in fact the movement, if any, is in the other direction, I can wholeheartedly and impulsively reach for it. It is as if I could not really love and want anything I was offered, anything, that is, in and for itself, but must value it chiefly for its inaccessibility, for the fact that it does not want me.

This reasoning, though reason is the last word that belongs here, explains, Kenneth Burke says, the otherwise inexplicable fondness writers have for their failures, the books which no one else can read. These they defend as the best thing they have ever done, their great undervalued masterpieces. Why? Because they scorn the words, the themes, the scenes they conquered in the books that succeeded and that others praise. Only this, the meaning that eluded them, the character that never came to life, the words that refused to flow, they honor. They honor what is beyond them, the bird on whose tail they were able to shake no salt. A crazy, false humility. I should like someday to write a hymn to that undervalued bird, the bird with a salted tail.

In life, as literature, there is no royal path to happiness. But the tendency, if it can't be controlled, should at least be understood. I understood it well enough as I told Stuart, "No, no. That's impossible. I'm going to the University of Washington week after next, for one thing. For another, the novel. For another, I do not want to be mixed up any more with those Quakers in *The Friendly Persuasion*. Any further relationship with them is incestuous. And I don't want to be mixed up with the movies, either."

Stuart said: "This would not mix you up very much. Just to talk for a few days with Willy."

So I told him I would think it over and call him back. I didn't think it over. I put it out of my mind until this morning. Then I asked Hannah to call Stuart and find out exactly what it is that I am turning down. I hate phoning, particularly if anything important is involved. I like a filter to subtract the immediacy from the occasion.

Hannah phoned and I didn't listen. She came back after a while and said, "What you are turning down is five hundred dollars, princely living quarters, and the opportunity to talk with a genius."

"Who's the genius?" I asked.

"Willy," said Hannah.

"I bet Willy would die if he knew the way Stuart cries his name in the wilderness."

"Maybe he *is* a genius," said Hannah.

"Name some geniuses," I told Hannah.

Hannah hasn't spent twenty-five years in school for nothing. "Dante, Homer, Shakespeare, Leonardo, Mozart, Beethoven . . ."

"I think Willy is talented."

"Five hundred dollars is peanuts," said Hannah.

"It is not peanuts to me," said I, "but it is peanuts to the movies. I read movie magazines."

"They probably don't know you do. They probably don't even guess it."

"Small impecunious colleges pay me five hundred dollars for a week."

"They don't know this either," Hannah said. "My impression is that Hollywood doesn't know much about life on the outside. You read movie magazines. But they don't read college bulletins."

"It is not worth my while to go," I told Hannah. "I'm going to the University of Washington next week. I'll see a real genius there—Ted Roethke. Ted, with all the geniuses I've met around Stanford this week, is all the genius I can take for a while."

"The princely quarters!" exclaimed Hannah. "You cannot say these quarters are princely." She looked about my chintz and wicker basement.

"It was good enough for Auden and Spender and Elizabeth Bowen," said I, "and princely quarters are quarters where princes have lived. Name me some better princes."

"I wonder what Hollywood calls princely?"

"Something that costs too much."

"It would be a pity never to know," said Hannah. "Wouldn't it?"

"Never to know what?"

"What they call princely."

I phoned Max and told him what had happened. "What shall I do?" I asked.

Max is able to say yes to what approaches him.

"Go," he said, "at once. Of course. What's to be lost?"

"Time. A whole week of time."

Max went "tsk, tsk," and I said, "The Copes! What will happen to the Copes if I play fast and loose with them this way?"

"The Copes," Max said, "you have always with you. You can't always go down to talk with Mr. Wyler."

"It may turn into more than talk," I said miserably. "I'm already getting too interested in these Quakers."

"Take a chance," Max said.

"Henry Volkening and Ned Brown will fume and fret if I say yes without consulting them."

"Fuming and fretting," said Max, "is what agents are for.

70

Tell Millar you'll come down, if Henry doesn't say no to the terms."

"I'm not talking to Millar," I said.

"What d' you mean you're not talking to him? How're you carrying on these negotiations?"

"Hannah's doing the talking."

"Well, for Pete's sake," Max said. "Let me talk to Hannah."

Max talked to Hannah. And when they finished she said, "Max says to send a telegram to Henry saying that if he doesn't object to the terms, you are going. Then he says to call Millar and say you'll arrive in Los Angeles on the Owl Monday morning and for him to meet you."

"He didn't say for Willy to meet me?"

"He would've if he'd thought of it, I expect."

"Hannah, how would you like to have a husband selling you down the river to Hollywood this way?"

Hannah didn't answer that question. Instead, she said, "This way, if you hate the whole thing you can blame Max for getting you into it."

"And you, Hannah, too. I can blame you."

Hannah asked, "Whom shall I call first? Henry or Stu?"

I said, "Send a wire to Henry. 522 Fifth Avenue. New York. Then phone Stu."

She did, in that order. Now I can't wait for Max to get here. How can he be so calm and so late in the midst of this mess I'm in?

# II

## On the Owl

Poor maligned Owl. Bird, not train. This train could not be maligned. Except that it is nocturnal, nothing could less resemble that silent flyer. Murchie, the man who wrote about winds, taught me about owls too. Their feathers are so arranged that when they fly they absorb more sound than they make. This Owl, no flyer, but a nightly traveler between San Francisco and Los Angeles and vice versa, makes more sound than anything whatsoever could absorb —let alone itself or its passengers. I often think that they put engineers on the Owl for the purpose of practicing bumps, jerks, false starts, and precipitate stops; for perfecting grinding, grating, and lurching techniques. "Men," somebody in charge of young engineers says, "it is impossible to recognize the good without knowledge of the bad. Take the Owl out tonight and show me you know the difference." These are engineers with a conscience. They know the difference.

They have taken the dining room off the Owl and replaced it with a snack bar which serves hamburgers, chile con carne, fried eggs, packaged breakfast foods, and canned juices. The Negro waiters who run this bar are all statuesque men with scornful faces. They hate running a hamburger stand and are scarcely able to tolerate its customers. This morning, a seven- or eight-year-old colored girl, dark and sweet as licorice in stiff blue organdy, with brown-purple pansy eyes and spike curls shining like polished steel, asked for "a soft fried egg." This, I thought, would melt the hauteur of these big fellows. It didn't. The egg was fried, and slammed down, with the same efficient dislike with which we were all served. They, at least, are free of race prejudice. We are neither black nor white to them, but eaters, all of us stupid enough to put up with this kind of makeshift roadside feeding arrangement.

The Owl is my second home. I have traveled on it since graduate-student days in Berkeley. One of the waiters recognized me this morning. "Making the trip again," he said accusingly. I nodded apologetically. Ordinarily this would have been the end of our conversation, but the fact that I was Hollywood bound must have shown in some such way as to make me more than usually noticeable. Though not noticeable in any manner which I could easily or happily have anticipated. "You're a nurse, aren't you?" he asked. "A trained nurse?"

There is nothing I would like less to be taken for. Florence Nightingale was obviously filled with charm; but in my long experience with trained nurses she must have been the last, as she was the first, of her kind. Perhaps association with the ailing makes nurses what they are. Perhaps, instead, there was inherent in them from the beginning those qualities of domineering hardness which, as calculating sadists, they early recognized could be more fully expressed in the sickroom than elsewhere.

I took corn flakes, tinned juice, and coffee, very downcast, to a table and tried hard to act unnursely. Two things kept me from asking the waiter to elucidate. The first was that I feared hearing even more unpleasant facts. The second was that he was a man. My upbringing was such that I cannot easily converse with men as though they were normal human beings. They are too special for that. God knows how much knowledge and insight and sense and nonsense I've missed because of this.

I love train travel, even on the Owl. Perhaps especially on the Owl. You know you're traveling when you're on the Owl. It's probably nearer to the stagecoach in motion than any public conveyance still operating. I never sleep so well as when rocked and jolted on the Owl. I don't know much about Mary Baker Eddy but I respect her for one thing. She, too, liked being rocked, and instead of saying, when she was grown, "I am too old for rocking now," she said, "I like rocking," and had an adult-sized cradle built and got into it and rocked. I am ignorant of *Science and Health* as a manual, but as action this seems to me healthful and unscientific.

I first rode on a train at the age of six, when we Wests came to California. My next trip was at the age of twenty-five, New York bound to catch a ship to England. My sorrow at leaving home and husband was so great that I cried constantly en route. My fellow passengers believed me bound for a funeral which would put most of my family underground. I spoke to no one. Through ignorance and too proud to ask, I drank all the way east from the tank containing the tooth-wash water, though iced water would have been a blessing. It was summer, it was before air conditioning, I was traveling tourist in a car without screens and filled with numerable mothers and innumerable babies, all moving eastward to spend the summer with Grandma on the farm. The babies screamed without ceasing. There were only two nonmothers (in addition to the children) in the car. I and a handsome Australian. Alas, he was male, which made it impossible for me to talk to him; though he, in desperation, bored with the heat, the nursing mothers, the drying diapers, and the squalling children, tried again and again to strike up a conversation. I stared him down. He asked me where I would be staying in New York and I gave him a false address, proud of the quick-wittedness with which I circumvented his advances.

Mama had packed fruit for my journey in a hamper the size of a washtub. It took up all the space between my seat and the seat I faced. In addition to being bereaved, the passengers considered me a food faddist of some sort. Mama, thinking quite rightfully that I would try to live on ham sandwiches, peanuts, and popcorn, had attempted to balance my diet with some less desiccated objects. I was, or thought I was, a Stoic in those days. I read and adored Seneca. I was not a convert of his. Rather, on reading him, I felt that he was a follower of mine. By what chance of environment or temperament I had fallen into the drunken pleasures of doing without, I know not. Intoxicating those pleasures are, though. To live hard when you can live soft inflates the ego and exacerbates the nerves by which one experiences the world. On this trip, though I could have afforded it, I scorned those who took lower berths, traveled first class, and ate in the dining car. At home I hated heated rooms, people who had doctors when ill, people who permitted themselves to *be* ill, or wore bedroom slippers; I hated people who stopped, once even, to rest on five-hundred-mile automobile trips; I despised people who used iodine or mercurochrome, who bandaged blisters or wounds; I thought there was a weak strain in persons who wore sweaters, rubbers, raincoats, took warm baths, paid the slightest attention to what they ate, and couldn't chin themselves; I especially mistrusted people who read moderately. I once heard a woman say that she had never in her life lost a handkerchief, and thereafter I avoided her as inhuman. I never owned a handkerchief or a pair of gloves as a young woman. This does not mean that I wasn't mad about clothes. I was and had far more silks in richer colors than was either necessary or suitable for a girl on a ranch. I could have *them* and remain a Stoic because *they* weren't necessary to me. My policy was to spend all for luxury but not one cent for necessities.

I understand very well the power the ascetic feels, how everything he does without, which his neighbor requires, fills him with a raw festering sense of superiority. The superiority of the man who has vastly more than his neighbors is nothing compared with it. Abstinence is in the beginning, perhaps, a substitute and a compensation for worlds unconquered and which should be conquered. The persistent ascetic, who becomes dissatisfied with this substitute world of his own conquered appetites, is a dangerous man. Shakespeare spoke of him. Germany experienced him. I lived mildly for about ten years going without bedroom slippers and gloves and iodine. Tuberculosis changed all that for me, gave me another substitute world to conquer, though one which had to be conquered in an entirely different way.

The hotel I lied to the Australian about was the St. James. I knew nothing concerning the St. James Hotel except that it had an unworldly name and advertised in the *Atlantic Monthly*. The ads said that it was an ideal place for women traveling alone. An ad in the *Atlantic* was the equal, in my mind, of a personal introduction by its editor, Henry Dwight Sedgwick, to the hotel's owner. And I knew Mr. Sedgwick would never entrust a young female subscriber to any undependable man. So I went to the St. James as perfectly confident as the young mothers homeward bound to grandmother for the summer.

The St. James was not what I had expected. In the first place, no one not brought up amidst the emptiness of western hills can imagine the frightful, crowding, deafening, roaring abundance of a great city. And the St. James was set down in the middle of some of the most crowded and menacing parts of this abundance. In addition, the ladies at the St. James were far from traveling alone. They could not, however, have been nicer. Many of them were actresses. Actresses were too far from any world I had ever known to suggest to me that I should find out *who* they were. Actresses belonged to a separate species like swans, peacocks, and leopards, and I would as soon have thought, traveling in Asia or Africa, of saying "Miss Leopard, what is your given name?" as of being personal with an actress. They sized me up very quickly and kindly, saw that I knew next to nothing, not even the directions. "Left, right, and straight up is about the whole of it," said one beautiful creature. She had the first painted fingernails I had ever seen. I could not take my unbelieving eyes off them. The St. James ladies wrote minute, explicit directions for me. "Turn left as you leave the hotel. Walk for five blocks. Turn right, walk for six blocks." Etc. With these directions I turned up where I wanted to go: the public library, Times Square, Tiffany's.

I had a little gold heart my father had bought at Tiffany's and brought home to the backwoods of southern Indiana when I was a baby. Tiffany's had been the highwater mark of his traveling, and I wanted to stand there where he had stood when he made the historic purchase.

Following the accurate directions of the ladies of the St. James, Tiffany's was where I found myself. They, very wisely, did not trust my ability to reverse their directions and so return safely home; instead, they wrote out in full carefully reversed directions. They asked me before I left the hotel at what time I would be back and were concerned if I did not arrive on time. All in all, the *Atlantic Monthly* and Mr. Sedgwick, though I doubt they had envisioned the ministrations of the ladies of the St. James when they accepetd the hotel's ad, could not have done better by me.

I walked everywhere. My reasons for doing this were not stoical but pusillanimous. I had never been on a bus, in a taxi or an elevated in my life, let alone gone down a hole in the ground to a subway. I tried once to get on a bus but bungled the whole business from boarding to paying so thoroughly that the bus driver abandoned bus driving to berate me—complete with some mild cussing. I had never in my life heard any cussing stronger than my father's "doggone it" or my grandfather's "oh sugar." To be publicly cussed was about as shameful in my opinion as to be publicly beaten. I myself said "hell" and "damn" out of sheer bravado; but I used these strong words only when alone and would never have directed them, any more than a bullet, at a living person.

I no doubt looked absolutely crazy to the bus driver; and my meekness, in addition, must have maddened him beyond all restraint. In spite of the fact that I was five feet seven and a matron of five years, I had a round freckled Mellen's food baby face. I had no idea of suitable traveling clothes or even, for that matter, of suitable street clothes. My idea, in dress, was to put on something pretty; and my idea of something pretty was plenty of color, plenty of ruffles, a low neck by the standards of twenty-five years ago and a snug waist. I had a small waist, and was proud of it. I disregarded the fact that cinching in my waist emphasized the fact that my shoulders were broad and my hips wide. Also, I liked big flowery hats. The bus driver probably thought I'd be better off locked up.

I met, or rather was spoken to, in the lobby of the St. James, by a man *I* thought should be locked up. I was sitting in the lobby reading, partly because I liked reading, partly because I wanted to have something to do with my eyes when people stared at me. I knew there was a man in the chair next to mine. I could tell if a man entered the hotel door fifty feet away. This man next to me suddenly turned to me and said emphatically, "There goes a fairy if I ever saw one."

I looked up to see a somewhat short, stocky, brown-haired, olive-skinned young man pass in front of me. There was something a little unusual about his appearance, though it would have been hard to say what; if fancifully inclined you might call him an elf or a brownie or even a gnome but no one in his right mind could see anything in that young man which could call to mind the gossamer wings, the star-tipped wand, and the general iridescence of a fairy. At this mad pronouncement I gave the man next to me a look of real fright, rushed to my room, and for the rest of my stay at the St. James steered clear of him. He was obviously a victim of delusions, possibly an ambulatory sufferer of delirium tremens, and would be seeing green snakes and pink elephants next—a person who could see a fairy in that perfectly ordinary, slightly plump young man was capable of any aberration.

We are passing through country that looks like one of my homes, for I have two homes: southern Indiana and southern California. This makes me, I suppose, a Southerner of sorts. I only live in northern California. We're lurching along downgrade through the dry hills south of Bakersfield. The landscape of childhood is, for me anyway, the yardstick by which I judge other landscapes. When I say "I don't like it," I only mean "It doesn't look like anything I knew as a child." I am like Marty's mother. When he tried to pin her down to some real reasons for not liking his new girl, all she could say was "She don't look Italian to me." "I don't like it" means, when I say it, "It don't look southern California to me." That is, the southern California of my youth, which was essentially a country of unobscured horizons, of few trees, of brown hills ringed by mountains and sea. I wait, always with some excitement, when I go south for the sight of the first orange grove. It signified for me the entrance to the heartland.

This will be an odd home-coming. Though Hollywood is only twenty-five miles away from Yorba Linda, where I grew up, it is as remote to me as Africa in everything except its mountail wall, its palm and pepper trees, its afternoon and evening breezes off the Pacific. I think I went once to Grauman's Chinese Theatre as a child. Once, one of those Sunday afternoon auto drives Papa and Mama loved, we went past a hillside where Ben Turpin was making passes at a securely tethered bull. Or at what we were supposed to believe a bull. Though there was no mistaking those energetically in-turned eyes of Turpin's. We didn't pause long. Motion-picture making, if that was a sample, seemed boring.

Once I sat in the Philharmonic Auditorium three or four rows behind Doug and Mary. They looked so much like themselves it was disappointing—I had as well have gone to the movies. Or better. The same looks there plus a story. Otherwise, except for my familiarity with the Hollywood of the beauty-parlor movie magazines, the town to which I go is as unfamiliar as New York was when I was twenty-five. And no ladies of the St. James to guide me. Only Stuart.

Last night the train got mixed up with a skunk, and skunk scent was pumped into my room for a while through the air-conditioning system. How sweet amidst the mechanical and the mechanized to be once again in touch with reality! I stretched in my berth with pleasure. I'm glad the skunk got the train—though I hope the train didn't get the skunk—but I accepted the smell as a good omen. Hollywood bound, but not yet divorced, completely, from the country.

Well, I'm on Wilshire Boulevard in my princely residence—a white apartment hotel, built in imitation of a pillared southern mansion. With my southern background I should feel at home. I do. I've been in many a good motel exactly like it. My quarters consist of sitting room with a kitchen alcove, bedroom, and bath. The place is so thoroughly and heavily carpeted, curtained, and upholstered that I feel like a stowaway in a dry-goods counter. I have lint in my teeth, and my finger tips are tingling with textures.

I'm on the second floor, twenty-five feet above and fifty feet away from the six lanes of Wilshire Boulevard. I've been trying to decide what kind of a car to buy, and this is the perfect place to look them over; hundreds of new ones go by every minute. It would be unfortunate to be here and uninterested in cars, for there is nothing else, except a couple of Hawaiian-style apartment hotels on the other side of the boulevard, to be seen.

My poor little Dodge convertible! It has served me faithfully for seven years, and I feel, sitting here at the window, like an unappreciative husband come to town to look over the girls. In addition to serving me faithfully it was my first car, so there's that special tie as well. But last winter Max bought so much hay for the horses he had to take over the garage as a hay barn. Some winters this wouldn't have mattered, but last winter was unusually wet, and my poor Dodge, already a little thin on top, absorbed considerable water. The continuous downpour, plus a winter warm as well as wet, brought up on the carpeting between the front and back seats not only a fine stand of volunteer oats but something far more exotic, a fine crop of fungi, toadstools or mushrooms, I never knew which. The idea of traveling about in a kind of Napa-version floating island appealed to me. When we had a dry spell I sprinkled, surreptitiously, my crop. People were pleasantly surprised when I opened the door, and I myself liked the adornment much better than a red rose in a vase held by brackets. My oats and fungi were indigenous. When the crop failed, as was only natural, at the close of the rainy season I did nothing to revive it. I desired nothing unnatural. I cleaned the car as best I could, a combination of uprooting, mowing, and sweeping, but since then the car has had the humid earthy smell of a root cellar. Passengers sniff, but I tell them it is nothing but last year's crop of mushrooms. Also, the top is mildewed and the seats are worn through to the springs; a mother mouse littered, if that is the word for it, amidst the foam rubber and horsehair of one of the convenient cavities in the back seat. Max and Fred have been preaching new car to me, and, until I saw Stuart's, I had begun to think I really

81

needed one. Seeing his, I remembered that mine still flew like a bird, that both doors opened, and that the top still went up and down. To want anything better seemed ostentatious. Looking out now on Wilshire Boulevard at these Cadillacs and Jaguars, I'm not so sure.

Stuart met me at the train this morning, the Stanford undergraduate look covered up by gray flannel. Mr. Wyler's mother was buried yesterday and he won't be able to see me until tomorrow. I was aware of Stuart's scrutiny as I came down the car steps and I knew what he was wondering exactly. He had seen me only in my own home and at Stanford, where I feel at home. He had talked with me only when we were both carried away, considering the difficulties and opportunities of making a movie based on *The Friendly Persuasion*. Now it was not home, nor inside that bubble of intense speculation about the making of a beautiful object. It was the clear light of a sunny February noon in a railway station, surrounded by brisk and businesslike people. Now he looked at me and said to himself, "Was I wrong to persuade this woman to come to Hollywood?"

I understood quite well how I happened to be here. Stuart had returned to Hollywood, after his visit to Napa, and had said to Mr. Wyler, "Willy, I think you ought to have a talk with the woman who wrote the book." Mr. Wyler had asked some questions, perhaps raised some objections, and had finally said, "All right, Stu, bring her down here for a week."

Now Stuart, who hasn't been Mr. Wyler's assistant long and who thinks Mr. Wyler is a genius, doesn't want to disappoint him. He doesn't want to confront him with an inarticulate housewife. Do I still have those ideas I had? Will I be able to express them to Mr. Wyler? Stuart wonders.

He said none of this and I asked him nothing; I like a cloud of unknowing in such matters. I'm not sure why, though I read a passage last night in Michaux's *A Barbarian in Asia* that seemed to fit my case. "The Hindus," Michaux says, "do not inquire . . . a word will suffice to prevent a lot of misunderstanding. No, they will not say it . . . so attractive to them is a situation involving density.

They like to feel it is a great act of fate rather than their small personal act."

I don't know whether my refusal to inquire adds to the density of this situation or not, but I like walking into it, wondering and speculating rather than knowing. Some things need to be thoroughly explained: how the stove operates, where the key to the door is hidden, which is the car's forward gear. All other activities are better entered into as wordlessly as possible, leaving the talk for afterward. A month from now I can say to Stuart, "Do you remember that first day you took me to see Wyler?" Or I can say it tomorrow, perhaps. To say afterward how it *was* is a part of action's pleasure; to ask how it *will be* is to subtract wonder and deny faith, which is half the pleasure.

Stuart asked me to have dinner with him tonight but I said no, partly to save him from feeling duty bound to keep me entertained while here, partly because I feel the need of a fix: a shot of my own drug, that dear intoxicant, solitude.

I have thought about going for a walk, though to venture afoot alongside that tide of cars below seems about as indecent as to walk naked into the surf at Long Beach.

By standing on the toilet seat in the bathroom and peering round the corner of an opaque window, made for obscuring not revealing views, I saw an unexpected sight: a slope of plowed land, topped with eucalyptus trees, and, through the trees, the spire of a church. This bare spot must be next door to the hotel. What an island of resistance amidst the flow of Austin Healys and Lincolns. I long ago discovered that public buildings keep their views for the bathrooms. I said good-by to the world from such a vantage point in a hospital at the age of twenty-four. Then, too, the view was of eucalyptus trees, with their aromatic scent stirred up by a slow-falling spring rain. I drew deep breaths, then went in and stretched myself out on the bed which was to be wheeled into the operating room.

My childhood was eucalyptus-scented. We were rubbed with eucalyptus oil when we had colds, and portiers made of eucalyptus pods hung between the living room and dining room, giving the whole house the scent of one of those gray-limbed feathery groves. This bathroom view of them makes Wilshire Boulevard familiar.

I called home. I have never outgrown the habit of calling the house in which Papa and Mama live "home." If I call Napa, I think of it as calling not "home" but "Max."

I called my brother Merle. He, beyond anyone I know, is the person to whom to tell good news. And since good news, not bad, is what I always need to communicate, I rejoice with him. What's to be done with one's bad fortune except to endure it? But happiness needs expression. And while many people pride themselves, and with no exaggeration, on their ability to hear with sympathy of the downfall, sickness, and death of others, very few people seem to know what to do with a report of joy, happiness, good luck. If they manage a dry "Well, congratulations, I'm sure," they have exhausted their feeling on the subject. The deep interest which a broken leg, a lingering illness, or a lost job called forth, peters out in the face of a report of good luck. But Merle knows how to rejoice in another's joy. His face begins to shine as he listens and when you have finished he does not congratulate you. He is not that far outside the experience. Instead, my feeling is that I have gained two voices with which to exult, two faces with which to smile, his and mine.

So I tell him I'm in Hollywood to talk about a movie based on *The Friendly Persuasion*, and we laugh at how crazy that is. To be fifteen miles from home, for *that* purpose! To have written about those old Quakers, of the time of our great-grandparents, and to have come, after living next door to Hollywood for most of my life, inside its most un-Quakerly gates on the strength of *that* ticket. It tickles us both. We say good-by, laughing.

I'm as drawn toward a bookstore as an alcoholic is toward a bar—only my case is really more neurotic. The alcoholic doesn't, I think, with a room full of bottles, feel the need of going off to search for the one perfect bottle which has, so far, eluded him. Actually, such a compulsion might be the alcoholic's saving—as it can be the reader's undoing. The alcoholic might spend so much time searching he would have little time for drinking. Less drinking is obviously good for the alcoholic. Perhaps less reading is also good for the inebriate of print. I have been sitting here looking down on this tide of prismatic automobile tops, fighting the desire to hail a taxi and go off in search of a bookstore. If others with my weakness had banded together for mutual aid, I might call a fellow inebriate, ask him to come sit with me, hold my hand and feed me black coffee until the longing was conquered.

I have two dozen books with me. Stuart was taken aback. "I hope you didn't think there'd be time to read all of these," he exclaimed, fearing, I think, that I planned to use this week as a period in which to prepare for next week's work at the University of Washington. I said, "No, I don't." The next question—"Why do you have them then?"—I didn't answer at once. I feel panicky—perhaps that's too strong a word—traveling without them. I don't even like to go from my room to sit on the lawn without taking a half-dozen books with me. "It's my insurance policy," I told him finally. "Insurance against what? Boredom?" I don't think of it that way. Though perhaps in the back of my mind there is the conviction that as long as I have my books all other evils (beside the loss of them, I mean) will be bearable. Perhaps I am like a person who, having once endured a famine, wants always to have a supply at hand. Though I never suffered from any real famine of books. Less than I wanted, perhaps; though that still seems to be my state.

I always take with me not the same books but the same variety of books. Half, usually more than half, will be books I've read before. A couple of Thoreau's journals. Some poetry new or old. This time I have Robert Graves, Elizabeth Bishop, and Thomas Ferril. I have Michaux's *Barbarian in Asia*, which I've read before, and Sackville West's *Inclinations* and Mumford's *Conduct of Life* and Welty's *Bride of the Innisfallen*.

Stuart took me to see Mr. Wyler this morning. We went to his home, and I had somewhat the feeling, though Mr. Wyler did nothing to foster this, of having been taken to an audience with the Pope. Had an editorial assistant taken me to see the editor in chief of a publishing house I would have had none of this feeling. Why the difference? Does a movie director "create" more than does the editor of a book? I suppose so. People often go to the movies to see the work of a particular director and I never heard of anyone reading a book because so-and-so edited it. So the movie director *is* more of a maker than the editor. Also, what he makes is seen by so many millions. And makes so many millions. Does this awe me? No, the contrary. Have I been affected by Stuart's two-week indoctrination? Willy, the greatest director? This, I think arouses my curiosity more than anything else. Was my feeling this morning, then, entirely personal, my inclination to tiptoe the result of an unseasonable lingering in me of the schoolgirl and her desire to please? Or a father fixation (of which I'm entirely unaware) which makes me overhonor masculine figures of authority?

Stuart, perhaps, feared some of these manifestations. He warned me as we clattered along in his car, which I have now discovered started life as a Chevrolet, that Willy hates yes men. "Stand up to him," he urged. "Don't agree with a thing he says unless you believe it."

Perhaps it was this revelation that there are people who do not stand up to Willy that, more than anything else, gave the call its papal character. Whatever the reason, by the time we reached the Wyler house I was following Stuart as if he were a papal nuncio.

The house, which is in the hills a mile or so beyond the Beverly Hills Hotel, is shut off from the winding road by a whitewashed brick wall. It would disappoint readers of movie magazines and visiting Europeans, both of whom find delight, for dissimilar reasons, in a strange, rich, and vulgar Hollywood. What I saw of the house was quiet and normal, though a living room where the Utrillos and the Riveras are originals has an undeniable degree of richness.

We went upstairs to Mr. Wyler's bedroom-study. The room is very large, perhaps twenty by thirty-five, and Mr. Wyler, when we entered, was seated at a desk placed at right angles to the wall opposite the doorway. If he had not risen to meet us, the papal illusion might have continued. He did rise and, moving twice as fast as we, met us two-thirds of the way across the room.

To women five feet seven, all men of five feet ten or less are short. Mr. Wyler is short, stocky, tanned, and

86

wears his thick gray hair cut close. Stuart said, "Willy, this is Miss West." Mr. Wyler said he was glad to see me, pulled up a chair for me, and seated himself at his desk. Stuart faced us on a nearby red sofa.

Mr. Wyler said at once, "I am deaf in one ear. As you see, I have arranged things here so that even if you forget it, you will have to speak into my good ear."

The deafness perhaps accounts for the intense listening look of the eyes. Perhaps not. They are eyes behind which a constant appraising, speculating, summarizing process goes on. The voice matches the eyes in this respect. It is a warm low voice which manages to be simultaneously tentative and incisive. It is incisive about its present discoveries and convictions. But there is a note in it which says, "If you have a reason to think that what I'm saying is not true, tell me." This tentativeness, this ruminativeness in the voice spoil it for platitudes.

He, apparently, was as little sure of what he had in me as writer as I was of what I had in him as director; with this exception: he has been dealing with writers for twenty-five years, while I have never seen, with the exception of Capra, a director before. He had experience to help him; I had only my wits. His experience, had he permitted it to make our meeting mechanical, would have been a handicap. He never did so. It is only now, writing, that it has occurred to me that our talk was not quite as unique for him as for me. That it did not occur to me as we talked shows where some of his strength as a director probably lies—the ability to respond freshly to old situations. The director (or writer) who can't do this finds himself becoming either hackneyed and trite, or, in his attempt to escape this (which is his normal manner with the normal), he becomes extravagant, exaggerated, mannered, arty.

As writer, then, I was an old story to him. As Quaker, I wasn't. As Quaker, he wondered about me. People are generally very uncertain about Quakers. Are they one branch of the Amish? Are they Dunkards? I have been served eggs instead of ham at dinner out of respect for my supposed scruples concerning the flesh of swine. I have had people worry about smoking in my presence and ask if it was "against my religion." Mr. Wyler evidently decided not to run the risk of getting tangled up with some-one else's orthodoxies. Or perhaps he, too, likes dense situations. In any case he asked no questions, offered me a cigarette, and, when I refused, lit one for himself.

Having discovered that I was a Quaker as well as a writer about Quakers, he needed to know whether or not I considered my writing chiefly as an opportunity to propagate the faith. If I did, it would be unlikely that our talks need run through the week. I thought anyone who had read *The Friendly Persuasion* would know that Jess and Eliza were human beings who happened to be Quakers, not vice versa. Relatives of mine have, in fact, felt that while the Birdwells were human a hundred per cent of the time, their Quakerliness was more intermittent. One cousin went so far as to write an old English professor of mine asking him to persuade me to use a more ladylike vocabulary in my Quaker stories. For a Quaker to use "ain't" and "duck dung" would, she felt, convince the world we were a vulgar, loutish lot. I am sorry to say that unaware as yet of the pressures familial and otherwise that can be exerted upon a writer I took out the dung. I would not do so today. "If you put goodness ahead of truth, you find in the long run that you have lost both," said F. L. Lucas. And that is a truth good people should try to remember.

I think Mr. Wyler decided that, instead of being a Quaker who writes, I am a writer who is a Quaker. This being settled, he went on to the book itself.

"Who have you thought of as the central figure in these stories of yours?"

"Thought of? Jess, of course. Sometimes I *made* myself give Eliza a little more space. Jess is the hero from beginning to end."

"Eliza? I was thinking about the boys."

"The boys! Those kids? They have characters of their own—I hope, but they're about knee-high to Jess in interest and meaning."

"Stu tells me you think, if a movie were made, it would have to center around the Civil War story."

"Everything else is either comedy, or has to do with the Birdwells when they're much older, or is very slight."

"Frank Capra had a script written which centers on

the Civil War episode. The last half of it has to do with the boys. Jess becomes an onlooker."

"In the one story, 'Battle of Finney's Ford,' that's true. But it's not true of the book as a whole."

"If you were to center the story on the Civil War episode, how would you get around this?"

"Invent something."

Mr. Wyler laughed as if he thought this easier said than done. And it is.

"What would you think of Gary Cooper as Jess?" Think? I didn't have to think about that. If Gary Cooper had been born a hundred years ago, a Quaker Hoosier, he would have looked like Jess Birdwell.

"Will Cooper play the part?"

"Not in this script. Coop says if he starts a movie he likes to be in at the finish. If all he's going to do is watch the last three reels, he'll watch it from a seat in the theater."

I wasn't worried about Mr. Cooper's space in the picture as a star, but I didn't want Jess to have less than his due, which to my mind was just everything.

"He is the whole book," I assured Mr. Wyler. "He must be in every scene."

Mr. Wyler answered in his exploratory way, which makes me disinclined to contradict him, "I don't think even Coop wants that much footage. When I first spoke to Coop about this part some years ago he wasn't interested in it. He said, 'I ain't ever played a pappy yet and I ain't aiming to start now.'" Mr. Wyler laughed and was quiet a moment remembering those words and the way Coop had looked when he said them, and how the saying had ticked him then and had continued to do so all these years since. One thing, at least, was apparent: Mr. Wyler liked Mr. Cooper. Mr. Wyler stopped remembering and said, "I think Coop's changed his mind about playing a pappy now."

There was a lot more talk. The windows from this upstairs room look out across trees—eucalyptus, pepper, palm, and the fancy decorative trees planted by landscape gardeners. A little mongrel dog came to the French doors which open out onto a porch, and Mr. Wyler shooed him away. Stuart sat on the red sofa, bursting with talk and keeping his mouth shut. His eyes, half-owl, half-cherub, half-Old Testament prophet—which is just the right proportions, since it gives him eyes a third again as large as most people's—showed the pressure. Once, he did start to answer a question Mr. Wyler had asked me, and then the papal tone was truly present. "Let Miss West answer the question, Stu," Mr. Wyler commanded.

Then a wonderful thing happened, and I can't remember what exactly led to it. We had been talking about the possible reception of a Quaker picture. Mr. Wyler wondered if I knew (and I did) that there are groups which believe that it is un-American to show or even speak of a people whose beliefs run counter to those generally held. Mr. Wyler didn't want me to have any illusions about himself—he was no Quaker. He had been in the navy during the war—his ear was deafened by gunfire. Evil, in his experience, had to be resisted with violence. Somewhere in the midst of this talk, I listening more than talking, there came to me an insight about the story. It came with a tightening of skin across the cheek bones, it came out of the talk, something that has only happened to me once before in speaking of writing—but then I have in all my life only spoken once before of the possible course a piece of my own writing might take. It came like a vision, a resolution of difficulties, a light on all those reels in which Jess had no part; but it came like a thing in itself too, it came like a person, and the only wonder was that I had not seen this person years before.

"Jess needs a friend, a man, no Quaker . . . someone who is a fighter . . . someone who opposes Jess and loves him . . . someone as strong in his own way as Jess is in his. . . . We can't really know Jess without him. . . ."

Mr. Wyler said, "Yes . . . yes . . . I see that. . . . It could be. . . . Perhaps you're right. . . ."

I don't know how much longer we talked—we parted I don't know how. Stuart drove me back to my princely quarters and all the way my face remained tight with this idea.

"What now?" I asked Stuart.

"Write," Stuart said. "Write it all down. Write your ideas about this."

"I can't write 'ideas about' things. I have to write the

thing itself. I don't care 'about.' I don't want to describe this man, I want to hear him and Jess talk."

"Write a scene, then."

"I don't know how to write a movie scene. I don't know how to say what the cameras are doing."

"We know all about what the cameras are doing. Tell us what these two men are doing."

"Write it like Shakespeare?" I asked.

"Willy will be very pleased to have you write it like Shakespeare," Stuart said, and I got out of the Chevrolet and walked up the steps, between the columns of my antebellum super-motel, to my little fabric nest.

I just called Merle at the plant. When anyone asks me what my younger brother does and I say he owns a furniture-and-rug-cleaning business I can see that this, in their eyes, severely limits him. Limited? He is as unlimited as Raleigh or Drake or Montaigne. Like Montaigne, anything that concerns humankind concerns him. I write my life. He lives his. The people I make up he encounters, twice as real, sad, and funny.

He thought he wanted to be a rancher. The idea of himself alone under the blue skies appealed to him. He bought a ranch and went round and round on his speechless tractor under skies blue, but silent, domed like a bell, but muter. He took his two-year-old son with him for company, though tractoring was bouncy for the little boy, and the conversation, which Merle was after, was not much improved by the child's presence. Where were the riches of people, the treasures of human idiosyncrasy, the give and take of talk with the funny word dropping into the one inevitable slot which had waited forever for it? Not amidst the furrows, not over the wheels of the manure spreader, not behind the Fordson engine.

He sold the ranch and bought a dry-cleaning establishment. (That is the word for it. Establishment.) Here was quirkiness indeed. Treasures of human idiosyncrasy that gave you the backache to contemplate, let alone experience. Here were people raising hell over one missing button, over the price for cleaning the corpse's suit, over there unremoved unremovable telltale lipstick. Merle wanted people on some larger scale, worrying about something besides their fig leaves. But their homes! That was different. Merle likes homes. He does not mind having people worry about making their homes nicer. He worries with them.

I asked him if he and Elizabeth could come over to have dinner with me.

He has three small children, has worked all day, will have to drive thirty minutes in one direction to reach home, then an hour in the opposite direction and through the worst traffic in the world to reach me.

He said, "If it's O.K. with Elizabeth, I'll see you at 7:30."

I asked the desk clerk where there was a fancy place to eat—a place with good food that looked like Hollywood. Thick steaks, thick carpets, lots of people. This is no night for a well-bred quiet hole in the corner, fruit and cheese for dessert, and a main course more sauce than meat. This is a night to find out—by having too much—what is enough.


*Wednesday*

I wrote twenty pages today in spite of the fact that I've been dead with headache and drugged with headache killers. The man's name is Sam. He is dark, he is heavy-set, he is a widower. He has not Jess's subtlety but is perhaps freer to act because of this. He loves Jess and honors his convictions.

In a scene . . . but it's written . . . and I can't rewrite it any more than I can relive a day.

I've sat here all day in bed, in my pajamas, writing and taking headache remedies. Now the stuff goes out to be typed and I'm going to have a bath and take a few more pills.

## Thursday

I would not choose to have a four-Optalidon, four-brain-shrinker-pill headache on the day I meet Gary Cooper. Quite likely, though I feel dimmed, he won't notice the difference.

Stuart called to say Mr. Wyler had read the typed script, liked it, and was sending it to Cooper to read. And that I was invited to the Wylers' for dinner to meet Mr. Cooper. All I ask is that the hot-water bottle doesn't make a blister on my forehead.

## Friday

Nothing to do today, except see Mr. Wyler this afternoon, pack, catch the northbound Owl tonight.

Last night a couple whose names I never did learn picked me up and took me to the Wylers'. I had been told that the man was a script writer, his wife a former actress. Both were lean and handsome and talked about their children, their garden, their dogs, their children's school. I felt quite blowsy and Hollywood beside them. I saw at once that if this lady was properly dressed for a Hollywood dinner party, I wasn't; not that I had on anything very flamboyant. But this lady had on a wool street dress. I don't think it is an absolute breach of taste to wear a dinner dress to a dinner party, but if that wasn't done in Hollywood, I was going to be conspicuous.

The minute I saw Mrs. Wyler I knew I was going to be conspicuous. She is very pretty, blue-eyed, delicately boned, has a fair skin, wavy brown hair, a slight Southern accent, and the spiritual strength, it was obvious, to run a Southern plantation single handed. Mrs. Wyler's dress was not a smart street dress. It reminded me of the dresses Mama used to wear on Sunday afternoons, an in-between dress; not an out-and-out church dress, but plainly a Sunday dress. Mama's dress would not have looked right in a store, just as Mrs. Wyler's dress, while not a dinner dress, would not have looked right on the street. Mr. Wyler greeted me. I met Cathy Wyler, a girl of sixteen, the person she will be still lost behind round cheeks.

Then I noticed entering the living room a man, the sight of whom gave me a very odd sensation. I had known him all my life though I had never seen him. Or was it the other way around? I had seen him all my life but I didn't know him. There was nothing to do but stare. I disdained pretending that it was not an extraordinary thing to be in the presence of a man whose face I had attentively watched for twenty-five years.

We grow accustomed to the faces we see every day. Habit blinds us to them. Also it is not often necessary to deduce from the expression of that daily face the drift of a crucial sequence of events. In the first place, the drift is not often crucial, no kingdom is going to be lost, no bridge blown up, no girl tortured. And even if the drift is crucial, no talented script writer, playing the will-he, won't-he for all it is worth, has so arranged events that we must watch the face opposite us for a telltale clouding of the eye, a preliminary stiffening of the upper lip to answer our questions: "Does he know?" "Does he care?" "Will he kill him?"

Domestically, these questions do not often come up, and when they do, there is not usually any attempt to "sustain suspense." Everybody talks at once and God alone knows what expressions are being "registered." In the movies things are ordered differently. Suspense *is* sustained, expressions *are* registered, and from outside we enjoy the predicaments of our heroes; we watch their faces closely, not only out of sympathy but out of curiosity as to what their next move will be. One of the pleasures of watching drama is this crossing of wits with the dramatist, this effort to outguess him. The dramatist's problem, as Elizabeth Bowen says, is to make all action appear unpredictable as seen and inevitable after it has been seen. The courteous dramatist lets us pick up a few clues, for without some helpful telltale scents we might give up the chase altogether. And one of these clues is the expression of the actor.

So it may easily happen that we have given a closer, a more anguished and concerned attention to a face seen on a screen than to any "living" face whatever. And suddenly to see that face, whose darkenings and lightenings we know so well, but whose owner, so to speak, we know not at all, is very strange. It was very strange to me to see Gary Cooper enter the Wylers' living room.

He differed, in some ways, from the image I had seen on the screen; he was larger, grayer, younger. But chiefly I was startled by two facts: first, the likeness of the man to the image; and second, the aliveness of the image, a real flesh and blood man, blowing his nose, smoothing back his hair, carrying a drink. I had never before seen a great movie star, so had not understood how much they are myth to us, how little human. Nor had I anticipated the degree to which it might be a comedown to have love, adventure, justice, and fortitude become a man in a gray striped suit. Man into myth is a process in which we enjoy having a hand. Myth into man (though it has its attractions for the mean-spirited) demands from all others a courageous taste for reality.

Somehow, too, I had supposed that the flesh of the star-in-the-flesh would radiate a special quality of livingness which normal flesh never has. Cooper, guided by Mr. Wyler, moved toward me very normally. His suit, unlike those of the businessmen of Napa, was tailored so that the fact that Mr. Cooper had a body was not hidden. This doesn't mean that the suit was tight or padded or exaggerated in line. It means, I guess, that it fit, and that Mr. Cooper, having run neither to belly nor bum (as the rhyme says human beings to the age of forty come to) had nothing to hide.

So he came toward me, looking very much like himself, fully alive, known and unknown, and I scanned his face with the close attention twenty-five years of movie-going had trained me to give it, alert to detect in a movement of the long upper lip or a narrowing of the dark-lashed eyes the hero's intentions.

The hero's intentions were plainly good will and the hope of discovering a topic of conversation about which we both had some knowledge. The topic I proposed was Gary Cooper. I asked him if he understood how strange it was to meet a person at once familiar and unknown.

He didn't know it from my side, as the viewer, but he knew it from his side, as the viewed. Men in railway stations have rushed up to him, clapped an arm around his shoulders and said, "After all these years! How delighted I am to see you again, Charlie. It is Charlie, isn't it?"

"Charlie," Mr. Cooper told me, "would be the name of a character I'd played."

Other people had arrived, a woman in a real evening dress, all black satin and white shoulders, and this, with my quickly picked up Hollywood sophistication, I considered flagrant overdressing. Small town, I thought. Looks like Napa, and I twitched my own sober brown skirt demurely. We sat in the living room with our drinks. Mr. Wyler has a table which, if touched here or turned there, becomes a variety of objects. By demonstrating it, he gave a center to the group of disparate persons. Though Mr. Cooper was our real center. This was his party; his lawyer was here, a woman who had gone to school with his wife was here, a director who wanted him to star in his picture; also a woman who had written a book and thought Mr. Cooper looked like its hero.

He was aware, of course, of this focusing of attention. But his very lack of innocence permitted him to be himself. And he had a self to be. That was the important and comfortable thing about Mr. Cooper. Somehow the years of adulation, the cameras, the women's voices scarcely able to convey the weight of admiration they felt without breaking, had not engulfed him. He had made no effort to conform to the image the screen projected of Mr. Adventure, Mr. Romance, Mr. Love, Mr. Probity. He had stayed Mr. Cooper and, with none of the yupping and nopeing of his publicized trade-mark, he sat down beside me and bestirred himself to be agreeable. One subject which he knew at first hand, and I second, was hunting, and we talked pheasant and deer and duck and bear and quail.

I was placed next to him at the dinner table. He spoke of his daughter Maria, who wanted to go to U.C.L.A. and to be a biochemist, "if her grades were good enough."

"You can send her to Napa Junior College for two years," I told him, "if they aren't."

"Ah, no," he said, "Maria is a home girl."

Mr. Wyler, Mr. Cooper, and I stayed in the dining room for an hour or so after dinner talking about *The Friendly Persuasion*. "There comes a time," said Mr. Cooper, "when the people who see me in a picture expect me to do something."

"You mean pull a trigger?"

"Deliver a blow," he said. "Fist or bullet. Or sword. They expect it. They feel let down without it."

"What people *always* get, they soon fail to notice. I saw you in *Vera Cruz*. That was a stupid picture. It was a great waste of ability. *Who* you were didn't matter. All the part took was a trigger finger. I could've played the part."

"I stank," Mr. Cooper said.

"It had as well all been done by automation. It is a pity for you not to play a complete human being. Alive in all his senses, but wanting to be a good man."

"I would like to play a part like that. But I don't know that I'm very well suited to playing a Quaker. They're fine people. I met two young Quakers in Mexico. They were spending their summer working without pay, helping put in a sewer system or something in a Mexican town. I've not forgotten them. They had something you don't often see. They weren't thinking about themselves at all. But I don't know that I'm the right man for a Quaker." Mr. Cooper's hands were folded together, the attitude prayer-like. "My life hasn't been very Quaker-like. This man, Jess, is a very good man."

When we rejoined the guests in the living room, Mr. Wyler explained our absence. "Miss West, Coop, and I have been telling stories." We were an unlikely trio for after-dinner stories, and everyone laughed.

I thought that Cooper must surely recognize his likeness to Jess, that the part was made for him—or vice versa. I wished he would say so. What kind of conversation can you have with a man who does not accept elementary facts? The sun shines. Two and two are four. Birds have wings. If there is a difference of opinion about matters like these, words are going to be wasted. And agreement needn't mean that he wanted to play the part. Cooper never admitted any likeness whatever, and on the way home the writer's wife said, "I was very amused to hear you, with all your enthusiasm, urge Coop to admit he thought the part a suitable one. Coop's far too wily for that. Stand there before Willy, who is doing his best to sign him, and say, 'The part appeals to me greatly.' He would never do that. What he must say is, 'This is an impossible part. Me play a Quaker? Don't be funny, Willy.' "

I hadn't thought of that. But I know something and would never have asked Cooper the question if I hadn't known it. Mr. Cooper does not consider the part impossible. He likes it. He would like to be more than a finger on a trigger. Though I suppose it's possible that he might like to be a Quaker with his finger on the trigger. Have his cake and shoot it too.

Napa bound on the Owl, my downy bouncer, my old Southern Pacific home. Five thirty and nothing between me and my cradle except chili con carne or a hamburger covered with catsup squirted from a plastic bottle. It looks like a baby bottle, complete with nipple. Take it to my rocking berth and I'll feel that infantile regression has set in for sure. It is already dark. Burbank, Saugus, Lebec behind us and the climb toward Bakersfield ahead.

I suppose it is crazy not to go directly to Seattle. As it is I'll get to Napa at six thirty in the morning, leave for Seattle at eight tomorrow evening. But I want twelve hours at home. I want to examine my soul, I want to sit in the Barwa Napper underneath a madroña tree, listen to the quail and ask myself if I am going to be a script writer.

Stuart took me to Mr. Wyler's this afternoon. He was out and we waited for him in his study-bedroom. We took our former seats, as if assigned to them, Stuart on the sofa, I on the chair by the desk. Not talking, I saw things I hadn't seen before: bound copies of the scripts of all the movies he's made—*Little Foxes, Sister Carrie, Wuthering Heights,* twenty-seven, altogether; pictures of his wife, his children, the little son who died. I examined the room as one examines a shell to discover the nature of the occupant. This shell told me its occupant was a man, a family man, a movie-maker, no great reader, liked warm colors, was practical, pragmatic, and unpretentious.

Stuart had no need to examine the shell. He has known Mr. Wyler since he, Stuart, was a boy. Stuart's father was Mr. Wyler's publicity agent for some years. What Stuart wanted to know was how the party went off last night. Who was present? Who said what? Did I have a good time? What did I think of Cooper?

"Could you fall in love with him?"

"I didn't."

"That isn't what I asked you."

"You mean could I imagine a situation in which I might fall in love with Mr. Cooper?"

"Mr. Cooper! Don't be so standoffish."

"The woman who feels herself incapable under certain circumstances of falling in love with Mr. Cooper ought to see a psychiatrist."

"What's so enthralling about old Coop?"

"Are we still talking about falling in love?"

"No. Just the man and his face. And whatever there is behind Cooper's face that's made people want to keep on looking at it for twenty-five years."

"I don't know what's behind Cooper's face. But I know what it seems to be: it seems to be a promise of intensity. It swims up more nakedly into his eyes than into the eyes of any other human being I've ever seen. He is alive in the eyes. In a dead-eyed race, that's something to watch."

"Am I a dead eye?"

"You're so live-eyed all the time degrees don't register."

"That all Coop's got?"

"He's got the tenderest mouth and upper lip."

"Coop sign you on as his press agent?"

"Nope."

"So that's Coop. A live eye and a tender lip!"

"I don't know what Coop is. You know that. But I've thought about the durability of that face too. I think there's a contradiction in the face that keeps people looking at it. Or a contradiction in the man which the face shows. The promised intensity, the apparent tenderness are there; but before they can win out an innate reserve, and even shyness, have to be overcome. Cooper's movies can be pretty static and the audience will still be interested.

They can watch the battle in the face. He's got a built-in will-he, won't-he, and the audience, if it doesn't give a hoot who gets the gold or the girl, and a lot of the time it doesn't, is still interested in Coop's face. Will it keep its promises? And which of the promises will it keep?"

Stuart said, "Gosh! I'd sure like to hear Coop say 'yep' or 'nope' to this."

"He'd say yes."

"You Coop's alter ego?"

"I wrote Jess. And Jess is Coop. So maybe I am."

Mr. Wyler came in and took his seat at the desk, bad ear to the wall. Without preliminaries he said, "Write me a script."

I didn't say yes and I haven't said yes. I didn't say no either.

I said, "I don't know how to write a script."

He said, "You know how to write a story."

"Yes."

"Write me the story of what the camera sees."

"In a real story . . ."

He interrupted me. "In a real story you mean, as opposed to the unreal story a movie tells?" Mr. Wyler laughed. Some people seem to be more themselves doing one thing rather than another. Mr. Wyler seems to be wholly himself laughing. He becomes more transparent then. Then, and when something you say has taken hold of him and he has begun to develop it. The core comes up to the surface then.

"No. I mean the story told with words alone. In that story, the eyes that behold the action belong to someone I know. Whose eyes are the camera's? I don't know. I could learn, but I mightn't be able to learn fast enough."

"Work with someone then. Stu, here, if you like."

"I couldn't work with anyone. How could I ask Stuart, 'What do you think Sam does next?' No, you'd better get someone else."

Mr. Wyler pointed to the roofs we could see from the window. "Under every roof is a script writer. In two hours I can have twenty-five here. They don't know Jess and Eliza though. You do. Write me their story."

Stuart took me to the train. "See you next week," he said. But I have made no promises.

Now I'll go squeeze that catsup teat.

And I'll look out of the snack-bar windows on to the dark countryside I have traveled over so often and which is always, mile by mile, so unremembered. I traveled this route when I was returning to the sanatorium and had to be carried onto the train. I traveled it with Frankie's body. I have passed these lights and bridges and hills in love and out, in pre-Christmas anticipation and in after-Christmas relief. I have traveled it to tell my father he had cancer, and I have traveled it to be made a doctor of letters. Or laws or literature, something that begins with 1, anyway; I always forget just what. I have lived, imaginatively, with dozens of Mexican families in their pumpkin-colored Southern Pacific houses. I have been how many Mexican women at twilight, standing with a baby on my hip and a dog playing London Bridge with my ankles? How many Mexican men with still enough valor to defy gravity and perch a battered hat on the downward incline of the head's backside? How many? And now a putative script writer who will become in the dining car a trained nurse.

*Napa*
2 P.M.

I'm so glad I didn't go straight to Seattle. Here I am, having twelve hours of a little summer. I am outside, stripped to the buff—though I do not know what or where that is. The sun has a puckery bite. The trees are still leafless. I get the sun directly, a bare-knuckled fighter. Such beautiful warm blows. I am sad for people who do not like to be in the sun. It's a free intoxicant. Mama, who will heat a room to ninety, cannot bear the sun, whether as fact or idea I'm not sure. That the sun is warmth seems never to have occurred to her. She will hurry away from it to sit by a fire. She was raised on an Indiana farm where success in life was measured by the degree to which you escaped the elements. Exposure meant defeat. A sun-burned woman meant a woman who "worked in the fields." When I was a child I had to wear buttermilk masks

101

to fade the freckles, and even now freckles and tan are more than pigmentation to Mama. I like the sun as heat, apart from what it does to my skin. I can remember at twenty-six, already far gone in tuberculosis, though I didn't know it, choosing for the first time to sit in the sun. Now, I thought, I am really old. I couldn't remember ever having felt cold before, and feeling cold was, in my experience, a characteristic of the aged.

I am covered with sweat, which seems to me a fine accomplishment. This pleasure in sweating dates from my fevered tubercular day when, with the thermometer in the room at 110°, I lay, my skin dry as desert sand, envying my cheerful, perspiring visitors. To sweat is to be feverless and to be feverless is, for the ex-tubercular, health.

There was rain and wind here while I was gone. Eucalyptus leaves were blown into the driveway and they still lie there, gray and purple like fossil fish. The jays are very loud. Robins have returned to harvest the last of the red berries. A train is whistling far away, fainter and fainter, moving out of the valley, carrying wine and hay and dried fruit.

— The garden is filled with flowers: daphne, daffodils, Chinese lilies, camellias, red-hot pokers, primroses. Max, who is sound asleep beside me, has a flowering peach petal on his face, just like Galsworthy's hero. This petal doesn't move either, though the reason, thank God, is not the same.

Max and I don't agree about flowers and, since I do nothing about the flowers except to cut them, I am not entitled to a say as to what shall be planted. I do not care for big invented flowers. I admire them in the same way I admire big pastel-colored electric refrigerators. How bright! How big! How extraordinary that it should exist at all! But love it? Max can love the new. We argued for years on the subject of brooms versus vacuum cleaners. I never recognize myself in the European pictures of the American housewife, the mechanized woman who constantly badgers her husband for more stainless-steel equipment. I was the last woman in the world to own a vacuum cleaner and, except for Max, would still be raising dust to the tune of Sousa's "El Capitan" or "The Stars and

Stripes Forever." Sweeping is a lovely occupation in itself —but done to a Sousa march it is almost as good as quickstepping off to war, and is, I suppose, the Quaker's substitute, not only for that but for dancing. "A partner like a broomstick" is a familiar saying; my partner *was* a broomstick, and, oh, how I hated to give him up for an Electrolux who, crawling snakelike on his belly, hasn't a dance step in him. I love the motions of sweeping, the push and swoop of body and arms, as much as I love shining floors. Is there anything more beautiful than a room you have cleaned yourself? A shining, harmonious light-filled and light-reflecting room, made that way by your own dance with a broomstick? There it stands, a picture you painted. But it is also a dance, a congealed dance. You danced the room clean, you painted your picture with the movements of your body. No wonder women don't paint more pictures on canvas. They are dancing pictures all the time, pictures that make love visible, dancing a dance that makes motion permanent. No other art is so enrapturing—for a woman.

I am very warm, very happy, and my eyes are closing.


*Two hours*
*outside Seattle*

What am I going to do about writing this script?

Reasons for doing it:

1. If I go to Hollywood I'll see a world I know nothing about.
2. I may learn how to do something new.
3. I will be a part of what is one of the characteristic phenomena of our times.
4. I will combat the hermit in me.
5. I will combat the coward in me.
6. I will make money.

Reasons why these reasons are not valid:

103

1. There are many worlds you know nothing about and which your ignorance doesn't justify exploring: shoplifting, dope pushing, six-day bicycle racing.
2. Instead of learning to do something new, why not learn to do something old better? Like writing short stories, novels, poetry?
3. Strip teasing, sky writing, and skin diving are parts of our time, and probably unsuitable occupations for you.
4. Why combat the hermit in you? Thoreau didn't. He cultivated that hermit, fed that hermit, listened to that hermit. And now we listen also.
5. Doing what you're afraid to do, and for that reason alone, will soon make a flagpole sitter out of you.
6. If money is your object you might, quite probably, make a lot more sitting home writing a good novel. Everyone talks of "selling out" to Hollywood. Unless more money is spoken of than has been, I won't be selling out to Hollywood, I'll be shelling out.

*Seattle*
*Friday*

I am leaving for Napa tomorrow at noon. I wired Mr. Wyler I would accept his offer.

Last night Alex and Sue Gottfried gave a party for me. One of the guests was a lawyer who had spent a year or two in jail as a conscientious objector. He was not a Friend at the time of his jail experience but has since become one. Sue and Alex thought we'd like to talk, and I, at least, did. People's faces often seem unfitted to their reputations and professions. The holy cardinal looks like a spoiled baby; the able financier, a country-store dolt; the lyric poet, a longshoreman. This man had a face to match the spirit which had preferred jail to abandoning his convictions.

He has what it called a "pure" face, though I am not sure what we mean when we say that. A "pure" face need not be, as this one was, spare, close to the bone, stronger in eye and brow than in jowl and cheek. Though this helps.

It is easier to *see* the purity in such a face. "Purity" in a face is an outward reflection of an inner oneness. The face is "pure" because inside there are no contradictions. Reality has become appearance. Such faces rest and reassure us like natural objects, like clouds and stones and pools of water.

A devil, if he is at one with his devilishness, may have a pure face too. If he has truly said, "Evil be my good," he may look out at us with the clearest eyes from under the most unclouded brow. Iago, perhaps, had a pure face; while St. Paul may have had an impure face, a face stained with conflicts. This face reflected the resolution of conflict. It was an odd face to encounter in the midst of a party; it was a place of quiet.

He said to me, "Alex tells me you're going to Hollywood to write a script for *The Friendly Persuasion*."

I told him no, I had not yet decided to go.

He was very surprised. "But you must go," he said. "Jess and Eliza were wonderful people. You mustn't miss the chance to help make a movie that will let millions of people who have never read the book know them."

When I told him that the movie would probably show some Quakers fighting, he was undisturbed.

"If a man has a sword in his heart he must pull it out and use it," he said. "You must do this," he urged. "Don't think of saying no."

Am I going to Hollywood on the word of a stranger met at a party? No; he only externalized the words I myself was speaking.


*Napa*

Packed, once again, for the Owl. But I am going to see if I can't come back here to do my writing.

It's a drizzly day. "Mizzling" was Thoreau's word for it. I've been sitting by the open fire. Back East it was called a "grate" fire.

Everything enhanced, as always for me, by the prospect

105

of leaving. There is sickness in that. Happy natures love what they embrace, not what they turn their backs on.

Dolores came over to sit with me by the fire. She doesn't like school.

Me:  What don't you like about it?
D:  Singing. I don't like to sing for an hour.
Me:  I hear you singing at home.
D:  I don't like to sing for an hour.
Me:  What else don't you like?
D:  Beginning to read. Beginning to read is silly. "See Dick. See Sally. I see Dick. I see Sally." That's silly.
Me:  What's silly about it?
D:  If I see them, I see them.
Me:  What else?
D:  Recess.
Me:  What's wrong with recess?
D:  Monkey-bars. You got to go on the monkey-bars. There's nothing but monkey-bars and they blister my hands.
Me:  Couldn't you just walk around and play hopscotch —or something?
D:  No, you got to stay with the kids and do what the kids do and that's monkey-bars.
Me:  Isn't there a single thing you like about school?
D:  Lunch.

As we sat together, she bewailing school and I the necessity of leaving, she said philosophically, "Things are things." And that includes monkey-bars and script writing, leaving home and singing for an hour at a time.

Private Eye, as we sat by the fire, came yowling to the door. Dolores, meanwhile, had taken up some kind of banging operation with the fire tongs. After the duet had continued for a minute or so, I said, "For loud noises you and Private Eye take the prize."

Dolores, without pause, said, "What's the prize?"

What can Hollywood offer me that will recompense me for the loss of Dolores?

# III

Back in my Wilshire Boulevard ante-bellum mansion, prepared to buckle down to my bellum script.

Stuart met me at the train; he has a press pass and is able to get clear to the tracks. He carried my basket of books for me. The guard, who also recognizes me by this time, has *his* conjectures about my life and occupation.

(Note to myself as script writer: Please keep in mind, when writing, this universal desire to make inferences. Most movies err in leaving us too little to infer. The mind and imagination of the viewer rackets around with nothing to grind on. Everything has been too thoroughly Pablumized.)

What the guard wondered about, seeing Stuart helping me, was our relationship. Said he, "I see you have your big boy to help you this morning?"

I was startled. Not to be thought old enough to be the mother of anyone as large and bearded as Stuart, but to be thought a mother. I scan faces constantly without being able to read them. But I always attribute to others greater powers in this respect than I have; and for this reason I have believed that my childlessness could be seen in my face. Perhaps a face is as marked by what has been wished for as by what has been accomplished, and the child hoped for also leaves its marks of motherliness.

Anyway, while I was busy mulling over my unexpected motherhood, Stuart answered the guard, "I'm just her youngest, sir." I hope the guard didn't believe *that*.

My return had made Stuart proud of his gifts as a prognosticator. "I knew you'd be back," he told me. He was also proud of the welcome he had arranged for me. A welcome that *was* Hollywood. I now have a more luxurious apartment, with windows that look over the pool, and Stu had made it sweet with flowers. Yellow roses from Mr. Wyler, white snapdragon from the management, gold tulips from himself. The full treatment, as they say. There was liquor in the cupboard. "The Scotch," Stuart said frankly, "is for me to drink." He can have it.

"Look out of the window," he bade me. I did. "See the green convertible? The one with the cream-colored top?" I did see it. "A new Oldsmobile. Yours while you are here."

I walked about the apartment relishing the improvements. "How much does this cost?" I asked.

Stuart looked as if he had not expected such venal interests from a Quaker. I told him of the Eastern potentate who voiced his approval of the Society of Friends thus: "I like the Quakers. I have always found them to be a businesslike people with no religious nonsense about them." Stuart didn't laugh. I think he doesn't relish jokes about Quakers.

"This apartment costs three hundred and seventy-five dollars a month," he said.

"You've been cheated!"

The apartment is shaped like a boxcar, somewhat wider, and considerably longer, but it wouldn't look too strange hooked behind a locomotive. It is divided three ways. One enters the sitting room. To the left is a very small kitchenette, to the right, bedroom and bath. "None," said Thoreau, "is so poor he need sit on a pumpkin." This place is furnished with a couple of poufs that look and feel like pumpkins.

"In Napa," I told Stuart, "this apartment would not bring you seventy-five a month. Even on Stonecrest."

"Who wants to live on Stonecrest? Rent free. We're going to the Beverly Hills Hotel for lunch. Are you ready?"

I always forget the difference between the pine and the palm; that while winter still lingers under the northern oaks it has never properly come to southern hibiscus and bougainvillaea. I had packed *all* of my winter wardrobe, but the thermometer in Los Angeles was in the eighties.

"I have nothing to wear," I told Stuart. "I brought nothing but winter clothes with me."

He had the solution. "Go to Robinson's or I. Magnin's and get yourself a couple of summer dresses. Put them on your expense account."

This was really Hollywood, boxcar or no boxcar. This was the genuine gilded legend. I felt as delighted as one who discovers that the gingerbread house he has read of is not only real, but iced.

"I'm not suggesting mink," Stuart said, "but a couple of cotton dresses around a hundred."

"Apiece?"

"Can you get them for less?"

I didn't say another word. I'm not sure he meant it, but either way I didn't want to know the answer. Let the situation be dense with charge accounts. This was the final touch to the Hollywood legend, to the flowers, the liquor, the convertible, the pool, and the overpriced boxcar. I would not have changed a thing except the weight of my suit. We had lunch in the sunny patio of the Beverly Hills Hotel. To eat good food amidst flowers under a warm sun! Night dining, no matter how good the food or luxurious the surroundings, can never equal it. We had hot curry and a cool wine. Magnin's was staging a fashion show, and models, bird thin and bird bright, drifted past us in varicolored plumage. They broke out into the open from under the shelter of the oleanders and gnarled olive trees like pheasant, and Stuart, an alert bird dog, his specs clapped quickly on for better seeing, all but pointed as they went by.

As one girl neared us, he whispered, "Wouldn't you like to ask her about that dress?"

"It's not the right style for me," I whispered back.

He shook his head, disappointed me. "*She* was the right style for *me*."

It was a fine sunny time, all of my decisions behind me, none of my responsibilities yet assumed, simultaneously warmed and cooled, bird models amidst the real towhees and linnets, fantasy and reality mingling. I had a sudden desire to run, thinking I had experienced it all in my imagination; no need to stay for the hard work and the disappointments.

I didn't run, though. I had a date to see Mr. Wyler at four thirty. Until then, Stuart suggested that we visit the Allied lot where "our" picture was to be made and the Paramount lot where we could watch Cecil De Mille directing *The Ten Commandments*.

Three things, no, four, happened this afternoon that, if I were writing a story, couldn't be mentioned. The reader of a story would consider them symbolic. But since I am living my life, not writing a story, I can put them down. The question is: Is my life a story someone else is writing? If so, should I myself pay some attention to these symbolic signposts?

We left the Beverly Hills Hotel and rode north on Sunset Boulevard toward the Allied Studios. I'm going to have to drive to the studio alone presently, so I tried to memorize the route. Sunset Boulevard, while no more garish than many other highways outside large cities, has a particularly shameless public look because of the number of public names which one recognizes in connection with it. Here Crosby sang, Sinatra swung (a fist), the Mitchums reconciled, Dean and Jerry feuded, Judy Garland wept, Rita Hayworth danced. I was amazed at the number of businesses having to do with the movies. I felt a little frightened. These were the professionals. Here was a machine that had been meshing for a long time. True, it depended upon people like me for material; but if spider, as well as web he had spun, were pulverized in the gears, the machine would never know the difference.

Stuart had warned me that Allied was a very small studio. I was without standards, having never seen a studio before, and an undersized one could have been presented to me as normal or even colossal. Allied is on a bungalow-lined street off Sunset, a street that reminds me of those of the small Orange County towns of my high-school years. Those towns have become modernized, while here, in the heart of Hollywood, was a living fossil, the 1920's preserved. The sight made me feel tender and skippy, like someone in sneakers and middy blouse.

How could such an anachronism have been preserved? Brown bungalows covered with shingles, gray bungalows covered with clapboard, an occasional opulent Swiss chalet. Bungalows with four-by-twelve porches scaled by the eastern farmers who had built them to hold rocking chairs. But the farmers had found that they didn't really care for rocking chairs. What they wanted to sit in was a Hupmobile or Graham-Paige or Overland. But their chairs still remained, on the porches. In my day we, the kids, filled the steps while our grandfathers were off touring. For us the porch was a home and a world. Meadowlarks were our neighbors in the vacant lots next door; the moon rising over Saddle-Back Mountain lighted us, and inside, the Victrola played Hawaiian music.

The TV has replaced the phonograph, but inside these bungalows all is familiar to me: dark wood, Mission furniture, a fireplace flanked by mantel-high bookcases. The dining room is still dominated by a built-in buffet, with leaded-glass doors and a mirror to reflect the cut glass kept on display. So we rattled up to Allied through my childhood and parked on a side street in front of where I used to live, complete with Gold of Ophir roses smothering the front porch and pampas grass on guard with plumes and spears beside the garage. Which way was I moving, forward or backward, in coming to Allied? How should my first symbol be read? I got out of the car and turned my back on what was so familiar and entered the studio with Stuart.

He asked me to wait while he made some phone calls. He is always doing this—making phone calls—and I don't know whether it is a characteristic of his, of Hollywood's, or a necessity of both. While I waited for Stuart, I could hear a man, out of sight beyond the half-opened doors of an office, engaged in a phone call of his own. He was talking to someone he called "Captain" about someone he called "Ludy."

Ludy was in trouble. In fact, Ludy was in jail. He had been picked up the night before by the police. The papers had run a story on it, exaggerated, of course, but which, if they were to be believed, would have Ludy involved in a series of extralegal activities, the most innocent of which were being drunk, being drunk in a car, speeding, resisting an officer, and attacking an officer.

"Captain," the voice went on, "you know this series Ludy is appearing in and how it's registering with the kids. They really look up to Ludy. He's a kind of hero to them. What he wears today they go into the stores and ask for tomorrow. Give him some special slang today and they're all using it tomorrow. He's a real idol to them, and if they hear he's got clay feet it won't help them any. I think our first concern's our kids and the impression we give them. I think we've got to keep this in mind. Besides, Ludy's a fine boy. Of course he gets under tension now and then and blows his top. Who doesn't? But he's a fine boy, Captain; all he needs is a little mothering and fathering. He doesn't need any publicity or a tough sentence to teach some other fella a lesson. He just needs mothering and fathering, and, Captain, if you give it your personal attention I'd be glad to see that a bottle of Scotch found its way to you."

I heard the phone click into place, the speaker sigh, and then say to himself, "Just a little mothering and fathering." He didn't say this cynically, but like a man uncertain as to where his own supply of mothering and fathering was coming from.

Stuart, who had overheard the last two sentences, said as we started our tour, "I'm afraid that's a bad introduction to movie making."

"The management will like me," I said. "I never speed, get drunk, or hit policemen."

"You can if you want to," Stuart said. "Writers aren't that important."

So there would be no mothering and fathering for me, even at the price of a bottle.

Symbol number two.

Stuart led me out of the office into an open square enclosed by a variety of shops: a drugstore, tailor shop, barbershop, café, a dentist's office, a hardware store. I took a letter I had been carrying all day (letters, so easy to write, so difficult to mail) to a postbox and lifted the metal flange.

112

Stuart grabbed my hand. "Drop that in there and it will be lost through all eternity. That's a movie mailbox."

"You mean it's a fake?"

"It's a real mailbox, all right. The trouble is, no one takes out what you put in." Only then did I see that I was on a movie set and that the shops were false fronts built across the faces of the Allied offices.

Symbol number three.

At Paramount, where we went next, I saw movie sets that *were* movie sets, sets that even I recognized. They looked like the movies, like Cecil De Mille, and even remotely like the valley of the Nile. There were mountains of canvas and sunsets of paint, and palms of crepe paper, and fountains of real water, all covering acres. It was fascinating to have this double vision, appearance and reality, present simultaneously. Which was real? Or neither?

Neither, according to Stuart. De Mille is not his hero. Willy is, and he spoke to me of all the ways in which they differed and how all the differences made Willy the superior director. Of these differences the only one which he regretted was that De Mille made more money. The set, large as it was, was filled with people, many of them in costume. Yul Brynner and Anne Baxter were there, looking like themselves in spite of their costumes: gods like men once again.

Although there were so many people, the set was very quiet. 'That's a difference between De Mille and Willy," Stuart whispered. "Willy won't let a mob of visitors on a set of his, but the people who are there may talk when he's not actually shooting. De Mille likes an audience, but they've got to follow his rules."

"What's going on now?" I asked.

Stuart pointed to De Mille, a short bald-headed man, who was seated watching a girl in Egyptian costume toss some gauzy material in front of a great reflecting disk of copper or brass. Occasionally De Mille spoke to the girl in a low voice, words I couldn't hear, and the girl tossed her gauze in a somewhat different fashion. Once she tried tossing green instead of purple gauze. But this was no good. She went back to the purple and, for the time I watched, stuck to this color. De Mille did not watch the girl, he watched the reflection of purple gauze in the copper mirror.

"They're rehearsing," Stuart said. "De Mille is a very patient rehearser."

"Why does he watch the mirror instead of the girl?"

"The picture will be of gauze reflected in the mirror. Not the girl."

I don't know how long we stood there, endlessly it seemed, as the girl continued to toss gauze and as De Mille continued patiently to instruct her how to toss gauze better and as the cameraman inspected the scene in order to be able to photograph most tellingly this well-instructed girl's best toss of gauze. It wasn't like watching darts or quoits. I didn't know a good toss when I saw it. I didn't know whether the girl was improving or going stale. Once De Mille had the copper circle polished and this, too, was without visible effect. He had the girl put on a different headband and, while this afforded a pleasant break, it did not alter the manner in which the gauze was tossed. Meanwhile, we were all as silent as an audience watching a performance of *Hamlet*.

I began to feel that I might scream in order to determine whether or not I was entranced and De Mille, some old Merlin, who had put us all under a spell.

"Let's go," I whispered to Stuart, and we tiptoed out into the real, the non-Egyptian sunshine.

"How long did we watch that?" I asked, my voice booming unnaturally in my ears after all the whispering.

"I don't know," Stuart boomed back. "Thirty minutes or so, I guess."

"Wasn't that awfully long to give to the reflection of purple gauze in a mirror?"

Stuart grinned. "Don't worry," he said. "They probably won't use it anyway."

Picture which will not be used of gauze reflected in a mirror. Fourth and last symbol of the day.


I was disappointed with Mr. Wyler's office. The movies have taught us to believe that executive suites are more resplendent. Perhaps in the movies everything is more so than in life, and the real difficulty, when it comes to filming a story of the Quakers, won't lie in any effort to jazz

114

them up but in a constant tendency to make them more Quakerish than any Quakers ever were.

Mr. Wyler's office was certainly not threadbare, but it was not lavish either. Here, as at his home, his desk was so placed that he was able to keep his bad ear to the wall. Mr. Wyler has a very collected face. It might be so in any case, or perhaps in a business of directing faces to show emotion he compensates for the excesses of others by his own quiet. No use trying to outmug professional muggers. Whatever the cause, his "basic" face is full of reserve. This may account for one's pleasure in watching his face for the "breakthrough" of interest or amusement. And one takes personal credit in affecting the breakthrough. "I made him smile." The face (mine, I think) that is continuously responsive affords no one this pleasure. But, contrary to popular opinion, it is this "open" face that hides more than the "closed" face. What is the significance of movement in someone with St. Vitus's dance?

We read of persons who look "all broken up." And there are certainly faces that appear to be right on the verge of that, of shattering with laughter or disintegrating with a grimace. I can't imagine Mr. Wyler's face "breaking up." In soup kitchen or police line-up, if some turn of fortune brought him there, I think his face would remain much as it is. I think he has already, imaginatively, contemplated life's misfortunes. Such conclusions may show only how little I know of life or its misfortunes. I have had no acquaintance with persons who have gone from good fortune to police line-ups, no knowledge, even second hand, of concentration camps. Those who have might tell me that, under certain circumstances, there is no face that doesn't "break up."

I've often wished it were possible to see the different faces one might have—and I am sure they are innumerable. What if we had lived without any envy, meanness, duplicity, fear, or sloth? With what kind of sunburst radiance would we face the world, finally? What would be the result if identical twins were, from birth, encouraged in dissimilar responses to life? Would their faces remain identical?

Mr. Wyler's face, as Stuart and I entered his office, said, insofar as I can read it, pleasure. When we were seated he

115

told me that Cooper had agreed to play Jess. Cooper was, in his opinion, the only person for Jess. For Eliza, he had a list of twenty-four possibilities.

"Have you had any idea about Eliza?" he asked me.

I told him I thought that the actress who played Eliza should be the last person in the world anyone would think of as a Quaker minister.

Mr. Wyler laughed, "That's easy. Marilyn Monroe. Seriously, what would you think of Katherine Hepburn?"

"I think she would make a fine Jess."

Mr. Wyler didn't laugh. But lank and blue-eyed is the way I've always seen Jess. Eliza I've seen as small, plump, black-haired, white-skinned. Visually, I'd seen Eliza as Olivia de Haviland or Jane Wyman. I mentioned these names, and Mr. Wyler said, "There are some actresses who might play Eliza well enough, but combine them with Cooper and the public won't be interested. Another combination and excitement is communicated. I don't know that it can be explained. But it exists. Apart from the story, audiences like to watch a certain byplay which they think they detect—and perhaps they do—between an actor and an actress. I think an audience would enjoy the combination of Cooper and Hepburn."

Like the shoemaker who sees the world in terms of the shoes it wears, I had seen the movies in terms of their scripts. How important was casting? Could a good actor "but wrong for the part" ruin a movie?

"What, in your opinion, must the actress who plays Eliza convey to the audience?" Mr. Wyler asked me.

"First of all she must be lovable. Pretty. Appealing. She's so cocksure of herself; she must be that or no one will believe that Jess could put up with her."

"Is Hepburn pretty enough?"

Hepburn was pretty enough, though a round, dark Eliza was hard to give up.

"How would you describe the relationship between Jess and Eliza?"

"They're in love—after twenty years. But there's an edge to their feeling for each other. Maybe that's the reason they still are in love."

"What's the edge?"

"Eliza will wear the pants if Jess doesn't look out. She

116

doesn't want to. She won't love Jess if she does. But she's intelligent and energetic and if he isn't more of a man, constantly, than she is, she will take over."

"You don't think Hepburn could play that part?"

I began to feel that I had been describing Hepburn.

"And you don't think that Cooper isn't the man to be constantly more man than she is?"

"Oh yes, I think that."

"And you think the audience wouldn't relish that duel?"

It would, all right.

"The trouble is," Mr. Wyler said, "I think Hepburn's unavailable. So we'll have to find someone else who can do the same thing. How do you see Jess's friend, Sam?"

"Well, as a kind of younger, more rural Donald Crisp."

I am beginning to catch on to a few things. First, the importance of casting. Also the way in which known actors are used for purposes of defining characters in the script. They are used as chemists use the elements to describe. Thus, water being made up of two parts of hydrogen to one of oxygen is $H_2O$. And the formula for Sam might be $I_2C$. Two parts Burl Ives to one part Donald Crisp.

*Thursday*
*9 P.M., at home,*
*Whittier*

In bed and broken, every bone in my body aching. And it isn't what I did but the way I did it that broke me. I was broken by all my feelings of despair, anger, bewilderment. And now I am being revived by feeling. Irony and amusement are saving my life. Now that I am no longer victimized by it, my own stupidity fills me with as much amazed wonder as if I were seeing it displayed in a play. "The poor silly fool," I say to myself. "She ought to be committed." And I relish the fact, too, that, deserving commitment, I have escaped it and lie here in this upstairs bedroom listening to the dry desert rustle of the palm trees outside my window. Sweet sound! Sweet desert quiet! And I long, after what I've been through, for slow desert

117

camels moving soundlessly, without benefit of lane or signal, sign or cop, from one motorless oasis to another.

That cursed convertible sitting under my window all week began to prey on my mind. I'd been too busy to use it. But yesterday I swore I would stop work at three today and drive out to the ranch at Whittier. Actually, since Papa subdivided, it isn't a ranch any more, but I suppose that even when it's reduced to a nubbin the size of a city lot we'll still be calling it "the ranch." But ranch or no, I did stop work at three and head toward it.

I've been accustomed to thinking of myself as a fine driver. I've driven since I was twelve and I can't remember learning to drive any more than I can remember learning to read or to walk. I haven't always obeyed the traffic laws but I've never been caught disobeying them. So, besides being good, I'm lucky.

Today I discovered that I may be a good and lucky driver in the country but in the city I'm a poor, unlucky driver. In the country we drive fast but the roads aren't congested with a lot of other lunatics doing the same thing. The sensation on the freeways, with eight cars abreast, is of tandem driving: all the hazards of Ben Hur in a chariot, and none of his controls. He, after all, had a rein to each horse. We control only one; the other seven are freewheeling in every sense of the word. In spite of this lack of control, we must synchronize the movements of our steed with that of the other seven. And what those movements will be, one man's guess is likely to be as bad as the next's. In addition to all this unpredictable movement on the freeways, there are the unpredictable freeways themselves. At sixty miles an hour, and that's as slow as it's safe to go without danger of being run down from the rear, it is often impossible, in the time you have after seeing the sign announcing the turnoff, to get into the proper lane for the turnoff. So you miss it. You can't stop.

Though last week the papers were filled with the story of a man who did. He pulled up in a center lane, turned off his engine, set his brakes, turned his face to the automatic window wall, and gave up. When the officers arrived he said, "The freeways win." The ordinary poor conforming citizen can't, stop, however. He has no choice but to continue, hurtling indefinitely at breakneck speed

118

often in the wrong direction. The sensation while he does this must be as near that of damnation by predestination as a modern man can achieve.

There are elements of Catholic indulgence as well as Protestant hell in the situation. This wayward path may land him, instead of in the ditch, in Anaheim, Pomona, San Pedro, Azusa, etc. Not destinations, God knows, he had elected. Still, after spending some time in these places, he may find ways of turning around and making a new start.

With all of this in mind I decided to avoid the freeway and go to Whittier by Beverly Boulevard. Some foe of mine had told me that this was a good direct way to get there. What he hadn't told me was that for several blocks in the heart of Los Angeles, Beverly Boulevard, with no warning of any kind, simply ceases. With that false humility which I abominate but which often rules me, I immediately decided that it was not the boulevard which had left me but I who had left the boulevard. I managed to get off the street I was on (a real job, since the Oldsmobile is not only larger than the Dodge, but I had to manage its largeness in spaces much smaller than those to which I'm accustomed) and to ask how to get back onto Beverly. I was told, I got back, I drove with one eye on the road, one on the signposts, determined never, never again to lose Beverly. Well, I never did. Which was a pity, since the direction I was going was wrong. At about the time I should have been seeing the San Gabriel River I began to see mountains. Instead of Pio Pico's mansion, the Tahitian Hut. Everyone has been telling me that southern California has changed so much I wouldn't know it. How right they were, I thought. I would never believe I was entering Whittier. I wasn't. I was leaving North Hollywood, headed north. I had been an hour and a half on the road and was still ten miles farther from the ranch than when I had started. It was five o'clock; evening traffic was at its heaviest. I had bypassed all purgatories and arrived in hell itself. Humble but persistent, I turned around once more.

I got through Los Angeles and was finally on the Whittier side of that city. Up to this time I knew the mistakes I had made. They were big mistakes, but simple and explainable. From now on they were smaller, more numerous, and less explainable.

I passed a stopped school bus, I drove forty-two miles an hour in a twenty-five-mile zone. I drove the wrong way on a one-way street. I received three tickets. It took me three hours to get here. It wasn't the three hours that broke me. It was the anguish. Merle says that what I need in the car is a built-in teleprompter. "Prepare to turn left in four blocks. Slow to twenty-five miles per hour. Signal for turn."

In the country I have a built-in teleprompter which takes care of country hazards. Here I will have to develop a new one. Thank God for a day in which to recover before I have to attempt the return journey. I shall go by the freeway. What happens there at least happens fast.

*Sunday*
*Whittier, 9* A.M.

Sunday-school bell ringing in the Friends' church down the road. Everything in that sentence would have been wrong to my grandparents. They were in revolt against making, by name or deed, one day more holy than another. For them there was no Sabbath or Sunday, only a day that began the week and that, for convenience's sake, was called First Day. The building in which they met for worship they refused to call a "church," as if there could be anything holy or special about any edifice, a mere collection of boards, shingles, plaster, etc., put together to give man some protection from wind and rain. A place where Friends met for worship was a "meetinghouse" and nothing more. And what took place there was important, not the boards under their feet or the shingles over their heads.

There were no bells in early meetinghouses. Partly because to have a bell properly hung a steeple or spire was needed. And steeples and spires were characteristic of churches, temples, cathedrals, abbeys, buildings that, so the early Friends felt, emphasized objects rather than men, means rather than ends, outwardness rather than inward-

120

ness, the world rather than God. George Fox called churches, derisively, "steeple houses." And the bell in itself was a worldly contraption. A man shouldn't need to have the memory of his God or his desire to commune with Him clanged into his ears by the pounding of clappers against metal.

This bell, ringing down the road, was given to the Friends' church by members of my family in memory of Elizabeth Griffith Milhous, my great-grandmother, a Quaker minister. There were still those who thought it unsuitable to hang a bell in a Friends' meetinghouse, so there was a period when the bell waited, uncrated, until the control of the meeting should pass into the hands of its younger members. Little Frankie, listening to this same Sunday-school bell, used to tell us what its ringing said. According to him its message was: "Be good, people. Be good, people." George Fox, I suppose, would have believed that Frankie, aged four, should not have needed bells to remind him of this.

It is an odd thing that Hollywood should be the means of making me more thoughtful about Quakerism. A birthright Quaker (*Collier's* once said I was a "birth rite" Quaker: something like a Scottish Rite Mason, I guess) whose forebears were birthright Quakers when they arrived in this country in the seventeen-hundreds—some with William Penn himself—I have tended to take Quakerism for granted. One needs to be a convert, or as Quakers say, a "Friend by conviction," to be sensitive to one's religion. And I not only have the disadvantage of taking Quakerism for granted, but the Quakerism I take for granted is unlike that anyone cares to believe existed. No one wishes to believe that the Quakerism I knew as a child in southern California had little to distinguish it from shouting Methodism. We sang the rag-time hymns, listened to sermons long on rhetoric and short on reason, and had revivals that tore all but the most stolidly built emotionally among us right apart at our spiritual seams. We had revivals that put all of us in a "weaving way." I have seen a Quaker minister, an uncle of mine, pace the platform, singing, and, in time to the music, alternately smack the songbook to his palm, and toss it with an equally loud bang against the ceiling. The timing, at least, was remarkable. We may have had no spires on the outside, but inside the Quaker meetinghouses I knew as a child, a level anything but dead prevailed. Richard Nixon's father was my Sunday-school teacher and the father put into his Sunday-school teaching all of the vigorous verbal polemics the son displays in politics.

Lee Vernon, the Presbyterian minister in Napa, was a member of the Friends' church I attended as a child. He wanted to be a Quaker minister, but the Quakers of Yorba Linda then believed that "the second birth," that is, a "baptism by the spirit," and "a death to the world," rendered an individual for ever afterward incapable of sin. Lee never felt himself quite incapable of sin, and for this reason the Quakers rejected him as a prospective minister. The Presbyterians, people who have never lost sight of man's ability to sin, welcomed him; and the Quaker loss has been the Presbyterian gain.

The kind of Quakerism I knew as a child and young woman is horrifying alike to Philadelphia Quakers and Hollywood movie-makers. Neither, though for different reasons, likes to think that Quakers ever sang, listened to sermons, or clapped hands in a revival. But Quakers were not, in the beginning, a moderate people. They were nearer Hollywood than Hollywood knows. They, too, flung off all their clothes on occasion to get attention. I went with one of my household helpers (it is nonsense to try to pigeonhole such women by calling them "maids") to an Assembly of God service. I thought that I was much nearer primitive Quakerism there in the middle of that fervor than in most present-day Quaker meetings.

When I was in London after my first silent transcontinental train trip, I went to the Meeting for Worship of the Friends in London. The congregation was silent when I entered, many with heads bowed. Prayer had just been finished or was about, I decided, to be forthcoming. I bowed my head and waited. Nothing. Nothing, indefinitely. I began to wonder whether or not I had stumbled into a meeting of deaf mutes. I lifted my head, opened my eyes, looked about, and realized that I, the birthright Quaker, the offspring of Quaker ministers without number, was in the midst of my first silent meeting. I also realized that I was unprepared for it. I missed the spank of the songbook against the ceiling, the clip-clop of the organ, the exhortation, the vigorous congregational singing. "Oh that will *be* glo—*ree* for me." Worship *was* these sounds and sights. Alone, silent, surrounded by silent people, I was like a nonswimmer deprived of his water wings.

People believe, Mr. Wyler believes, that I have experienced the life depicted in *The Friendly Persuasion*. I am as innocent of first-hand knowledge of the life depicted in that book as he is. Perhaps more so, since, for all I know, worship in a Jewish temple may be nearer the practice of the Philadelphia Quakers than of the Yorba Linda Friends.

*The Friendly Persuasion,* insofar as it is anyone's experience, is the experience of my great-grandparents as remembered by my mother from tales told her by her parents. This is about the right remove for fiction. The facts are very few—except for one fact which is really responsible for the book: that is Mama's love (amidst the barley fields and the seedling orange trees and the shouting Quakers) for, not *the* old-time Quakers, but *her* old-time Quakers, the people of her own blood. In her opinion there was never anyone like them. This doesn't mean that she was in any way against singing or barley fields. Though she never, to my knowledge, opened her mouth in church to sing, pray, or testify. This silence was the result of no condemnation of a pastoral meeting. There were—and now I conjecture, for who is so strange to us as our parents? —there were three reasons for her silence. First, a real timidity; second, a real intuition that religious insights should lie too deep for words; and third, and perhaps most important, a real arrogance. She was and is full of pride. She scorned to speak without excelling. She had none of the self-forgetfulness of a real religious.

Someone has said that of all people the Irish are the least suited to Quakerism. Yet Mama's people were Irish and Quakers when they arrived on these shores. It is as if a person should elect a wound, marry an irreconcilability. The Irish nature, which can, as Shaw said, live on hatred, which loves words and glories in contradictions, which can be tickled by a straw and cast down by a shadow, must, when it embraces Quakerism, forswear its own nature. These Irish Quakers, possibly in an effort to match tensions, married Welsh Quakers. This is no easy heritage:

123

the "right" by birth of Quakerism, the necessity by blood of Welsh and Irish emotionalism. Mama has never given up trying to subdue the "necessity" by means of the "right." The spare mold of Quakerism, as envisaged at the turn of the century in the backwoods of southern Indiana and a little later in the barley fields of southern California, cramped a lavish nature. Yet it is difficult to imagine her of any other faith. The Irish, emotional and romantic as they are, put two and two together very coldly. And there is a hard clear rationality about Quakers—and, indeed, all mysticism, which, once experienced, makes other ways appear indirect, childish, and crude.

She no longer tries so hard to reconcile the Irish and the Quaker. I can hear her downstairs playing a Sousa march, "El Capitan," I think. She is seventy-three, has had two strokes, but a corps of fighting men could step out to the beat of this music with no sense of age, invalidism, or, I'm afraid, Quakerism to slow them down.

The strokes have not impaired her physically in any way. The first robbed her of her ability to give objects their proper names: hats were pills and pills were hairbrushes and so on. The second restored this ability, but took much of her memory of persons and events. Though what she has felt, she remembers. We are all perhaps what we have felt, not what we have done. She can recall the sensations of love and hatred, though she may have forgotten why and for whom.

I cannot speak of Mama to anyone without making her state appear either worse or better than it is, either wholly tragic or wholly happy. It must be tragic to drift unknowing amidst persons, familiar yet unidentifiable, a real existential hell, where nothing is re-experienced, but everything must be accounted for anew minute by minute. Mama begins every day unable to remember that her children are her children, her husband, her husband, her home, her home. By evening she remembers more.

She says to me, "You remind me of Jessamyn. Not in your looks so much. She is a good deal younger than you. I don't mean to say you're old. I expect you're right in the prime of life. But Jessamyn was a girl. She always carried an armload of books in the same way you do. You would have liked her, I expect."

If I give her a certain smile and say "Wonder if she would have liked *me?*" Mama will clap her hand to her forehead. "You *are* Jessamyn. Oh, I feel like fainting."

But when she is involved in minute to minute happenings, not caring to whom she speaks or in need of remembering the past, no one is wittier or more capable of happiness.

This morning for instance, she asked Papa, as she always does at the beginning of the day, "Are we married?" When Papa said "Yes, for more than fifty years," she answered, "So long ago? No wonder I can't remember it."

To me, privately, she said the other day, "I'm not really married to that old man. But everyone takes for granted we are and when we visit they put us in the same bed. At first I didn't know what to do about it. But I've always liked to sleep with someone. My feet and back get cold if I sleep alone. So I sleep with him. He's a perfect gentleman and everyone expects it and I'm more comfortable, so I don't see any harm in it, do you?"

I told her it was the only thing to do under the circumstances.

Since she no longer reads easily, she likes to look at pictures of any kind, old family photographs especially. Going through some of these last night she came upon a nephew's efforts at a still life—the snapshot of a grass-skirted, South Sea island figurine. Without pause she handed it to Papa.

"Some member of your family, I suppose."

In saying this she was being witty, which anyone with wit can do. But she was being witty at her own expense, which takes a certain kind of—not humility, but security. She was remembering that she had always twitted Papa about the Indian blood in his family.

Recently, having made some notable gravy, I boasted, as the bowl went round the table, "I'll be content if you put on my gravestone, 'She was a fine gravy-maker.'"

Everyone except Mama agreed to this epitaph. "No," she said, "we'll not do that. We'll put on your tombstone, 'Standard G. M.'"

"Standard G. M.? What does that mean."

"Standard Gravy-Maker, of course."

So how is one to describe her state, how sum it up? It

cannot be summed up. The minute I speak of laughter I remember the tears. People who hear such exchanges as the standard gravy-maker substitute epitaph cannot believe that the same woman walked down the street weeping, saying "I am looking for my mother," to passers-by.

Now she is playing "Old Folks at Home," slowly and sadly. Extending all those notes of longing and past time, of places and persons alive in memory alone. She, without memory. And yet she doesn't play it as she did the Sousa. What does it mean to her? What comes to her as the piano says "home" and "old folks"? She, who lives in the house where her father lived, but who asks each morning when she comes down the stair, "Will we be here all day?"

I hope she lives to see the movie *Friendly Persuasion*. She started it. The other day when I told her I'd met Gary Cooper, she asked, "Is Gary Cooper Jess?" She didn't mean will he play Jess, but I said yes without attempting to explain. Maybe he will be.

If I'm going to church I've got to run.

NOTE: Hamlin Garland in *Boy Life on the Prairie* written in 1907 uses the word "bushed" with today's meaning. I thought it was new slang.

Mockingbirds sing here. Over on Wilshire electric razors sing the only morning songs.

Memories of this house when I was a child:

1. The wind blowing—paper and tumbleweeds roaring, it seemed down the orchard rows. Excitement and fear.

2. The new piano. How wonderful! But not as wonderful as the box it came in. The box could be *anything* —boat, house, prison, church. The piano was always a piano.

3. The orange celluloid ball, pitted, even, like orange skin, a gift on an ordinary day. Not a birthday or Christmas. The best gift of my life.

4. Eating, little by little, every bit of Grandma's ice cream, when ice cream, because she had cancer of the stomach, was all she could eat. The worst sin of my life.

5. Making valentines. The mystery of the arrow drawn

so it appeared to pierce the paper heart, but actually did not.

6. Grandma's rose glycerin lotion.

7. Alone with Grandpa. The sight, sound, and smell of the coal-oil stove when he lit it to heat the milk for our milk toast. He made enough toast at one time to last several days. But the milk was fresh and hot. Then he played the accordion.

8. Grandpa's truss. Trying to figure out what its use could be. He seemed ashamed when he found I had seen it. Something evil evidently.

*Napa*

I haven't written here for two weeks. I never do when I'm spending eight hours a day on other writing. Though that is just the time when thousands of ideas come to me. I always hope they'll return.

There was no sense staying in Hollywood at this stage of the writing. Mr. Wyler wants everything fast, also very full. He said, "I like choices. I like room to turn around in in the dialogue. Give me more than I need."

I'm not accustomed to doing this. I don't write more than I need, then cut. True, this happens, though usually I discover redundancy sentence by sentence and paragraph by paragraph and eliminate like an earthworm as I go along. My plan always is to write exactly as much as is needed.

"I want all your ideas," Mr. Wyler said. "Who knows which will be most valuable?"

Well, usually, I do. I have a conviction, at least, whether I "know" or not.

Mr. Wyler is going to Japan soon and would like to see a first-draft script before he leaves. The day I left Hollywood he said, "Forget that you have home or husband, mother or children, and write, write, write."

Since I'm working by the week, not by the piece, it might be thought that Mr. Wyler wants a lot of work for as little money as possible. If he does, this doesn't upset me. Without wanting this he'd probably never get a movie made. He also wants it good and he wants it fast. Whether good or not, I don't know. But fast, yes. I sit outside in my sun trap, so still and unmoving, except for my fingers racing across the page, that a cock pheasant walked past me not more than six feet away.

Stu called today to say "hire a cook, hire a maid," do whatever is necessary in order to be able to write full time.

Someone mailed me a clipping from Hedda Hopper's column in which she said that, though I was not a script writer, Mr. Wyler wanted me to write the script. Also that I had headed back to Napa to do the writing.

Fred read this and shook his head. He was very sorry for me. I asked him why. "To have something so unflattering written about you."

"But how is it unflattering?" I asked.

"To say, right out, you're no script writer."

"But it's the truth. And besides, I'd rather be called a novelist or short-story writer."

"Script writing is the top," he said flatly. "Everybody knows that. Also 'heading back to Napa!' as if you were too small-town to get along in Hollywood."

"That may be the truth too."

"There's a lot of truths," Fred answered cryptically, "that it's not very flattering to have the newspapers publish."

Fred does not greatly relish my return, flattering or not. I take him off the hamburger train and put him back on a work schedule. Fred has his own reasons for wishing I would make the grade in Hollywood.

Max, bless his heart, welcomes me and is more interested than I in the way Hollywood works. So far, I can't give him much information, except about script writing.

"What's the difference," he asked, "between writing a script and writing a story?"

"To see more with the eyes and hear less with the ears."

"What else?"

"To tell less. The actor can say it with his eyebrows."

"I don't think Cooper's got very agile eyebrows."

"You've never watched him the way I have. The most difficult thing is to decide who the camera is."

"Who? You mean where, don't you?"

"Where is who. Sometimes it is Jess looking at Eliza. Sometimes Eliza looking at Jess. Sometimes it is God looking at the whole shooting match. When it goes close things slow down. When it pulls away they speed up. When it goes close you want the audience to know what the actor feels, to feel the need to scan his face in order to see what he will do. When the camera pulls away you want the audience to watch action, not faces. Stu says Mr. Wyler is famous for getting both at the same time, depth in action, the movement and the significance of the movement."

"How?" Max asks.

And I get mad. I don't know the answer. How can I know so much so soon? It seems unreasonable of Max to think I could explain such a thing.

"How? How do I know how? I'm not a director. I'm a beginning script writer in the third week of script writing. Don't ask me such silly questions."

But if I *had* known, I would have been mad if he *hadn't* asked.

Why am I so irritable after long hours of writing? Is it because in writing one puts down only the questions one can answer, and gets out of the habit of saying "I don't know"?

Nothing can be well written without complete openness. Openness to the people about whom one writes. Does Jess love music, yearn for it? Yet is able to hear so little and that only at the expense of Eliza's disapproval? Does Josh think he has no courage and believe that he must test it? Is Mattie falling in love for the first time? None of this can be put down without the most complete openness to these people and to their emotions. None of this can be known —known by me anyway, without love.

One spends a day, then, in this openness and love. One is exposed. Writing might be defined as the constant practice of self-exposure—and not in the sense that the finished writing exposes the writer—but in the sense that the writer lays himself completely open to the world he is creating. At the end of a day of writing one walks, full of this openness, which anticipates nothing but a like openness and love, into a world where the day-long practice has been a protective closing, a striking back. The blow one receives then, one can't dodge. The particle flies into an eye trained to stay open.

One can write out of love or hate. Hate tells one a great deal about a person. Love makes one become the person. Love, contrary to legend, is not half as blind, at least for writing purposes, as hate. Love can see the evil and not cease to be love. Hate cannot see the good and remain hate. The writer, writing out of hatred, will, thus, paint a far more partial picture than if he had written out of love.

I have begun, sometimes, to write out of hatred, but, since writing is a way of learning for the writer, as I began to know more about the hated person, my hatred lessened. Finally I became the hated person. Then I no longer hated, for I do not hate myself. But perhaps I forgave the hated person too much, as I forgive myself too much. Though I do not hate myself, I have hateful characteristics. "To know all is to forgive all." Forgive, yes. But not to forget. Not to forget that there is evil in the world. If I'm going to do that, better put down the pen and start selling Good Humors . . . tinkle, tinkle, little bell, tell the world I've sweets to sell.

Also, please to remember, J. West, that the openness after you have been writing doesn't show. Others don't know you've dropped your guard. When you put your pen down, lift the mitts, please. Protect yourself a little.

*Monday*

Max and Fred off to school early. Gray, quiet day. Birds with voices like water. Protective vocal coloration, since the streams are still fairly loud. Frogs still croaking. I mark the seasons here by whether I hear frogs or insects at evening. Frogs mean the season of water. The season of water means winter, no matter what the month. Insects, cicadas, katydids, crickets, all the dozens of little shelled jumpers and complainers whose names I don't know mean sun and dryness to me. And sun and dryness, no matter what the month, is summer. So we may have summer in December and, in a wet year, winter in May. Thoreau dates spring from the hour in which he hears the first peepers, and the first katydids tell *him* that frost is only six weeks away. Three thousand miles change the messages.

I have been walking about the house in my nightgown, "setting things to rights," picking up fallen tulip petals, sweeping the ashes back into the fireplace, putting the little magazines on top of the big ones. What is this strange secretive delight of being alone in a house? Walking like a burglar on tiptoe through my own rooms lest someone discover me stealing something. What am I stealing? And from whom? What is solitude? The theft of the self from others? Who wants me now? No one, as far as I know. No one in the world feels deprived because of my absence. But do I make solitude a sharper sweet by some unconscious pretense that I am putting something over on the world? Is it the "putting over," the defiance, the living "in spite of" that really pleases me rather than being alone?

I like all the words for making a house tidy which convey something short of a thorough housecleaning; words which say that the house is already clean and needs only the flick of a dustcloth, the rearrangement of a vase of flowers, the stirring up of a fire to make it perfect: words like "setting to rights," "straightening," "redding up," "brushing out."

Walking about the house this morning "straightening up," I felt momentarily like a girl again, filled with the desire to surprise Mama when she returned, with my gift of love in an unexpected orderly house.

The gifts of love one wants to make change, but the desire to make them remains the only real happiness I know anything about. I am not speaking of joy now, which comes unbidden and is unaccountable, but of love and its accountable accompaniment. And this happiness has nothing to do with being loved. "Being loved" is something that happens to someone else. Loving is what happens to you. Without it and the desire that always goes with it to make gifts of love, life is maimed, mutilated,

131

deprived, depravèd. Without it, life is soured at the source. With it, anything can be borne. To live without being loved is sorrowful. Without loving there *is* no real life.

## Thursday

Max and I went to San Francisco last night and ate at the most expensive and fashionable restaurant there. We remembered the old days of walking by, dreaming, desiring, but not daring to enter. I try to remember why, what our feelings were about the place, why we would not enter. Partly fear, fear that in so fashionable a place we wouldn't know the ropes. Partly concern about money, an exaggeration in our minds of what "expensive" meant. And partly we were kept out because of our stupidity and narrowness. We had never in our lives dined in so elegant a place and had not enough intelligence or imagination to see ourselves doing so. And we were satisfied with the little world we knew. Proud of it even. We had no desire to increase our experience. It never occurred to us to ask about prices instead of deciding, without knowledge, that they must be beyond us. It never occurred to us to look inside to see if, actually, we would like to eat there. We accepted the legend both of the desirability and the unattainability. When either or both might have been false. We had the fear of the poor and the ignorant that we would reveal our poorness and our ignorance. Both honorable states which need not be hidden; and yet we did yearn to enter.

If I had money I think I'd set up a "Small Pleasures Foundation for the Young." The grants would not be money and there would be no attempt to allot them according to desserts. They would be handed out by an administrator who gave them for no better reason than that he liked the person who made the request. These grants would never cost more than a hundred dollars and they would consist of: theater tickets, beaded handbags, elegant meals in renowned restaurants, beautiful books, slippers made of anaconda skin, intricate side rules, ivory chess and domino sets, rare perfumes, pedometers, the world's most famous champagne, hunting sticks, recorded music, hundred-dollar tickets for campaign dinners. The preference would be given to those who wanted to "do" rather than "have" things. But the "Small Pleasures Foundation" would try to take care of both.

*Friday*

Dolores here this afternoon. She moves me more than any other natural wonder—except the wind, and the brown hills—and almost as much as the unnatural wonders: poetry and prose. I'm tempted to enshrine her like a sibyl, a junior-size sphinx.

We heard horses coming down the road. She said, "Listen! They might be beautiful! They might be white!"

She said (Dolores is no either-or person), "I am going to be a nurse, an amplayne flyer, and a dog-seller."

She said, "We can't use our milk. It smells like gasoline."

I said, "Maybe you can use it in the car then."

She said, "Oh, no. Milk is a liquid and gasoline is clear as water."

She said, "Do you want to know a funny story? Humpty Dumpty sat on a banana peeling."

I said, "Is that funny?"

She hurriedly improvised some more. "Humpty Dumpty sat on a wall *and* a banana peeling and fell clear to the ceiling."

She looked at me beseechingly, which she almost never does. What she thinks, ordinarily she thinks, and I can take it or leave it. She made me feel like a producer refusing to laugh at a first-draft script.

She asked for a pencil and paper and sat beside me writing, while I wrote. She said pensively, "Nobody knows what I'm going to write, not even you, but I will tell you."

"What?" I asked.

"I have to tell myself first."

Now she makes me feel like me.

133

What do I hope for this picture? It can clearly never be a *Hamlet* or a *Farewell to Arms*. Though that wouldn't be such a bad title for it. Mr. Wyler, talking about possible titles, once said that if it hadn't been used before he'd like to call *The Friendly Persuasion* "War and Peace." I hope it won't be a "Ma and Pa Birdwell" or an "East Lynne"; though if it were another version of either of those it would be very popular. I hope it will be a movie about people whose fate interests the audience. That from the beginning the audience will say, "I want to know what happens to Jess and Eliza." And when the movie is over, I don't want them to say, even though they may have been on the edge of their chairs every minute, "So what?" I want them to say, "I must think about this some more. I must remember it. It had some meaning."

Here I am, wondering about the audience and what it will think of the movie. I never do this about a novel or short story. Yes, I do try to write in such a way that what I feel and see in a story will be accessible to readers. Or rather to a reader. I can't think of plural readers.

Will this sense of an audience make the writing of a script different from the writing of a story?

*Evening*

An hour-long call from Stu today. I'm going down to Hollywood tomorrow evening. He said two things that make it impossible for me to write another word until I know definitely what he means. And if what he said means what I think it does, I must find out whether he is speaking for himself alone or for Mr. Wyler.

The two sentences which trouble me are these: "Jess

must go through hell and high water" and "Jess must undergo change."

Now there are all kinds of hell and high water. Some kinds Jess will certainly go through. No Quaker in time of war with a son enlisting is going to be in heaven and on high ground for the duration. But if Stuart means a hell of physical action, of Jess himself engaging in some hand-to-hand fighting, that I'd better know, because I am not the person who can write it.

And if he means by "change" that Jess, who starts the picture as a pacifist, ends it by becoming the doughtiest fighter of them all, that I'd better know too. Because I can't write that either.

I am suspicious of the "switcheroo," a change in the fundamental nature of a character in any literary form; but especially in the hour-and-a-half movie. There, more than any place else, it appears to mirror the author's need, rather than the character's necessity. All audiences see and evidently delight in these unreal switches: the plain prim girl who becomes, when she takes off her glasses, beautiful and seductive; the coward who mows down the bully; the adolescent who "faces up to life" and becomes "adult"; the wastrel who looks at a good woman and puts away his bottle and the girls who aren't good. Such rightabout-faces are, outside of a few real conversions, extremely rare; but it is almost impossible to depict even a real conversion in an hour and a half in such a way as to make it plausible.

If the story we are reading or are looking at on the screen is a fairy tale, then fine and good. Coward-to-hero, prim-to-seductive is what we're entitled to. We'll feel cheated without it. But *The Friendly Persuasion* isn't a fairy tale. We're going to have to tell it straight.

Nor do I think that *Othello*, for instance, is the story of a "good man who becomes a killer," nor *Hamlet* of a "weak man who becomes strong," nor *Macbeth*, "a steadfast man who became ambitious." Othello was a jealous man confronted by circumstances which aroused his jealousy. Hamlet, a man who could not act except spontaneously, and who finally did so act. Macbeth, an ambitious man, who did not lose his ambition when all that stood between him and the throne was the death of a king. All the best writing has been of those who become more and more themselves, of the discovery by the hero of himself.

"Anyone who arrives at self-knowledge through desperation is the raw material for a great play," Kenneth Tynan said, and I shall go down to Hollywood and quote him to Mr. Wyler.

## Beverly Hills Hotel

My favorite room at this hotel is a room looking over the kitchen gardens. By kitchen gardens I don't mean plantings of parsley and chives and sage, but the gardens at the back of the hotel onto which the kitchens open. The planting is the same here as in front, gardenias and old olive trees and trailing geraniums. But the cars and the guests are not to be seen. Cooks and cooks' helpers, maids and factotums whose functions are unknown to me, step outside for a cigarette and a lazy quiet word. Their voices are low. They are enjoying the sun, the rest, the silence. Their attitudes are easy as they lounge for a minute against a tree, or sit, feet extended, on a bench. It's a very warm day, a couple of hours before sundown. The day seems over—though perhaps not to them, with dinner ahead. A man in a cook's outfit puts a geranium behind his ear. Their smoke drifts up to me very sweet, warm, and summer-afternoon smelling. My feeling in this room is of staying in a great Irish house, a very grand Irish house, I suppose, if a staff of this size is to be accounted for. I have no knowledge of Irish houses, grand or mean. But this room with its faded chintzes reminds me of Bowen's Court as described by Elizabeth Bowen.

I had lunch here today with Mr. Wyler and Stu. We ate in the sun, but without white wine, birds, or models.

I am glad I came down, though I've simply replaced the old worries with new ones. But I know more about the nature of the new ones, and they do not involve any writing in which I don't believe. I quoted Tynan and Brunetière to Mr. Wyler. He listened with that rare (in human beings, not in him) listening look. Tynan's hero called upon "to answer the unanswerable," he liked. He agreed that this was Jess's position. He was less convinced about "change" in characters. He admires John Huston's *The African Queen*. He finds dramatic and agreeable (I'm not just sure how it should be described) the change we see in Katherine Hepburn as she plays the missionary's daughter in that picture.

I asked him what change there was in the princess as played by Audrey Hepburn in his own *Roman Holiday*. Stuart began to answer this and Mr. Wyler silenced him with one flashing look and two sharp words. I was uncomfortable but Stuart seemed calm. Mr. Wyler thought the princess did change. At the end of the picture she refuses her usual hot milk, rebukes her lady in waiting, etc. Was this not change? No, this was development. He thought I was perhaps quibbling with words. I thought not. Development is the opposite of change. It is becoming more of the same. There is no reversal in it.

We were, theoretically at least, in agreement finally. Jess's "hell and high water" need not be one of physical participation in conflict. There need be no worm-turning twists. I am not sure whether Stu, in his talk with me over the phone, was advocating hell and reversal or whether he was warning me that hell and reversal might be the order of the day. I didn't ask him. Keep it dense.

These were the old worries cleared up. The new ones uncovered are these: Mr. Wyler said that the script would undoubtedly need, before it became a "shooting script," the assistance of a professional. He hasn't seen what I've done yet and I told him that what I was doing so very fast and so full was not finished, that it was a raw first draft which I would expect to make much shorter and tighter when I revised.

"You are not writing a 'shooting script,'" he repeated.

"If I have a collaborator everything I have put into the script that is not in the book will be attributed by the audience to him," I said.

"That may be the case."

"I will hate that."

With my hatreds Mr. Wyler did not want to be involved. Very wise too. Argument or sympathy, either one, might, at this stage, have made me cry. And movie making could be washed clean away, no doubt, on the floods of female tears a director-producer encounters. Mr. Wyler's business is to avoid the erosions of such floods.

So here it is, almost evening now, and I feel fine. How can I, faced with the possibility of this damned collaborator? I feel fine because I came down here and said what I thought, made my stand known. I suffered having to do that. But pain purges. I feel as I do after I've done my duty, gone to the dentist and been hurt. I walk out of the dentist's office as refreshed as any flagellant by my pain. No, it is not the pain that refreshes but the sudden concentration and focusing of one's being to meet the pain that refreshes. Pain is a substitute monomania. Monomaniacs, in the pursuit of their mania, float on a tide of exultation, and it is the focusing that supplies the power.

It is this achieved focusing that makes the air so golden now, the Nicotiana just opening so sweet—and one other thing—the fact that I put my feelings into words. A man might kill my mother and father, I'm afraid, plagiarize my writing, betray my love, defile all I valued most, and if I were able to tell him all I felt about his actions, he would be in no further danger from me. Because the words would have drained off all my animosity? Hate can thus be drained away by words. Can love? Having told the hated one of my hate, I am hateless. If I tell the loved one of my love, am I loveless? Are words substitute action? No, not for me, I think. They do, in the case of hate, at least, permit other action. Let the words take care of the hate and acts are freed for other purposes.

I feel Irish in my Irish country house above my Irish garden. I'll go home and finish this script as I began it, prolix, and hope for the chance to prune. I feel at once peaceful and belligerent this evening.

Stu asked me to have dinner with him, a Stanford friend, and the Stanford friend's girl. I know and like the Stanford friend, a young man who walks on his toes, distends his nostrils, and chews his smile. But I'm through talking for the day. I want to eat alone. I'm going down to the dining room, get a table where I can sit with my back to the wall, and have a two-hour glut of watching human beings whose problems I do not have to dovetail dramatically for a two-hour cinema.

## Napa

For a minute or two tonight I thought like a horse. I knew that Dandy was going to think about a tractor parked up the road before he did. I also anticipated rightly his reaction to the sound of water newly turned into an irrigation pipe. Of course, the minute I thought, I'm a human being thinking like a horse, I abandoned equine thinking. But I had a flash of understanding of what it takes to make a real horseman. Our three horses are as unlike as three persons. Perhaps more so, since they don't read, listen to radio or TV and hence aren't imitating any horsey models. They don't try to talk like Flicka, walk like Trigger, or eat like Silver.

Dandy is a gelding, twelve years old, cut quick and too early so that he never developed some of the stallion traits and musculature he should have. His neck's too thin and his nature's too amenable—so far as the two mares are concerned. They boss him, eat his hay, chase him when he doesn't want to be chased, and bite him, out of boredom. With humans, though, Dandy can't be pushed around. He's as obstinate as any old bachelor, set in his ways and finicky. He is not at all feminine, notionate, passionate, or unreasonable. His reasoning is a horse's, of course, and reasoning this way he considers it folly to leave the stable fast or to return in any other way. He takes a spur going out and a firm hand coming in. But going out or coming in, his gait, even for a Tennessee Walker, is unbelievably creamy. It is like waltzing sitting down. He has the Tennessee's head-swinging manner, and to see him, a burnished bay homeward bound through the mustard fields and down the eucalyptus-lined lane, is almost as good as riding him. He can outsprint six-year-old Judy, the fat black Tennessee Walker mare and keep up, for the space of a sprint, with Cheyenne, the five-year-old thoroughbred mare. Judy makes me feel like arguing, all her faults are feminine, greedy, nervous, willful, over-charged. Cheyenne's faults if she has them, are equine, not feminine. She is too much horse to argue with. She is enormous, affectionate, and eager, and could unseat you out of sheer willingness to please you quickly.

Dandy is my darling. He has the great eyes, the flaring nostrils, and long switch tail of the classic horse. I once bought a book because of one line about a horse. This book was *Pictures and People* by Naomi Royde-Smith and Roger Hinks, and the line was: "It is a record in bronze of how a man once loved a horse." I've forgotten what horse this was but I remember that "the record in bronze" was contrasted with a Chinese painting of a horse which was just "a portrait." If this distinction is a true one I think I'd take the Chinese painting. Though why not be like Dolores and take both? I love Dandy and it seems to me that one could become more attached to a horse than to any other animal—even though, as we now live, horses can't share our tent or bedroll. Horses and cats, these are my animals; though alas, I have even watched a mosquito rubbing his forelegs together like a brittle old man in front of a fire and wished to spare him. And if he hadn't begun his infernal hum, I would have. I spare all quiet animals—spiders, ants, and the like. But noisy animals—mosquitoes, flies, ducks, woodpeckers, and even those herons—are in danger around me. I can forgive an animal wanting to eat me; hunger is understandable. I can forgive a frightened animal wanting to kill me; fear is understandable. But why should an animal want to hurt my ears? That's plain maliciousness.

*Sunday*

1. The attack—Josh hurt.
2. The horse returns. Scene between Jess and Eliza.
3. Josh inching along.
4. Little Jess's report. Purdy, the cocksure Quaker. Sam's talk with Eliza. Jess leaves.
5. Maurauders.

6. Sam dead. Jess goes on.
7. The fight. Josh kills and is hurt.
8. Jess finds him.
9. Meeting with Eliza.
10. Final scene.

That's about it, I guess.

VI

# IV

*Beverly Hills*

I am out of the habit of writing here. I wrote "Beverly Hills" and couldn't think what next. Everything ending at once. Last pages of this volume of my journal, my convertible, which I'm going to sell, mushrooms and all—and the script. It is going into the script hopper.

It never, in the beginning, occurred to me that I would not have a chance to rewrite the script. Would I have gone so fast, written so fully, if I had known that I was writing final—as far as I was concerned—words? No. Stu came up to my apartment to get the manuscript. I put it into his hands like a baby. This was before the script-hopper news. I said, "This may be my last caress," patted the pages, which are baby-thick, and sat down and read Sheldon's *Varieties of Delinquent Youth* as if my life depended upon it. Sheldon can tell more about a boy in five hundred words than many novelists tell in five hundred pages.

I saw Mr. Wyler this morning in his office. The manuscript was on his desk. He touched it occasionally, but I had the impression he hadn't read it. He had looked at it, and saw (even I could have told him this) that he did not have a shooting script. He had a surgeon's kindness in separating me from my manuscript. Quick, incisive, businesslike. I was filled with emotion. He asked me if I would be a technical adviser, come back to Hollywood and stay with them until the picture was finished. He said he would match the largest sum ever paid anyone at Paramount as technical director if I would. They plan to make the picture in Indiana and he asked me if I wouldn't like to go. I said yes, it was a beautiful state. He said, "Wait till you see it on VistaVision," and I got rid of the ache at the back of my throat.

"I don't know what is the usual price for technical advisers," he continued, "but if you'll stay with us I'll see that you don't lose money. Run out, Stu, and ask the accounting department what's the most they've paid."

When Stu came back with his figure Mr. Wyler looked a little surprised. "I'll meet that. If Allied can't—they're not a wealthy studio like Paramount, you know—I'll do it myself."

I said I'd come back.

"Now," Mr. Wyler asked, "would you mind talking with Mr. Kleiner? He's the man who's going to work on your script. There are things he needs to know and that only you can tell him."

I said I would. Then I wished Mr. Wyler a happy time in Japan and we shook hands; but I saved my last glance for the two hundred typed pages on his desk.

Stu and I had lunch with Mr. Kleiner. Mr. Kleiner is a small, white-skinned, rather tight-faced man in dark glasses. There is no more glare in Hollywood than elsewhere in California, but they combat it here more vigorously. Even Stu has the specs for his nearsightedness darkened. I begin to feel that dark glasses are on a par here with clothing. Though I am not sure with what garment they should be equated; whether when they are removed the gesture should be considered a discourteous vulgarism or a flattering invitation to greater intimacy. Stu and Kleiner confronted each other through lunch, though we ate inside where no sun penetrates, dark glasses to dark glasses. I, only, ate bare-faced, like an emancipated woman.

Mr. Kleiner struck me as being an earnest, pleasant man determined to understand Quakers. His questions showed me a tension or "conflict" which he thought might be injected into the script.

"Mrs. Birdwell is the real Quaker, isn't she?"

"What do you mean by 'real'?"

"The good one."

"Oh no. Jess is a far better Quaker and person than Eliza."

Mr. Kleiner seemed dismayed. "But she's got the Book."

"The book?" Amidst the luncheon clatter I wasn't sure I had understood him.

"I mean the Bible. She's got the Book, hasn't she?"

"They *all* have it."

"But she's got the official one, hasn't she?"

"Hers is no more official than anyone else's."

"It's bigger, isn't it? She carries it to the pulpit."

"There isn't any pulpit."

"Look," Mr. Kleiner said, "as far as the audience is concerned she has the Book. She's the authority, she's the head."

"All right," I told him. "Let's say she is, for the audience. What then?"

"Jess strays, doesn't he?"

"He does some things, certainly, that strict Quakers of his time frowned on."

"O.K., O.K. He strays. I see a big final scene. The white church. The congregation. Eliza with the Book. Jess has strayed. He is filled with shame. He has wandered. He hasn't seen Eliza since his fall. He hasn't slept. He's not in Sunday clothes. He hears the church bells ringing. He stumbles into the church and Eliza opens her arms to him. He is received. His wife forgives him. His church forgives him. He lifts his head."

I could see this scene, and I thought, Perhaps I'm too much of a Quaker to write about Quakers. Perhaps I don't take things big enough. I said, "It's something like the return of the prodigal son, isn't it?"

I would not tell a writer that a scene of his reminded me of a scene in another book. But my impression is that in Hollywood it is reassuring to remember that what one is trying to do has succeeded before. So Mr. Kleiner agreed with me. Prodigal son with sex, since this is a man returning, chastened, to a woman.

Down to the desert in April like a real Hollywoodian, only I wear my rue with a difference. A real Hollywoodian does not come down to visit his sister who lives in a real date garden, one of the oldest in the valley, in a real adobe house set beside a swimming pool that is half reservoir. Though I'm not really at Carmen's, but a quarter of a mile down the road in a motel. The motel serves breakfast to Max and to me; we eat fruit for lunch and go up to Carmen's for dinner—or earlier if we feel like it. This is visiting without tears, so that we enjoy all the pleasures of hospitality and none of its responsibilities.

If Carmen still had her roof bedroom I would accept the responsibilities also. Actually her "roof bedroom" was no more than the roof of their house, with beds on it. The wooden steps by which one reached the roof have fallen into disrepair and now support ivy; the beds have been taken away. Too many people liked that roof too much. Carmen was becoming an unpaid motel-keeper and she felt this unfair to the professional down the road.

I used to wake on that roof to heaven, a heaven that was first one sound, then two, and presently a scent, and finally, as I opened my eyes, and before I burrowed more deeply under the blankets to sleep some more, a vision.

The first sound was the far-off cry of coyotes. A coyote sings more sweetly to me than any bird. He pushes the horizon back with his voice. He makes a gift of space. He says that something is still hidden. He reports escape. He acknowledges himself. He celebrates survival. Who will build us a mechanical coyote when this fellow is hunted and poisoned off the earth? What voice, recorded earlier for our convenience, will cry at dawn with the same assurance of an ancient and secret world? Assurances our ears so long for. Who can fabricate that foxy grin, those shrewd eyes, smiling, that sidewise lope when he is gone? But ten years ago, from the roof of the adobe house set in the midst of the date palms, he wakened me each morning. And immediately afterward and almost as if he were their alarm clock, the Mexican workers who lived on the ranch began to sing as they chopped wood for their morning fires. Then these three sounds mingled—Señor Coyote, Mexican voices, ax on mesquite and greasewood. It was a perfect trio for that hour and place. And the Mexicans' songs, like the coyotes', said, "It is morning, and we have survived the night and darkness but we do not forget them. There is light and warmth and food, but we do not count on them." At the back of their songs was this sorrow and it was the sorrow which made the happiness so sweet.

Before these sounds had stopped, the fires had been started by the women and the scent of smoke was in the air, and, as I inhaled this, I opened my eyes and saw the desert shining like an empty polished shell and surrounded by mountains which begin their morning blooming with the colors of smoke and flowers.

Now it is five in the evening. I'm alone outside Carmen's house. Doves are calling. When I was a child I confused the cry of the dove with that of the loon. I had read somewhere that the loon's cry was the loneliest in the world, and since I could not imagine a sound more lonely, a dove, calling, was a loon to me.

Looking at the desert is like reading Proust. I have to absent myself from such felicity for a while. If I do not, if I continue to look or to read, my feeling is that I'll die of a surfeit of pleasure. I suppose I'm tougher than I think and could actually read and look all day.

I know the reasons for my feeling about Proust better than the reasons for my feeling about the desert. Why is the desert more beautiful to me than mountains or forests? Because I like spareness more than fullness, earth colors more than growth colors, far horizons rather than near ones? Sun rather than shadow, wind rather than rain, big stars rather than small ones, silence rather than sound?

*Next Day*

Afloat in my room, cradled in movements of light and shadow, supported by a basket of shifting patterns. Little dry sounds of dry grass in a small evening wind, a blade-sized blower; spring running out like a tide into the big warm summer sea; silky waters flowing about me; living in them like a fish or an eel or a maggot. The shadows run back and forth across my bare legs, across my paper. I stab a shadow with my pen point but I can't pin it down with ink. I am bathing in light, and the light is not still. I am taking the weight of the day on my body. "O let my days be loaded and fragrant." Emerson wrote this upstairs in his white chamber and I write it here in my sand-colored motel room.

Virginia Woolf wrote in her diary: "I shall feel some triumph if I skirt a headache this summer." I feel some triumph every day I skirt one, and my triumphant days are few. But I try not to let this become a record of headaches. When I reread such headache journals I have too much self-pity. Poor, poor girl, I think, how did you ever survive? And as a matter of fact, I don't know how you do, you poor, poor girl.

*Friday*

Going home tomorrow to the rain and the oaks. I wonder how Kleiner is getting on. I think the story, whatever else may now happen to it, is permanently out of the realm of Quaker versus non-Quaker and into the realm of Quaker versus himself—where all good drama lives—if it lives. Now, having aborted, I shall go home and see if my abandoned child, the novel, has also died.

Some persons have a kind of unexplainable magic. In their presence one expects revelation. It doesn't matter, really, whether or not they ever come—the magic lies in the expectation, not the revelation. It is a stroke of luck to have a sister about whom one feels that.

*Napa*
*April 10*

I am going to ration myself on this dope of journalizing, make new rules: No writing here until after the novel-writing stint is over.

*April 16*

I thought all day of a beautiful bouquet in shades of pink and lavender and this evening I made it, a big summer-rich, winey bouquet: peonies, last of the lilac, two purple tulips, pink syringa, iris, small cluster of azalea, three or four sprigs of lavender stock, forget-me-nots, some Cecile Brueners, a couple of black pansies. I am no flower arranger, but I keep all vases filled. A room without flowers is barren to me. Sometimes I think of summer and all those vases to be filled and feel tired. But I can't resist filling them. Max is a gardener and there are always flowers to pick. I wonder sometimes what I would do if he were not. Would I, to get flowers, put seeds in the ground? I'm afraid not. I would fill the empty vases with big-leafed weeds and silky grasses. I don't know how it is that, liking the outdoors so much, I have so little farmer's blood in me. Perhaps the reason *is* that I like the outdoors so much. The world looks good to me wild. Indoors I am always conscious of dust and rugs askew and ashes piling up on the hearth, and I feel responsible. Outside, nature takes the responsibility.

Max asked me, seeing me staring at a blank page, if I

were mourning the lost script. Yes, I am. I started living in that story again and I suffer displacement outside it. I also mourn or resent the relinquishment of an unfinished piece of writing. I tell myself I have learned a lesson and that the lesson is this: One must please the writing before one pleases persons. This is a lesson in inhumanity and one almost impossible for me to learn.

Kleiner called today and talked with me for an hour about the script. They do really believe me inhuman down there, to be able to talk of the script with such good will. To say nothing of not resenting the irritation of the hour-long interruptions.

Kleiner wanted to talk with me about ways of showing that Eliza, in spite of being a Quaker and a minister, was *human*. He felt that the audience would need to see her engaged in neighborhood good works and jollifications to understand this. This continuous demonstration by good works of Quaker saintliness was just what I was at pains to get out of that early script. Kleiner thinks a barn-raising would afford a picturesque background for good works and jollifications. The neighbors working away, Jess, too, of course. Then, at noon when no one expects it, Eliza arrives with pies, say; she has spent the whole morning baking, and we see that though she has the Book, she also has a heart and a light hand with the pastry.

What Kleiner wanted to know was how he could account for a barn-raising in a settled neighborhood.

"Strike the old one with lightning," I told him. "Burn it to the ground. Very common back there in summertime."

He was also in a quandary about the "thees" and "thys." Mr. Wyler feared—and this was something he had spoken about to me—that the audience was never going to be able to swallow that kind of talk. Especially from Gary Cooper, that old, hard-bitten two shooter. Kleiner had an idea about reducing the thees and thys.

"When the Birdwells are with other people they will use the Quaker language. But when they're home they'll relax and speak naturally."

I told him he was going at a thee and thy reduction wrong end to. "Theeing and thying was natural to Quakers a hundred years ago. You might account for their dropping it with outsiders on the grounds that they didn't want to make strangers feel ill at ease. But at home, when they speak naturally, they'd use thee and thy."

"How about having just the women use it?"

"If you do that you'll have the audience constantly aware of theeing and thying. I'd use it all the time—or drop it entirely."

"It's too quaint to drop entirely."

"It's your problem," I said.

I talked with Stu for a while after Kleiner had finished. "How are things going?" I asked.

"Swimmingly, swimmingly," Stu answered shortly, which is unlike him. Ordinarily he likes to say what swims and how and where.

I don't enjoy hearing about my lost child. I want to forget it. There's a new baby in the house, a baby named Cope, not Birdwell.

*April 27*

There are situations the reality of which can be conveyed only by forgoing realism.

Why has everyone always sympathized with Hansel and Gretel and never given any thought to the troubles of that poor old witch plagued by those two noisy children? I look speculatively at my talkative visitor and wonder if she would fit in the oven. Too large, I fear, but I think that, with a quick sharp shove, I might ram her into the dirty-clothes closet, slam the door, and lock it.

Whenever I start writing paragraphs, it is a sign the larger writing isn't going well.

Another call from Kleiner. I think I should do whatever I can to help him, Wyler, or anyone else. But I feel queasy after these conversations. What is it? Jealousy? The sensation of watching another woman fondle your husband?

151

*May 1*

My May Day basket to myself is a new car. It is agony for me to be suspended between choices. Once having made a decision, I can, with my horrible adaptability, be content with anything—learn to love it even. But until I decide, I am required to hold in my mind every model of every car in the world and to weigh their merits and defects. And am even required continuously to debate with myself whether to get rid of the convertible at all. It still runs; true, it smells like a cellar, but it is fragrant with memories of good trips. True, there are holes in the top, but what's the point of a convertible anyway if it's not to let in the sky? True, the original yellow paint is beginning to show through the blue repaint job. But this is a year for two-tone cars, isn't it?

Sustain the tension, Jung says, as long as it is fruitful. Yesterday I felt the tension would bear no more fruit and I bought the last car shown me for no better reason than that I liked its color. "Gold and platinum," the salesman called it—tan and cream or khaki and unbleached muslin or foothill and desert would be more accurate.

It has power steering, and this cheats me of the feel of the road in my arms as I drive. I drive for exercise as well as transportation, and driving now has become a carrot-peeling job, no exercise beyond the second joint of the fingers. Steering is now a job for the eyes, and what the eye sees—other cars eye-steered—is no treat.

*May 10*

A phone call from Stu this morning. No talk about the script. He was calling, he said, because a very good costume designer had been hired, Dorothy Jeakins, a wonderful person, and he wanted to know if I would be able to come down to Hollywood at once instead of waiting until June first when I was scheduled to begin work once again as a technical adviser.

"What can I do now?" I asked. "Technically."

"You can talk to Dorothy about costumes."

"She probably knows all about them already."

"She's a wonderful person, Jessamyn. You'll enjoy talking to her."

"Stu, I'm not going to come down there just to talk to a wonderful person. You know I can't do that."

"You said you'd be technical adviser and the job's beginning now."

"Am I coming now to stay until the picture's finished?"

"That's right. You will come, won't you? This is very important."

I said I'd come. This time I'm packing to stay until the shooting's over at the end of August. Stu will meet the Owl tomorrow morning. Max will bring my car down in a couple of weeks. I hope I will be able to keep my mouth shut about the script. Sometimes I think this picture is a maze in which I'll wander the rest of my life, unable to find my way out. Worse still, perhaps, grow to love maze wandering. It is, in its bemusing way, a happy activity. It resembles travel; the substitution of small surmountable difficulties for life's real unsurmountable ones. Each day, traveling, one feels successful because one has gotten the room with the view, lost no money, and made oneself understood. One makes ends of means, in this way, gilds the squirrel cage and goes to bed falsely weary but able to sleep.

*Beverly Hills*

Stu has just left. I've just called Max. Just called Merle and Elizabeth. It's unbelievable. My pen won't stick to the line as I write.

Stu met me this morning with a poker face and coal-bright eyes. We both played the density game. "Glad to

153

see you back." "Nice to be back." We walked through the station, and Stu, who is ordinarily anxious to get me down to Mr. Wyler, said, "How about some more breakfast?"

"After Owl pellets—I could eat some more."

The dining room at eleven (the Owl for once was on time) was as deserted as a railway dining room ever is. When everything was on the table and Stu had swallowed some coffee, he said, "You're going to be asked to come back on the script."

I heard him, but "come back on" might mean anything. "What does that mean?"

"Do what you wanted to do. Revise it. Make a shooting script out of it."

A ripe red strawberry became tasteless in my mouth. "What about the new script?"

"Terrible. Willy wants you to come back on the script."

"You said everything was going swimmingly."

"What did you expect? With Kleiner at my elbow. Besides there was a chance it might go better."

"And it hasn't."

"It hasn't. This is final. He's a good writer. He has written some workmanlike scripts in the past. He muffed this."

"Willy could've saved a lot of time and a lot of money if he'd discovered this earlier."

"He made a mistake."

"Perhaps I should refuse. Perhaps I should have too much dignity to be writing according to stop and go lights."

"You never did stop writing."

"You and Kleiner never gave me much chance."

"Do you want to keep on? Or do you want to be dignified?"

"I want both."

"You can have both."

"How did this happen? Mr. Wyler told me ten times at least that there were ten thousand script writers here. Why me instead of one of the nine thousand nine hundred and ninety-nine others? Kleiner isn't the bottom of the barrel."

"Do you really want to know?"

"Consider yourself coaxed."

"You are here, Miss West, because of Willy's brother, Robert."

"Have I met him?"

"For two seconds one day going into Willy's office."

"He is smaller than Mr. Wyler?"

"A little, I guess. Robert read your script and told Willy, 'There's nothing wrong with this script. It's too long. It's not a shooting script. With some revision it could be. I could help Miss West fix it up.'"

"What did Mr. Wyler say to that?"

"Willy told Robert that you hadn't wanted to write a script in the first place. That you didn't want to work with anyone and for all he knew you might be hell to work with. And Robert told him that he knew from reading the script that you would not be hell to work with. That no one could write such beautiful scenes and not be a good, intelligent person to work with."

"I guess I love Robert Wyler."

"Robert is older than Willy—and he had a reputation before Willy. Now his reputation is much smaller. It's hard for two brothers to be equally regarded. People want life to be dramatic. They want reversals. They like the idea of the earlier and older being replaced by the younger newcomer. It satisfies a streak of cruelty in them too. But Robert is a writer and Willy isn't. He wants to work with you . . . if you're willing. This script has to be ready by July fifteenth. That's two months. Robert knows all the stuff you don't know, technically, about a script. Together you could have it ready by that time."

"Does Mr. Wyler know you're telling me this?"

Stu laughed. "Probably not this much. He'll tell you himself. But I thought there were some things I could tell you he couldn't and that you ought to know. Now that you know them, what're you going to do?"

"Write. I'm going to write. I'm going to finish this job."

I'm in the same old boxcar apartment with the same old view of the swimming pool. But because it is now my home I feel quite different about it. I am putting up books and pictures. I brought a picture of Grandmother and Grandfather in Quaker dress; of Mama at fifteen in embroidered white ruffles and wearing on her finger the borrowed splendor of her mother's wedding ring. That hand rests on a velvet pillow, ring finger slightly elevated. Her large eyes are bright, imagining a world that contains jewelry and marriage. She is trembling with anticipation inside that ring. In her mind its circumference is as large as the earth's; larger, since there are no limits on her imagination.

Everyone stops to look at that picture. Looking, they move back into their own dreams for a minute. Stu looked and said, "This is Mattie, isn't it?" Stu is still young enough to tremble inside rings of his own imaginings. But it was wise of him to know by looking at a picture of my mother as a girl that she was the visual model, at least, for Mattie in *The Friendly Persuasion*.

I talked with Robert Wyler this afternoon. He shares a bungalow with Stu and a secretary. The bungalow is one of a series of identical bungalows on a street of bungalows in a neighborhood of bungalows. This one has front yard, climbing roses, porch. I cannot enter it as I do a "real" office in a "real" office building. Memories of macaroni and cheese, Christmas tinsel, and the monthly payments still linger here. This seems a place of life rather than business. I have trouble accepting this office as official. I expect to hear a sewing machine in the back bedroom.

William Wyler's office is quite differerent. Allied prepared a new office for him while he was in Japan, and I went with Stu when he inspected it. The air conditioning, the intercom, the carpet, the curtains, the davenport? Did Stu think that Mr. Wyler would be pleased? The colors? The position of the desk?

But Mr. Robert Wyler liked his own bungalow. "I am happy to be over here by myself," he said. And I could see that he was. His room was air-conditioned by throwing the back door open to the studio parking space behind him. When he did this a breeze from the ocean, slightly scented with gasoline and lubricating oil, blew through.

Mr. Robert Wyler may very well have been the most beautiful young man in France at one time. He is smaller, frailer, grayer than his brother. William Wyler's face looks solid enough to push through a situation. This doesn't mean that W. W. has a tough mug—but he does have a compact one. If the brothers' faces were hands—William's is a hand curved inward, self-protectively. Robert's lies open.

156

William Wyler, however, can focus, does focus more attentively upon the person who faces him. Robert is open but what he is open to is not necessarily the person in front of him. William either focuses upon you or gets rid of you.

I have the feeling that Robert somehow, somewhere through a process of withdrawal (of which I, too, know something) finds it more and more difficult to make the effort to communicate. This does not mean that he isn't talkative. He is. He is a courteous man and he wills himself to speak; but his speech *is* that: a speech; the outward presentation of an inward memory or dream. In his kindness he will turn himself inside out for you. Here is the memory, the phantasy, the rumination. But they are gifts unrelated to you, or the present minute, except as Robert gives them, like beads to a savage, to win your acceptance of him; his guarantee that while not savage himself, he is at least willing to play with savages. So much that he will hear from you, he has already imagined; so much that he will say, he has already said to himself.

When he spoke of the script, when the focusing point lay outside the personal, all his dispersal vanished. Then he was present, and nowhere else. He said something about his enjoyment of cards—gin rummy, I think it was—and I can see how this would be. It gives him a point of contact with another human being in the material world.

These impressions are snap judgments. I was not only a stranger to him, but strange. We waged what amounted to politeness duels, each deferring to the other.

When I got up to leave, he said, "We have all the time in the world. We won't let anyone push us. We have a good script of a beautiful, true world. "We'll work slowly, we'll put it in order, and my brother will make the best picture of his life from it. We will win honor and glory and remember these as the good years of our lives."

This, in the little macaroni-remembering bungalow, from the man who had once been the genius and had been displaced by his younger brother; breaking through whatever were the barriers into the veritable present, forgiving whatever there was in the past to forgive, and pinning his faith on a few words in which he believed. Robert made me wish for some non-Quakerish extravagance with which to express my extravagant feeling. I managed no more than "Thanks," and "Good-by."

Stu and I had dinner at the Cock 'n Bull, which has become our favorite eating place. It has the three necessities of an agreeable eating place: 1. good food; 2. people who appear happy to be eating; 3. enough quiet in which to talk.

I talked about Robert Wyler. I said that with many middle-aged people one is aware of the ugliness—physical and spiritual—added since youth. With Robert there is none of this. But I feel I have missed something in not knowing the young Robert. Is it the personal beauty, still visible? A feeling one is more accustomed to have in the presence of a woman?

Robert's pulchritude, past or present, was nothing to Stu. He was popping his glasses on and off for better looks at the pulchritude passing our table.

# V

*Wednesday*

The routine, the plan, evolves. I live here like Thoreau in his hut beside the pond. My pond is a pool. My bean crop is the word crop. My animals are the people. My Bronson Alcott is Robert Wyler. My Emerson is William Wyler. My younger brother is Stu. Where's Lidian and Aunt Mary and the Irishmen and the farmers? Nowhere yet. I live here more solitary than Thoreau. After all, he walked abroad each afternoon; often he went into the village. He passed the time of day with many people. Why he has been called a hermit I don't know. I have been sitting here two and a half days on this bed writing, without seeing a soul other than the maids. I bet Thoreau never did that in his life. And he was right. I'm going to stop.

*7:30 P.M.*

Things are picking up. Didn't see any muskrats or tortoises or measure the depth of any snow, but did go to the village—Westwood, not Concord—and saw the towns-people. I caught a bus, figured out how and where. I walked the village streets in the cold raw wind. I went to a bookstore and bought bargains. Received a compliment. Had a choc coke—a drink I had forgotten. Champagne of the candy-bar set. Returned home, not cast down by the bus driver's browbeating. I have conquered a part of my environment. Very gray, cloudy, windy. No weather for palm trees. I am very happy. One old lady and one woolly dog keep watch by the pond. I mean pool. Nothing in the pool but fallen leaves.

*Friday*

This is the way it works out. I write here in longhand. No secretary, no office. Portia de Lisle, who is Robert's and Stu's secretary, types my writing. Robert reads it. We talk about it. He suggests changes. If I agree, and so far we have seen eye to eye, we incorporate the changes then and there—if they don't involve much writing. If they do, I work on them at home. Robert then, if there is nothing more to be done to the script, breaks it up into proper sequences for shooting.

Stu took me down to the bungalow this afternoon. Just as I was about to step out of the car, he pulled me back in.

"Stay where you are," he ordered.

I stayed. But I wanted to know why.

"Kleiner and his secretary just went in."

This gave me a hollow spot in my stomach. "What's he doing here?"

"Still writing."

"How many people are writing this script?"

"Two. You and Robert. But Kleiner's contract has a week yet to run. If he knew Willy thought it was hopeless, what would he be able to do? Nothing. And we had as well have our money's worth of work from him. He's being paid well."

"A lot more than me, I bet."

"I wouldn't be surprised."

"Surprised? You know."

"Do you want me to tell you?"

"No. If I heard, I might not have the heart to write, either. And if Kleiner also found out, then where'd you be?"

"Ten thousand script writers in those hills, you know."

"What if Kleiner has an inspiration this last week? Writes about Quakers better than I can write about Quakers? Imagines a scene strong as Marlowe, sweet as Shakespeare, popular as Oscar Hammerstein?"

"It's not likely."

"But if he does?"

"It'll go in."

"What is this, an assembly line? Just rivet things together?"

"Shakespeare was quite a riveter."

"But *he* chose. The material was strained through his temperament."

"Willy chooses."

"Why do you protect Kleiner—when you didn't protect me?"

"Do you want it brutal?"

"I'd like the truth if you think I can take it."

"You were paid by the week. Kleiner's paid by the job. Also it's the truth—whether you believe it or not—we trusted you to do your best for the script, even after you knew you weren't going to be working on it any more."

"I'm too trustworthy."

"O.K. now," Stu said. "They're gone. We can sneak in."

"The trustworthy sneak," I said.

"You will be writing dialogue soon for Abbott and Costello," Stu told me, "at this rate."

"What is the rate?" I asked.

"High."

"Good-by, Stu, address me care of Abbott and Costello."

Happy as larks. Got a chestful of froth. Happy to be awake. It's a sweet life. Nothing very achey, able to do what I like—write—and what I like to do—my duty: make this script a good one. No conflict. Is that all I'm reporting? A very sweet, nasty, cold, murky day blowing across my pond and palm trees and me alive in it. Praise God, bare bones.

Last night I found my way through doors leading, I knew not where, to the roof. I walked up there more scared than can be told, though what the danger was I can't say. The height? The darkness? The sense of trespassing? A fear of falling through, off, over? I'll go up there again though. It's a wonderful place to be at dusk. Height makes a desert of a city and I faced Los Angeles like an Arab facing Mecca. Should have faced Hollywood, I suppose.

Yesterday I did a little lazy writing. Finished the scene of the Elders calling on Jess and Eliza. Put it back as it was in the book, so that Jess and Eliza don't know that they're coming. The original script, with Jess and Eliza morosely awaiting their arrival was unpleasant. Stu called last night to say that he thought it was wonderful. Stu kindles with what pleases him, and I bless him for it. That visible kindling is one of the pleasures of script writing —and one of the perils, perhaps, also. In nonscript writing one works alone and in the dark. If the story is bought, the book published, one concludes one has succeeded. But it is pretty much like pounding sand in a rathole—and not even a rat home to protest or applaud. Here, somebody laughs at the funny line; somebody says, "This is just what was needed." Here, there is a perhaps dangerous (to me) sense of community. Since I find it pleasant, perhaps I would in time be willing to sacrifice virtues in the writing in return for the warmth of "working with"— a pleasure I have never experienced before except as a child in a large family and never knew was possible in my own adult work. And paradoxically I have this sense of community while I live and work in the greatest solitude I have ever known. I went from a large family to a college dormitory to marriage. Never before have I had these long hours, in which I can count on not being interrupted, for writing. Nor have I, when I put the pen down, ever been able to elect so selfishly people and activities which relate to me and my work. Nor have I been able to feel that the work itself relates to a larger project. I go down to the studio in the late afternoon to talk with Robert and

I hand in the day's writing with the same kind of childish pleasure I had as a high-school girl handing in my composition to the English teacher.

Who would have expected these pleasures from Hollywood? And are they dangerous ones? Do I shed responsibility? Not shed, not yet anyway. But I do share.

I went with Dorothy Jeakins, the lure with which Stu got me down here early, to a lunch at John Houseman's. Dorothy is, as Stu said, a beautiful and exceptional woman. She belongs in the Haworth rectory. She is six feet tall, big for one of the ailing Brontës, but she has their intense fine-drawn look. I think, however, that she is more of a romantic than either Emily or Charlotte. How, I ask myself, thinking about that, could anyone be more romantic than the girls who dreamed of Heathcliff and Rochester? But under the circumstances, isolated on those moors and surrounded by curates, the most practical nonromantic, mind-saving therapy in the world was to invent demon lovers. Nor were the Brontës, I think, romantic, in their talk.

When I walked into Dorothy's house I felt as if I were stepping into my own past. Facing me on the bookshelves which separate the entryway from the living room were so many books I had loved and read as a young woman. The pantheist boys, Stu calls them. Richard Jefferies, Henry Williamson, A. E., *The Wanderer*. When I spoke of them she picked them up, touched them with love. I think they mean more to her now than they do to me, that she still can or does read them. I own them. I would not like to be without them, but they are a part of my past. I am removed from them. It strikes me, as I write, that these are the books with which the lonely young solace themselves. Having not yet found their "persons," they take the whole world to their hearts. "The wind is my wife," Keats wrote, "the stars my children." Dorothy's husband elected to remain in France after the war, a choice impossible to understand, but this choice perhaps helps to explain the warmth Dorothy still feels for these books.

She evidently never went on, to make her own, as I did, the perfect antidotes for these world-inflating, world-embracing books—the writings of the old hedonists, the old stoics, the old men, disappointed in life for one reason or another. These men also loved the earth but there was renunciation in their love. They knew *why* they loved it; life had failed them. I read in my twenties Amiel, Marcus Aurelius, George Gissing, Bardellion, Seneca, Grayson, Alexander Smith, every old codger with the melancholy, autumnal doctrine that though life had passed him by, it was better so; I read as if I, too, were an old pantalooned briar-smoking failure instead of a young female unwilling even to take the risk of failing.

The "pantheist boys" do not recognize that cloud love, while a solace, is also a substitute. The old men recognized it, but said, "It is better so." But the old fellows, for the most part, had had their life, as in their time—and their books formed no proper reading for me, who, before I joined them in their celebration of old books, old wines, and the daily sunset, should also have had my thirty years of living. Dorothy seems never to have collected these odes to resignation. Nor did she have Thoreau, who, though he loved the wind, licked his finger and held it up to see the quarter from which it blew.

Dorothy wore a heavy turtle-neck white sweater to the lunch. If I can only learn to wear to parties in Hollywood what I wear to basketball games in Napa I'll be properly dressed.

I met Houseman ten years ago when I was working on *A Mirror for the Sky* and made a mistake in his presence that still causes me embarrassment when I see him. I mispronounced "chorale," a simple word, God knows, but not one much used in the barley fields where I grew up. Houseman turned in complete mystification to Raoul Pène du Bois who was with us and said, "What *is* she talking about?" as if we did not speak the same language. Which, indeed, we did not. It is very easy to forgive others their mistakes; it takes more grit and gumption to forgive them for having witnessed our own. I tried to forgive Houseman this afternoon for his mistake in overhearing that one of mine—and I think I did.

Food and dress as usual were simpler than in Napa. I see that it would be possible for me to "go Hollywood" in some respects and never have the change, on my return, identified as such. Greet my guests in sweater and skirt, feed them a sparse meal, and explain it all by saying, "Oh yes, I've gone Hollywood." They wouldn't believe me. One thing is the same, Napa or Hollywood. Whenever, evidently, men of the same profession get together, they prefer to talk work with each other rather than talk anything else with a woman. Educators or producers, they collect in clumps coagulated by like interests. We women they have always with them, but a co-worker is a treat that they can't always count on. The thing to do if one is a hostess is to mix the varieties of workers. If a plumber can't find a plumber, he would rather talk to a woman than a male bricklayer. But give him another plumber and a woman doesn't stand a chance.

Simon Michael Bessie, an editor at Harper's, talked to me—but since we are both more or less in the same business, the talk may have been plumber to plumber rather than man to woman. "How's it going?" he asked me. And while I tried to think of the two or three words which would convey it, he found them. "Like work?" That was it, exactly. "Work" was writing, and it was going like writing, which also meant, as we both knew, that I couldn't ask more of it.

The Housemans have two small dandelion children, all fly-away hair and sunny faces. Dorothy embraced one of them, then said in her deep, emotion-filled voice, "Oh, I want to have another baby so much." It is strange how we can accept such statements from a woman, while, if a man were to make public in his resonant baritone like ambitions, we could not help smiling. Thus it is evidently a highly feminine exclamation. And it explains, I think, what I could not explain to Stu when I said to him, "I like Dorothy a great deal. But she makes me feel very masculine."

The minute I wrote this I saw that it was probably *not* true. What she makes me feel is, no doubt, very feminine; all the men present, though they would perhaps not care to hear such yearnings expressed by one of their own sex, find them entirely suitable and even endearing in a woman. Perhaps, too, I simply feel foiled conversationally by such sentiments. There is not much that can be said, by a woman, anyway, in reply to such exclamations. "Me too"

165

is a flat echo. "Why not?" is nosy. "Oh no!" is inhuman. "Try Lydia Pinkham's," old-fashioned.

I remember another conversational impasse, though of a more unconventional nature. At an official reception at a university, my hostess took me into the library to show me pictures of members of her family who were absent. Her own picture hung among the others. Though it was taken five or six years earlier, she looked less young and attractive then she did at the moment, standing by my side. I said so and she explained her wanness in the picture. "I was not having enough intercourse at the time."

This answer is less startling to me now than it was then; and famine of one kind is perhaps as suitably mentioned to account for a falling off in looks as is famine of another. But ten years ago this honesty silenced me completely. And I could not help looking with some speculation for the rest of the evening not only at her husband but at the other males present.

Now I have come to value honesty in conversation, a willingness to speak of what is central to one's being, even at the risk of making a fool of oneself, so much that, though I may be startled, I also bless. Virginia Woolf said in her diary that she had the courage to "beat up" out of conversations mechanical and life wasting, elements that were personal and real, and Stephen Spender in his autobiography describes her doing so. I honor and envy that doing. It is the action of someone with reverence for life. She will not waste any of it. She will go where meaning is. She will not permit herself to revert to the parrot, nor proceed to the tape recording.

*Monday*

This is the way a scene develops here. In the book, Eliza, when Jess brings the organ home, flounces down in the snow and says that she will not enter the house if Jess takes the organ inside. The script written for Capra followed my story. I thought that the story told in the movie would be more effective if the time it covered was shortened. All that was important to it happened in the summer months of 1862. The minute I decided that, I lost my snow and had to discover a new way for Eliza to demonstrate to Jess that she meant business when she said, "If that organ goes into the house I stay out." Should she climb the windmill? Perch on the upping block? Sit down in the dust of the summer driveway? I thought she would go out to the barn and say, "Jess, if that organ goes in the house I go to the barn." There were scenes showing her preparations to go, showing Jess's and the children's embarrassment when they have to explain to callers, "Mama's taken up residence in the barn." But there was no scene showing Eliza in the barn. I had thought about including one, but, with a script that should be around one hundred and twenty-five pages already running over two hundred, some scenes had to be resisted. I resisted Eliza in the barn.

Stu, when he saw the change, Eliza out of the snow and into the barn, was delighted. "But we must see her in the barn," he told me. "To know she was there and not be able to see her, prim amidst the hay and harness, would kill the audience." That was all the encouragement I needed, and the scene wrote itself. Jess went to the barn and, after he had promised Eliza to put the organ in the attic, Eliza returns to the house with him.

So the scene stood when Robert read the script. He wanted it expanded still further. But Robert also frequently feels, in talking to me, that he is face to face with Eliza herself, the woman with the Book. The other day he sidled up to a proposed change in so cautious, slow, and circumspect a manner that I was convinced that he was going to propose nothing less than a full-scale Hollywood seduction scene. He told me he well knew that if a sweet innocent girl ever lived she was Mattie. He told me that if there existed a sect more pure, honest, and devout than the Society of Friends he had never heard of it. He insisted that if there was a writer whose intuitions were more reliable than mine he had never met her. Still, he wanted to know if I were not of the opinion that Mattie was a normal young girl. That Quakers were often quite a lively, ordinary people. And I myself often of robust humor. I denied nothing of this. Well, then, he wanted to know, would I be adverse to, would I think it so unsuitable, if Mattie were to (and here I braced myself, waiting for a Hollywood roll in the Birdwell haymow) if Mattie were to say, when her mother refused to let her attend the county fair, "Mama, I wish thee would let me have just one real temptation in my life."

I told Stu about this afterward, and he said, "For a Frenchman like Robert, temptation probably has a more restricted frame of reference than it does to you." But even with the references restricted I felt I had been overprepared.

So Robert took an even longer time preparing me for his suggested additions to the barn scene. "Let's have Jess," he said, "when Eliza refuses to return to the house, decide to spend the night with her in the barn. And, when they emerge from the barn in the morning we learn that a compromise has been reached. She will return to the house if Jess will put the organ in the attic. To this Jess has agreed." And all this amiability, Robert warned me, might be attributed, he went daringly even further, would no doubt be attributed, to some love-making which took place during the night. What would I, what would Quakers generally, think of that?

For Quakers generally I couldn't speak. As for myself, I had always supposed that Jess and Eliza's children had been begotten in the normal way and that neither was so far gone in years as to have given up love-making, and that the end of marital quarrels, even among members of the Society of Friends, was often thus celebrated. Once I told a neighbor, speaking too fast as usual, that I belonged to the Friends church. Later I overheard her telling someone, "Mrs. McPherson is a member of the French church." My candor now has probably convinced Robert that I belong to the French church—not the Friends.

Though Robert ordinarily treats me as if I were the lineal descendant of Eliza Birdwell and George Fox, he forgets all of this when we are in the heat of trying out dialogue on each other. Then he goes flying across the office, all Gallic gestures and profanity, Quaker in spirit but not in movement and vocabulary.

"Eliza turns to Jess," Robert tells me, "and she says, 'Jesus, Jess, if thee keeps driving thy horse like a bat out of hell, thee'll bring the god-damn Elders down about our ears.' To which Jess replies, 'By God, Eliza, thee's right!' "

Casting is a part of movie making about which I have never once thought. Mr. Wyler is thinking about it continuously these days. He asks me in every now and then and uses me as a piece of litmus paper to help him judge a possible combination. He does so partly out of courtesy, I think—he wants me to feel a part of this enterprise —and partly in the hope that my opinion either as author of the book or as woman in the street will give him some helpful clues. Eliza is not yet cast.

Maureen O'Hara was tested. We all went to see Eleanor Parker in the worst movie I've seen in years. Today Mr. Wyler asked me, "What would you think of Jane Russell as Eliza?"

I sat down quickly, and Mr. Wyler hurried on. "She's a very pious girl, I understand. Goes to church, teaches Sunday school, sings hymns."

"And we can advertise her this way," I said. "See Jane Russell with her clothes on."

Stu, when I came out of Mr. Wyler's office, said, "Jane?" When I nodded, he shook his head despondently. His opinion of Willy is so high he suffers when he detects that box office rather than art is shaping Mr. Wyler's thinking. "Willy's out of his mind," he said.

*May 27? 28?*

Anyway it's nine o'clock. I know that. I had lunch with Robert today and he showed me the proposed shortening of the scenes preceeding Josh's leaving for war. I know they must be shortened. But not, surely, by a restoration of that early script's repulsive scene where Gard woos the sixteen-year-old Mattie by having her run through with him the desire-drenched lines of Antony and Cleopatra. Gard lies, his head in Mattie's lap, while she, ignorant of what she says, speaks of passions fulfilled. This is unconvincing, it seems a playwriter's contrivance, and it is repulsive in the same way that an adult, encouraging a child to use words whose sexual meanings he does not understand, is repulsive. There are those who think this sort of thing funny, and who would perhaps enjoy the sixteen-year-old Quaker girl speaking, without understanding them, Cleopatra's lines of sexual longing and fulfillment.

I didn't notice this scene at lunch, read it after I came back here, and didn't know, until Nicky called, how much I really hated it. I had asked Nicky to have dinner with me in honor of his twentieth birthday. If he were home, Carmen and Bill would have had a party, and I thought I would take him to Romanoff's or Chasen's, some place that would say Hollywood to a boy. He called to say he wouldn't be able to come. I hung up and began to cry as if my heart were broken.

Now, a nephew's failure to come to dinner doesn't ordinarily make me cry; and, presently, sobbing, I thought of this. What am I crying about? I asked myself. What has happened that is so terrible? What had happened that was so terrible was that vulgar scene, carpentered for snickers, as little able to show the delicate approach of young people to love as peep-show entertainment. And it is also the first time that Robert and I haven't seen eye to eye about a scene.

*Tuesday*
*June 7*

The Owl, my second home. 10 A.M. Back to peaceful Hollywood after the hurly-burly of Napa. Going through the Mohave Desert, full of hot, weak Southern Pacific coffee. Got home at seven thirty Sunday morning to find the house deep in dust and dirty dishes. And two hundred people due at four o'clock for Max's annual reception for the college faculty and the graduating class! The temperature was an even hundred. I put on shorts and a sun top and ran until three thirty, cleaning house. Barely got changed by the time the first guests arrived. They said they supposed that I was glad to be home to the peace of the country! They said they supposed I was having a glamorous time down in Hollywood, hobnobbing with the stars. I made as much as I could of meeting Cooper, of buying a pair of shoes sitting next to Jane Powell, and of eating at a table next to Mitzi Gaynor. I am going to lose face in Napa if I don't meet more stars soon, go to a few night clubs, or be subjected to some barbarous, lecherous treatment. Alas, such lechery as Stu, Robert and William Wyler, and Cooper may possess, appears to be directed elsewhere—and as for barbarism, I'm afraid they are entirely without it. I really rack my brain for something that will satisfy the appetite for Hollywoodania. Rich, scandalous events are no doubt taking place there, but I doubt if anything that happened in Hollywood the past week equaled, for real gaminess, the triangular mix-up reported to *me* of three Napa couples.

After the reception, I took off my finery and Max and I rode back into the hills. Yesterday I went to town and selected, at his urging, three suits and four sport shirts for him. Came home, cooked dinner for Fred, then went with Max to a faculty steak bake; home after that to ride again; then I caught the Owl at 10:45. Now, back to the solitude of the boxcar by the pool.

I've been reading Auden's *Shield of Achilles*. An odd place to discover that there are a great many kinds of lakes. Nothing like as moving as the names of winds, of course, but one man's meat etc. Lakes listed by Auden: moraine, oxbow, glint, sink, crater, piedmont, dimple.

*Thursday*

Death will be a surprise to me. Always, I think, there is a solution of even the unsolvable. The fire that won't start, the window that won't close, the cream that won't whip. God knows I am the least mechanically adept person in the world, and am not the one, as this list might seem to hint, who can repair either cars or can openers. But if they break down I can always find other ways of opening the can or of getting there. This belief of mine that there is no end to the possible solutions may only say that I have never really walked out to where the water was over my head.

I feel like a pioneer here in the city. Boone, lining out a bee tree, couldn't feel smarter than I did tonight discovering that delicatessens sell milk and cream.

I've spent the day making arrangements for Cooper to go to meeting with me. I didn't know which of the three Pasadena meetings would give him the best idea of a Quaker meeting of 1860; and I didn't like telling the studio people that there *were* three varieties of Quakers worshiping in a town as small as Pasadena. They all want to believe that the Quakers are flawless, and this evidence of disunity may convince them that Quakers are as petty and schismatic as any other sect.

The pastoral meeting is the largest; but Quakers singing and listening to sermons sound and look like Methodists or Baptists, so there is not much point in going there. Both of the other two, one Orthodox and one Hicksite, worship in silence. I talked with the office of the American Friends Service Committee and was told that the Hicksite meeting was so small that Cooper might feel that he was meeting with a Ministry and Oversight Committee rather than attending a church. So we're going to the Orthodox meeting, and I am as nervous as a girl taking a beau home to meet the folks; nervous lest the folks fail to put their best foot forward.

The studio has shown remarkable restraint. Cooper, worshiping amidst the plain people, is a subject wonderfully attractive to the publicity department, but they are going to let him do it without benefit of cameras.

Dorothy, Mr. Wyler, and I talked about costumes today. I hope they don't want to make them more severe and dark than Quakers ever wore. I understand the need, dramatically, to show by means of their costumes the Quaker's difference from his neighbors. But let's not de-gild the Quaker entirely. After all, he wasn't a Trappist.

Mr. Wyler worries every day about the theeing and thying. In his last days here, they had Mr. Kleiner going over the script removing thees and thys like rotten apples from a bushel basket. Kleiner has worked out a scheme which must have belied all fears that he would not put everything into the last days of his labor. The scheme, as reported to me (I have never been permitted to see the script) is so complicated that the audience would need a chart to keep track of the changes. They would think they were seeing *The Gold Bug* instead of *The Friendly Persuasion*.

*Sunday Eve.*

The momentous day is over. Cooper has been to meeting. I spent considerable time trying to decide what to wear. I wanted to be dressed with enough chic not to shame Stu and Gary. On the other hand, I did not want this fact to show.

Stuart came here, and we went in my car to pick up Gary. Even Stu, who thinks his car good enough for most people, decided that it would not do either for Cooper or the Quakers. Stuart and Gary in sober Quaker gray made me feel flashy in my yellow silk. But I, not they, resembled the other Friends when we arrived—a multicolored congregation, the women in flowered prints and many of the men in sport shirts. Gary, before getting in, remarked upon my car. "Very handsome," he said, "very Hollywood!"

"Hollywood! And you with a Mercedes!"

"A very drab little outfit compared with this rich job."

He got in, threw his hat, which he thought that Quaker formality might require him to wear, onto the back seat, and stretched. The rich job, as he did so, dropped the back portion of the front seat onto the floor like a wilted lettuce leaf and we were left sitting there bolt upright with nothing to lean against.

"I am an awkward ox," apologized Cooper, "wrecking your new car."

"Not at all," said I, "it's my terrible car."

Stu, with the wheel to hang on to, said nothing, but laughed and laughed, and we arrived at the meetinghouse on Orange Street with backs aching but, rigid and upright, decorum unblemished.

The worshipers were seated, as is the custom in Quaker meetinghouses, around three sides of a square. Half the congregation, thus, had a good look at Cooper as he came in. Whatever surprise they may have felt, they hid. The quiet, tranquil attentiveness was unbroken. They had centered down below the level of movie stars, and Cooper appeared to accept and enjoy the contemplative silence. The woman next to me, as the hour was ending, asked our names, saying it was the custom of the meeting to introduce strangers at the conclusion of worship. When the handshake of those on "the facing bench" announced that the meeting for worship was over, she rose and said, "We have had worshiping with us this morning, Jessamyn McPherson, Stuart Millar, and Gary Cooper."

I watched the faces of three or four teen-aged girls as this announcement was made. There was a discernible tremor of the eyelids but no more. After the handshaking, a very small old lady asked us to sign the guest book in which the meeting recorded the names of visitors. She used the plain language, something I haven't heard, except as a piece of rather conscious play acting, since the death, not of people of my grandfather's, but of my great-grandfather's age. It was obviously her customary way of speaking, and I was glad that Mr. Cooper was hearing her. Mr. Wyler's theeing and thying worries are related particularly to Cooper. Would he be able to use the plain language?

The little old lady's thees and thys were as natural as her breathing, and Cooper looked down at her (she came about to his waist) with that look of interest from the inside out which I cannot believe he fakes. It was not interest alone but amusement too, and what makes that look appealing is that he doesn't try to hide the amusement. The old lady responded to this honest blending of delight and amusement. Asking visitors to sign a guest book after having sought union in silence with God is about as unexpected, yet human an action, as can be imagined. Guest books? I thought What is this, a mountain lodge or a national monument? But the old lady made the request seem quite natural. She was interested in us. She was methodical. It gave her pleasure to keep track of those who visited meeting.

"Won't thee sign our guest book, Mr. Cooper?" she asked.

I think Cooper was, for her, only a visiting stranger.

"I'd be pleased to sign it, ma'am," Cooper said.

As she led him toward the guest book she asked him where he had been born, where he had lived, where he now lived. Cooper began with Montana, mentioned school in England and some intervening places of residence ending with Beverly Hills. She looked up at him when he finished and with lively benignity gave him a flattering title. "Thee is a real cosmopolitan, isn't thee, Mr. Cooper?"

Cooper, somewhat surprised, answered, "I guess you could say that."

There had been a second's pause before he said the "you," in which I could feel him considering a "thee." But he decided against it on the quiet understandable grounds of not wanting to be cute with something never intended for cuteness.

After he and Stuart and I had signed the guest book, a number of the members of the meeting came up to talk with Cooper. I asked one of the men if he hadn't recognized Cooper when we came in. "Of course I did," he said. "And so did almost everyone else. But we tried to give him a gift of privacy. That must be about the only gift anyone can give Gary Cooper."

While we talked a half-dozen little boys were running about, carrying on a sharp cap-pistol battle. I hoped that this sight of nonpacifist Quaker children would not convince Cooper that a little gun-toting wouldn't be amiss for him in the picture. There are still some ripples in the current of script writing that suggest to me that this possibility is yet to be thoroughly scotched. I saw that Cooper was watching the boys with amazement, and I myself was more than amazed. I was shocked. How could people who believed fighting wrong let their children buy toy pistols? True, if they don't have them the other children are going to think them queer. But as potential pacifists they had better be prepared for this.

I asked one of the men about the pistols and his answer,

175

whether in quotes or not I couldn't tell, was, "It drains off their aggressiveness."

On the way back to Beverly Hills we talked about the pistols. Conversation wasn't easy, since the front seat was backless and Stu was taking pleasure in swinging us around curves at sixty miles an hour. Cooper said it wasn't the pistols so much as the pistols in church that had amazed him—and that, at least, I could explain.

"A meetinghouse isn't any more holy to a Quaker than any other building. Whatever he does any place else he should be willing to do there. The building doesn't change the act, doesn't make it better or worse. The act of killing is no worse there than on a battlefield. *What* happens is important, not places. The building isn't holy, it's merely convenient. A garage or a hillside is just as holy. A cap pistol in the meetinghouse is no worse than it is any place else. Quakers don't want their children to believe that there is a difference in places and days. Be good on Sunday and in church and you can raise hell on weekdays away from church. It's always Sunday for a Quaker."

"Kind of sounded like it was always Fourth of July in there," Cooper said.

"I know it. But you mustn't think because of it that Quakers approve of war."

Cooper said, "Some Quakers have fought, haven't they?"

"A lot of them. Your son in this picture does."

"But not me?"

"Not you."

"Action seems to come natural to me."

"I know it."

"There comes a time in a picture of mine when the people watching me expect me to do something," he said, repeating what he had told me the first time I saw him.

"I know it. You'll do something."

"What?"

"Refrain. You will furnish your public with the refreshing picture of a strong man refraining."

"It doesn't usually film well . . . strong man refraining. Strong man puts hand toward doorknob, fingers quiver, then strong man lets hand fall from doorknob, shakes

176

head slowly, and walks away, head bent. That's not what I do best."

"How do you know? You always kick the door down."

"I reckon that gets old too?" Cooper asked.

When we reached Cooper's house he said, and I believed him, "I liked going to that meeting. Those people weren't holding themselves still and making themselves be quiet. They *were* still and they were quiet. I liked being with them."

When we left I told Stu to sit over. "I don't care if it is Sunday and I do look like your mother. I've got to have something to lean against."

"You could get over into the back seat," he said ungallantly.

"I don't want to. I want to talk. Get over. You don't need half the seat."

"What do you want to talk about?" he asked.

"I want to talk about Cooper and going to meeting and the ending of the script. Did you like meeting?"

"I liked it. I want to go again. Do you know what a friend said the other day? I talk about this picture and the Quakers all the time, and he said, 'Stu, do you know some of my best Jews are Friends?' "

"It's old," I told him. "I've heard it before."

"It certainly was nice," Stu said, "when you first came to Hollywood and all my jokes were new."

"Nothing is a joke any more. What am I going to do about Cooper's fans expecting him to do something? If 'something' means killing, winning the Civil War single-handed, you know he can't."

"You're the writer," Stu said.

"The writing's not hard. How am I going to persuade Wyler and Harold and Walter Mirsch and Cooper that this isn't another *Vera Cruz?*"

"Just persuade Wyler." Then after a while he added, "And perhaps the woman who reads scripts for Cooper and keeps track of the number of shots fired. She won't let Cooper appear in a picture in which he fires fewer shots than anyone else."

"Is there such a woman?"

"Yes."

"Does she really do that?"

"Yep. They can't be a smaller caliber either."

*Tuesday*
*June 21*

Midsummer day. Here in my little flower-lined garden back of the apartment.

I went to Napa over the weekend and am as usual taking the Hollywood rest cure: nothing to do but write and talk, and write and read and look at the sky.

This was graduation weekend in Napa, and since Fred was graduating and his father and stepmother and mother and stepfather were there for the weekend I thought it my duty to have them and some of his teachers for dinner Saturday night. I don't know whether Fred's pleasure balanced my pain or not, because all I wanted to do was listen to the herons clattering in the eucalyptus and watch the hummingbirds floundering hip-deep in the amaryllis. Not cook. I did manage to watch some. I saw a lizard yawn; and I saw a hawk, sitting on a bough scanning surrounding trees for fledglings, lash his tail like a cat watching a mouse.

Dolores came over and said, "I am getting bigger every day. Pretty soon I'll be too big to be little. What will I do then?" Dolores will know when the time comes. And what she does will be lovely, a hundred per cent Dolores.

Time passing, time passing! For me too. I have my first spectacles, and who but the middle-aged could guess the pleasure they give me. Specs! For me! It is unbelievable. I put them on like a small girl trying on high-heeled shoes. It is a kind of make-believe exercise wearing them. Do I fool people with these on? Convince them I'm middle-aged? I want to put them beside the bed at night like a new pair of shoes to be seen when I first wake up in the morning. And yet the novelty is one of deterioration. If I celebrate anything in these, it is the approach of death.

Stu came over and I told him about the closing scenes. I am too excited to put them down word by word yet, but I think they are right. Stu was elated. "It's terrific," he said. "I think you've licked the ending." I do too.

I had a long talk this afternoon with Robert and William Wyler about Josh's younger brother, Labe. Josh, smaller than Labe and doubting his own courage, goes off to fight. Labe, a big boy who likes to fight, thinks he shouldn't and doesn't. Actually, at fifteen, he's too young to enlist. He's an untidy, easygoing boy, while Josh is a careful, introspective worrier. Mr. Wyler wants to get Labe out of the script, and he marched up and down Robert's big bungalow office demanding that we tell him what Labe was doing in the script, what problem he represented, how he could possibly be cast, and if he wasn't just an echo of Cooper.

Stu stuck his head in the door occasionally. He, like Robert, is a great Labe lover and he couldn't resist defending the boy. I am given a pleasurable but odd feeling to hear Robert and Stu fight to keep Labe in the script—I think Labe is less real to me than to them; he is a part of me and hence I don't see him as objectively as they, nor feel that his removal is murder. If he makes the story, which is Jess's and Josh's story less effective, I'd take him out in a minute.

Mr. Wyler's arguments thus far I do not consider valid. Cooper is not diminished by having a brave son; and as for what problem Labe represents—one trouble with the movies is this insistence that all characters represent problems. Not only do the characters cease to be human beings when they all become "problems" but the audiences have become very smart problem-shooters. The minute they see a "problem" they know the solution. The fresh, shocking, mysterious treat for an audience is a human being who is not a simple two-times-two problem but a complex multifaceted man or woman who has no problem smaller than living itself—and this is a problem even a smart audience

179

can't solve in the first three reels. I told Mr. Wyler this. He said, "The audience is going to expect that boy to have a problem. They will listen and look and analyze and try to figure out what meaning he has in relation to the story you're telling. And you tell me he has no relationship."

"No, I didn't tell you that. I told you he had no specific problem. He can't be pigeonholed. Somebody in this story needs to be without a problem. There needs to be some contrast."

"Cooper is the contrast. Labe is in my way. There he is in every scene. And what does he do? Make me a list of the scenes in which that boy appears and a list of what he does in them."

Robert, when William left, flew around the office laughing. " 'The trouble with the movies is that every character has to be a problem,' " he quoted. "I was glad to hear you say that. I'm glad you told Willy. 'Every character has to be a problem.' Look, we'll make this list for Willy; he must save Labe. There are times when others speak when it could as well be Labe. Isn't that right? We'll give him a few more lines. For Willy's sake we must save Labe."


*Whittier*


Came over to say farewell to Mama and Papa, who start with car and trailer to make their annual summer trip. This time they are heading for the Gaspé Peninsula. At seventy-six and seventy-three, they do not have to wonder where the wonder has gone. They still have it. No sight so heartens the middle-aged as a happy oldster; just as no sight so disheartens the young as the middle-aged, happy or unhappy. By middle age, growing old is accepted. One hopes only to be able to do it happily. When young, one hates all reminders of decay; in fact, a happy old person (anyone over thirty-five is old) is a disgusting sight. Has he no sensitivity? Happy? Pudgy, bespectacled, short of breath? His happiness is only further proof of his disintegration.

Merle's son Mike has been ill. He kept his dog, Reddy, in his room with him while he was bedfast.

"I sure watched Reddy every minute while I was sick," he told me.

"Why?" I asked.

"Don't you know? If the master is going to die a dog always begins to howl. But Reddy just slept all the time so I knew I'd get well."

If Reddy had begun to howl I suppose the poor boy would have collapsed and died like any hexed savage.

I'm alone in the house, writing the final pages. Cooper will not be ready for shooting on this picture until August fifteenth, so we will not go back to Indiana after all. Mr. Wyler and Stu are leaving for New York next week, where they'll hear actors read for parts. The script will be mimeographed before they go, and for a month I'll be a technical adviser and not a writer. Less money, but also less work.

I can't believe we have arrived at anything so final as mimeographed copy. Robert laughs at me when I say "final." "You don't know Willy," he tells me. "When Willy comes back from New York he'll go over the script with you. Now we've got a good strong story line. Don't let Willy touch that. Willy gets carried away. He enriches the scene, but that scene, if it gets too big and heavy, will pull the whole design out of shape."

When Robert talks to me of the day when I must meet Willy alone with the script he fills me with a sense of great dangers to come. Great dangers, not little ones, for Robert admires his brother too much to suggest that anything he will advocate will be niggling.

I've taken Labe out of the script. It was quite clear when I had done what Mr. Wyler suggested, listed Labe's scenes and speeches, that he had nothing to do after the first third of the movie. So I invented a friend for Josh— who, because he is a friend and not a brother, can be on hand when we need him and absent when unneeded.

The title of the movie has been changed to "Mr. Bird-well Goes to Battle." This, Robert and Stu think, is a

181

publicity department echo of Cooper's success *Mr. Deeds Goes to Town*.

I was asked to tell my Quaker friends, in case they did not think "Mr. Birdwell Goes to Battle" a very suitable title for a story about a people who do not believe in fighting, that the considerations prompting the change were purely commercial. As if, as soon as it was explained to them that the title was being changed for the sake of money, all would be understood and forgiven.

Mr. Wyler asked me to meet Susan Strasberg and Robert Middleton today, two actors he is considering for parts in—I still think of it as *The Friendly Persuasion*.

Middleton read for Mr. Wyler. It was the first time I have ever heard lines of mine spoken by an actor. The coincidence of this large burly man sitting there, becoming before my eyes Sam Jordan, a man I had made up, was disturbingly magical. It was as if we had both simultaneously had the same thought; even stranger than that, he became my thought. I listened and watched with my mouth open. Mr. Wyler asked me, when Middleton left, what I thought of him. Under the circumstance, I thought he was a genius and said so.

The publicity department is worried about a line of mine. "Queen Victoria is getting kind of—fat." This, says the publicity department, will not set well with the British. Mr. Wyler is writing Alistair Cook, as the arbiter of what sets well with the British, for an opinion.

They are also, the publicity department, of the opinion that I cannot have one man call another a "shitepoke." "It sounds dirty." I told them the shitepoke was a bona fide bird, and that it was no dirtier to call a man a shitepoke than to call him a buzzard. "Sounds dirtier," they replied, and of course it does. That's the point of using it.

The publicity department also wants me to keep my eye on Southern feelings and have someone say, "Sherman was no angel when he marched through Georgia." He didn't march until two years after this picture. "We find twenty years one way or the other doesn't make much difference," they assure me.

182

We all sat in Portia's office at five tonight, congratulating ourselves and feeling good: Stu, Robert, Dorothy, and I. The first mimeographed pages were coming through. Everyone warns me there'll be a thousand changes yet, but this is the longest step so far toward finality, and I rejoice in it. Portia is a remarkable woman, able to keep track of all the day-by-day changes in the script, read my handwriting, absorb without friction Stu's driving and sometimes domineering energy, remember Robert's appointments with doctors, dentists, and bankers, keep Dorothy in touch with costume people, and at the same time never lose her interest in what seems to me, of course, the most important thing: the story itself and its meaning. We sat like people at the end of a day in a home and talked of what we'd done and had yet to do.

Dorothy's and Portia's jobs I not only couldn't perform but dislike even to think about. Dorothy has had to plan each costume, keeping in mind history, physical conformation of actors, scenes in which costumes would appear, relation of costumes to each other, relation of costumes to background, materials available, manner in which various colors and materials photograph, and the aesthetic whole —I'm not sure what she would call this—but what I mean by it is the appearance, aesthetically satisfying or not, of these people, regardless of story or scene or background. Doing this involves (horrible thought to me) assembling buttons, thread, samples of material; she has to measure actors, remember that Cooper's hips are small, Eliza's bosom ditto, and that pseudo homespun costs $7.90 a yard and real old Quaker alpaca, $8.20. I would rather break rock.

A little needle flashing in and out of a piece of linen, a little silver thimble going click, click, click, a little hem, worm-round and neat, following behind the click and flash, this much of sewing I enjoy. This is activity without thought and as pleasant as hopscotch or swinging in a hammock. But to have to think about sewing! When sewing requires this it asks too much of human beings.

I don't know whether or not this conviction dates from or antedates a high-school class in sewing. I was thirteen at the time, and I, with the rest of the ranch girls who made up the class, had to twine outdoor fingers around delicate

183

nainsook shaped into the minuscule garments of a layette. Perhaps the idea had been that layette making would transform these tomboys, bring out the maternal in us, soften our pitching arms, and gentle our mumblety-peg fingers. I have no statistics on the effect of layette making on thirteen-year-olds but I can't believe that it started any of that class to crooning cradle songs. Layette making was too much for me. Our teacher, as big and awkward in her right-handed way as I was in my left, became so entangled with me and the nainsook that we struggled together each sewing period like willing but unskilled lady wrestlers. At the end of the year I carried my layette home as grubby and worn, through the dozens of sewings, rippings, and re-sewings, as if a family of infants had used it. Mama, when she examined it, hooted.

"How in the world," she asked me, "are the babies going to get their heads into these things?"

The garments, some of them were called gertrudes, I remember, had little round holes at the top, frayed with hemming and rehemming, but no plackets (I believe that's the name) which could be unbuttoned to make the opening large enough for a baby's head.

"What was that teacher thinking of?" Mama asked.

What she was thinking of, I'm sure, in my case, was that a placket was beyond me. I kept that useless layette for twenty years, telling myself that when I knew I was going to have a baby I would fix those necks. Finally, without my ever having thrown them away, those unusable garments disappeared. Sometimes I think, as one does of happenings whose origins are beyond real knowledge, that if I'd made an act of faith, gotten those damned plackets ready for the babies, the babies would have been forthcoming. This kind of unreasoning, since obviously it takes more than a placket to make a baby, is a mixture of real primitivism and spurious Christianity. The amulet and the "faith like a mustard seed" is a self-defeating combination.

Mama could sew, though she took no pleasure in it, and I hounded her, as a girl, into making many an intricate dress for me. She made for my graduation from grammar school a dress of white voile, lace trimmed and heavily shirred. So beautiful, I thought, that when the curtain went up revealing us graduates it never occurred to me that the audience's audible gasp of pleasure was not wholly for my lovely, homemade voile.

Papa, as secretary or president of the board of trustees, was also on the platform that graduation night to hand out the diplomas. He had been afflicted all day with the summer complaint and, since he didn't want to miss giving his daughter her diploma, disguised his frequent need to leave the platform as a nosebleed occasioned by the intense mid-June heat. What with Papa clapping a handkerchief to his nose before rushing off stage and me in my gasp-provoking voile, the graduation was in my opinion pleasantly West-centered.

No wonder graduates, nowadays, hundreds instead of dozens, all dressed alike in cap and gown, feel the need to hurry to the city the minute the graduation mechanism has stamped them with its serial number. Somehow they must prove, by truancy if necessary, that they are not interchangeable ciphers. It is something, anyway, to have been the only boy ever to have watered every palm in the garden court of the Palace Hotel with wine brought from Napa Valley for that purpose—even if clapped in jail for it afterward.

I seem to be sorry for everyone tonight—today's kids, Dorothy making costumes. But Dorothy may feel sorry for me: all this work with words, second-hand objects, colorless, weightless, immaterial. I am the newcomer among them, and I asked tonight, as we sat in Portia's office, "Is this what movie making's like?"

"What do you mean by 'this'?" Stu asked.

"Where's the screaming and hating? Am I fooled? Are you hiding something from me. Or are we really sitting here enjoying each other's company?"

"We really are," Portia said.

"It's not always like this," Dorothy admitted.

"Are we special?"

Robert said we were.

"We're special because none of us are treading on each other's toes," said Stu. "Wait till Willy cuts your best scenes and Cooper says the pants Dorothy designed for him make him look hippy and Haworth builds that stone church."

So we're waiting.

185

I had a long talk with Mr. Wyler yesterday. When he comes back from New York he will work intensively on this picture. Up to this time, he has been finishing another picture, *The Desperate Hours,* while getting this one under way.

He spoke to me of his hopes for *The Friendly Persuasion.* Financial success, of course; without that, picture making stops. A picture that people want to see is a financial success. But why do people want to see a picture?

Mr. Wyler said, "I know it isn't fashionable to speak of pictures with a message. I don't suppose you care to be thought of as a writer with a message. But I believe that every good picture and every great book has a message; that when people call a movie good they do so because it has said something memorable. I have seen a lot of suffering and injustice in the world. I took part in the last war. I am a Jew. In my own religion there are practices that seem stupid to me. The separation of men and women in church, for instance. That's one of the reasons why, although you tell me it was customary, I don't like the idea of showing the men and the women in the Quaker meetinghouse separated. The Quakers, it seems to me, have been able to hit upon more that is honest and reasonable in their lives than most people. I want to show that. This movie can't be a sermon. No one will want to see it if it says in so many words, 'Honesty, love, and simplicity are best.' But I don't think it will be a success either unless, after seeing it, people say to themselves, 'Those Quakers had something worthwhile that maybe we have lost—or never had.' They quote Sam Goldwyn a lot for his mistakes in English, but Sam has made a lot of truths memorable by putting them in a form that people quote because they're funny. Sam said about one of his pictures, 'I don't care whether this picture makes a nickel or not. I just want millions of people to see it.' That's the way I feel about this. I'm not a pacifist, as you know. So that's not why I'm interested in this picture. I'm interested in it in spite of that. And I admit I wouldn't be interested in it at all no matter what its message if I didn't think it told a good story. That's why Capra bought it in the first place. Capra's always been a first-rate judge of a good story. But the Quakers honored other people's ways of thinking and doing. Jess, who thinks fighting's wrong, lets his son go to war. Eliza, who thinks music is wrong, lets Jess have his organ. This picture says that salvation isn't a mass product. It says that you save or lose your soul as an individual. When people go out of the theaters after seeing this . . . if we succeed . . . they aren't going to say 'so what.' They're going to say, 'That guy had guts. He did what he thought was right.' "

When I didn't answer, he asked me, "That's what Quakers do believe, isn't it?"

"That's what they believe," I told him.

I don't remember all he said. It was a very long talk. But that was the gist of it. I met Stu in Portia's office afterward. He asked me where I'd been all afternoon.

"Talking to Mr. Wyler."

Stu is still young enough, privy as he is to almost all the ins and outs of this picture—and many of which I know nothing—to be agog when some unexpected interview takes place.

"What's up?"

"Wyler's going to make a Quaker of me before this picture's over," I told him.

It's true. I am always being told by people on the outside looking in, what Quakerism means to them. Actually, I completely forget that I'm writing about Quakers or that these people are different from others. As a matter of fact I don't believe they are. But I was moved by Wyler's talk and told Stu so.

Stu said, "Willy's a great one to bring out the best in people working for him. He's won more Oscars for people working with him than for himself."

"Was that meant as cynicism?" I asked. "Are you saying, 'A little pep talk from Willy to put a bloom of spirituality on the picture'?"

"You know better than that," Stu said; and I do. Stu is not cynical about Willy.

"The trouble is," I told Stu, "I am so much more cynical than anyone else that I, expecting nothing, am able to recognize a gift of the spirit when I see it. The rest of you, knowing your own motives to be pure must be continuously on your guard and cynically suspicious."

It's the truth, but Stu wouldn't believe me.

Movie making is very quiet with Stu and Mr. Wyler in New York. I am now a technical adviser. Chief change so far is that I get a third of the pay I did. Even though I have been warned by Ned Brown that I must not write a word, if I can think of a way to better a scene, I am going to do it, writer's salary or no writer's salary.

One of my jobs as technical adviser I take to be an attempt to persuade Mr. Wyler that these Quakers should not be dressed too sedately; they were farmers and house-wives and dressed for their work. Also they furnished their homes with just as much Victorian luxury and bad taste as Methodists or United Brethren. I understand the dramatic need for heightening the differences between Quakers and others by stressing the simplicity and lack of color, etc., in their dress and homes. But there must be some color, some luxury, some bad taste, some frivolity. Nothing believable is ever a hundred per cent anything, not even a Quaker. I am going to Whittier tomorrow to gather up pictures, bonnets, and shawls, samples of materials which I hope will get the Birdwells down off their pedestal.

\* \*

I brought back a carload of Quaker effects all calculated to prove them a people less plain than they are usually pictured. I know that an audience *wants* to think of Quakers as very different from their worldly brethren. And in many ways they are. But we should know, in making the picture, what the truth is before we deviate from it.

I went first to the daughter of the red-haired hymn-tossing Quaker minister whose preaching gave me goose flesh as a child. She is eighty. No one would guess it. Her hair is still more yellow than white, her cheeks are pink, and her figure, while roly-poly, is womanly rather than aged. She lives in the house where her father lived when he was the pastor of the Quaker church whose Sunday morning bell now commemorates my great-grandmother —his mother-in-law.

I told Cousin Florence that I wanted pictures and samples of Quaker dress for a movie about Quakers. A movie about Quakers seemed the most natural thing in the world to her. She brought baskets of pictures, a quilt pieced with swatches of material from old-time Quaker dresses. "Mother was married in this." "Grandmother wore this to Philadelphia." Outside, the pepper trees shifted their dry lace in the dry summery air, and Grandmother, who was thirty-five at the time of the Civil War and approximately Eliza's age, listened, or seemed to, to the talk of what was the appropriate costume for her to wear in Vista-Vision. Well, it *was* suitable. These old-time Quakers were always getting a concern to travel to foreign parts and bear witness. This was only a more extended trip, and witnessing on a more universal scale.

"Cousin Florence," I asked, "did Quakers in southern Indiana always wear black or gray?"

"Of course not," she said. "Though when we went to church we wore gray or black or blue-gray or snuff brown. And I can remember that oil-red was very popular at one time. I don't know why it was called oil-red unless because it was darker than most reds—a red-black really, like a red rose that is beginning to wither. But at home—can you remember how hot it was in southern Indiana in the summertime?—we wore light-colored summer dresses like anyone else. They weren't low-necked and short-sleeved then the way they are now. But that was the times as much as the Friends. I'll tell you, Jessamyn, where Quaker women got in their fashionable licks—aprons. They had the most beautiful aprons, finished off with rich embroidery and crochet. When Mother changed from her morning apron to her afternoon apron it was a sign that the day's work was over. A change came over the whole house when she put her afternoon apron on; no one hurried any more and we all got politer."

I asked her about the color of afternoon aprons.

"White, always white. But no one, no man I suppose, since they are the ones who usually decide such matters, had thought to make any rules about aprons. So they were always very long, very full, sometimes of silk, and rich with handiwork.

"There was a revolt about bonnets in our meeting, I remember, when I was a little girl. The Quaker bonnet was adopted in the beginning because it was simple and cheap and wouldn't keep our minds on changing fashions and trying to keep up with them. But the Quaker bonnet got richer and richer in materials, and women got out of the way of making them. They had to send clear to Philadelphia or Cincinnati to get one, and they became much more expensive than ordinary hats. Here's a picture of Aunt Mary, who revolted from expensive bonnets. They said that when she walked into meeting with a straw hat on, perfectly plain as you can see, that there was more buzz than silence for quite a few seconds."

"Did Great-Grandmother have curtains in her house? Or pictures? Rugs? Upholstered furniture?"

"Do they think we were savages?" Cousin Florence asked.

"No, but they think you were very plain."

Cousin Florence went off for more albums—and I've brought them, together with blouses, aprons, and bonnets back with me. When Mr. Wyler and Dorothy look at them, at all this evidence of backwoods finery and Victoran vulgarity instead of the Quaker purity of which they dream, they may feel they are dealing with savages indeed.


What is "Hollywood" life? The life lived in Hollywood, of course. This, then, is Hollywood life. Waking at seven thirty. Going to the window to look at the pool, lonely as Walden at this hour, a few maple leaves still unskimmed and a Siamese cat, who makes the rounds before breakfast, pausing to watch their gentle rocking motion.

It is touching—oh, what do I mean by touching?—it is heartbreaking to find Thoreau, in his last house-bound days, tied to his couch and his window, refusing to make peace with a God with whom he had never quarreled, turning to kittens for his taste of wild life. He has more to say about kittens in the last pages of his final journal than in all the other volumes of the journal put together. Though he was never oblivious of cats, was full of health when he spoke of picking up the barn cat in winter and holding her to his face for her sweet haymow smell of summer. Now, dying, kittens had to be for him the woods and all the birds and animals. And he took them, without wishing them to be anything else, and contemplated them with that pure intensity which permits a kitten, as easily as a tiger, to be an opening into eternity.

Nothing is true from the outside. Not kittens, not death, not Hollywood. Thoreau entered into the first two without resistance. Had he come to Hollywood, would he have remained a homesick woodsman, or would he, tape measure and spyglass in hand have gone specimen hunting here?

Watching the Siamese, the rocking of the hand-shaped leaves, I think about this quiet, tiptoe life I lead and wonder if my own shell has grown too durably protective to permit any newness to enter.

Where is the Hollywood in this? I ask myself, making my own bed, picking up the petals fallen overnight from the flowers, plumping the cushions, putting the coffee on. I am living my own life here.

I sometimes wonder if cat lovers are catlike. Quiet; tidy, rather than clean; ruthless; lovers of places rather than people. Away from home I often get desperately homesick —but when I remember that this never happens except when I can't "keep house," the likeness to cats occurs to me. Is it really "the home," "the house," and the acts I perform as the "keeper" of a house, for which I long so painfully? For it is painful. In a hotel room where I have no chance to buy groceries, dust chairs, wash windows, fry bacon and eggs, I become so homesick that from mid-throat to mid-chest I ache continuously. Is this only the displaced person's longing for a familiar scene and familiar activities rather than for any individual? For homesickness and loneliness are different diseases. Here with a house to keep, I've never been homesick. Lonely, yes; but that can be dealt with by phone calls, letters, conversations with friends.

Since homesickness is more painful than loneliness, am I more affected by parting from places than people? Is what I do more important than who I am with? And how can housekeeping be so important to me when I hate it if I'm required to spend more than two or three hours a day on it? And also, I ask myself, what of the man who is my opposite number? Since all men were at one time men of the land, as women were women of the home, are there not some men who are "homesick" when separated from the land? What do they do in cities, these men with an ache under the Adam's apple for the lost farm, the lost ranch, the lost garden? Or was land only a means of making a living to most men and never as central to their lives as housekeeping is to women?

I ask myself these unanswerable—by me, anyway—questions as I make coffee and clean my darling boxcar. I write them down as I drink coffee right-handed, write left-handed.

NOTE: The "birdman of Alcatraz" is described as being "awkward, lonely, left-handed." Why was "left-handed" used to terminate that trilogy? Alliteration? Or does it in any way account for the first two states.

Robert and William Wyler both occasionally speak to me, each in his own way, of the same thing. And what they say silences me because I know I shall fail them. Both say, "When the shooting starts, the mechanical concerns, the concentration on the camera, the sets, the actors, the costumes, the colors, the salaries, the disputes, the heat, our own weariness and staleness will be so great that what this picture is about, man's spirit, may get lost. Help then, please, help then. The mechanics are not your concern. Stay open to what is going on with the spirit. Speak, when it goes wrong. Tell us when the tone is wrong. Don't let the movie get in the way of the living of these people."

I do not reply. A word, a line that seems wrong or stupid I can speak of; I can speak of what the characters wear and the houses they live in and the gestures they make; but I do not know how these things transfer to the screen; and what seemed wrong to me in the flesh might live with a trueness beyond reality on the screen.

I made my first visit to the set today. A long drive, an hour and fifteen minutes by studio car with Dorothy and Mr. Wyler, who is back from New York, out Ventura Boulevard to the Rowland Lee ranch. Up to this time I have thought it was the "Rolling Lea" ranch, but when I was introduced to the owner, I decided that Rolling Lea was a very unlikely name for a man.

Mr. Lee is a former movie actor who had the perspicacity to buy this tract of land and keep it free of power lines, telephone poles, paved roads, and other reminders of the twentieth century. Movie companies rent the place to shoot their period pictures without the labor of shooting around the anachronisms.

My first feeling, though the place was beautiful, was one of disappointment. How could this Western ranch of eucalyptus and olive trees, of dry brown hills and barley stubble, be made to look like a land of cornfields, green grass, domed clouds, and sycamores? And what *was* green—the shores of a little artificial lake—looked parklike rather than rural to me.

The corn was already being planted, Mr. Wyler said; the Midwest trees would go in; the camera would look the other way when a eucalyptus came in range.

The place was humming with studio carpenters and movie farmers. "Stone walls" for house and barn were being sawed. Both were already partially built. Telephone poles, or what looked to be telephone poles, rose like great mast poles from the center of the barn, and the barn walls, like masts but slightly more durable, were being attached to these. There has already been built what appears to be the stone tower of a Norman castle; but Ted Haworth, the art director of the picture, says it is a silo. This was attached to the barn structure.

"Surely silos weren't common in Civil War times?" I asked.

Ted whipped out a picture of a Civil War silo. I found myself feeling about barns as Dorothy and Mr. Wyler no doubt feel about Quakers: that we had better attempt no reformation of the public's concept of their appearance. I thought a barn must first of all, in anything that moved as fast as a movie, look like a barn. Neither audiences nor readers want to be told everything. The story on paper or on the screen is a set of clues by which a reader or a viewer can tell himself his own story. As readers and viewers we long to infer, to draw our own conclusions, and when we have no chance to do so, we lose interest. But one shouldn't have to spend any time wondering whether or not a barn is a barn unless the fact that it is or isn't has some bearing on the story. This barn is a barn, nothing else, and if an audience has to settle the question of what it is, before it can give its attention to the narrative, the barn is a handicap. If a husband whispers to his

193

wife, "I thought this picture was laid in southern Indiana," and she whispers back, "Shh," and he replies louder, "Looks like the tower where they kept the Prisoner of Chillon to me," and she says, "I thought this was Civil War times . . . but maybe it's the War of the Roses," and he . . . well, that's *bad*.

As technical adviser it was clearly my duty to say, "This barn looks wrong to me." As J. West this was a difficult job. I like Haworth. He told me he wept when he read my stories. Readers like that are rare. I wanted to love his barn. Besides I may be wrong. I consoled myself by thinking that my only responsibility is to say what I think. Mr. Wyler will make the decisions and take the responsibility. So I told Mr. Wyler, but he had already, and without my technical advice, decided against the tower and ordered it down. Up it goes, down it comes. Was there some way in which the unsuitability of this tower might have been envisaged before building? I don't know. Mr. Wyler, as producer-director, is a man in a hurry. He can't waste time salving our feelings when we make mistakes. He must concentrate upon correcting the mistakes.

"Pull it down," he told Haworth.

Haworth said, "Willy, I understood you to say you wanted Jess Birdwell's barn and house to tell the audience that he was a well-to-do, successful farmer."

"A successful *Indiana* farmer, not somebody farming on the Rhine. That looks like the tower where the rats ate the bishop. What's that fish doing over there?" Mr. Wyler pointed to a very large finned creature attached to a rod and leaning against the barn.

Ted brightened up at this. The fish was evidently a find of his. "It's a weather vane, Willy," he said. "Jess is a poetic, imaginative kind of man. I thought he'd be likely to have something kind of offbeat, not the usual horse or rooster on his barn."

"He's not that offbeat," Wyler said. "Get a rooster; the audience has got to do something else in the first two reels besides try to figure out this offbeat barn."

Somebody had been waiting for Mr. Wyler to look at the proposed setting for the horse race, and he strode off leaving Ted looking sorrowfully at fish and tower; fine

194

symbols almost anywhere else, but out of place on this Muscatatuck barn.

Dorothy, who had been with us during the barn discussion, had even more fault to find with it. The barn is what is called a sidehill or bank barn—haymow on top, main floor for farm equipment, lower floor, with the hill forming one wall, for animals.

"This will never do," Dorothy told Haworth. "It is a well-known fact that cows must be kept in an airy, well-ventilated place. How are they going to get any air down there in the basement?"

Now I was on Haworth's side. "That's where they kept them, Dorothy. Air or no air, at least they don't freeze in winter."

I begin to understand what Stu meant that afternoon in Portia's office. My toes, as technical adviser, aren't very tender; but Dorothy and Ted, he as art director and she as costume designer and color consultant, can really collide—and have. Fish or cock, tower or no tower, these are matters of opinion. But cows in a sidehill barn are a matter of fact, and we must look up cows or sidehill barns or air or southern Indiana in whatever is the appropriate book of knowledge and waste no more words and emotions arguing.

I left Ted and Dorothy and joined Mr. Wyler, who was inspecting simultaneously locations for the buggy race and the two churches, Methodist and Quaker. Jess, in his buggy, has to pass Sam at the Methodist church. Sam, unwilling to admit defeat, sweeps on down the road to the Quaker meetinghouse. So the problem is double-barreled: the locations suitable for worship must also be suitable for speed. Very easy to arrange in the script, but more of a problem on the Rowland Lee ranch.

Lunch with Stu. He said, "Are you satisfied with the ending?"

"What do you mean, am I satisfied with it? I wrote it. You said it was terrific. If you've forgotten that you said it, I can show you my journal. 'Stu says the ending is licked. He says it is terrific.' That's what you said. Robert likes it, except he wants the Home Guard to make that unreasonable march back across the river. Why do you ask? You make me queasy. It's as if you asked a mother at a hospital, 'Do you really like that baby of yours?' Is it going to be taken away from me again?"

We were at the Brown Derby, and Stu, who is dieting for a week by drinking nothing but fruit juices, had plenty of time to talk. "Don't be silly," he said. But he went on to say that he had talked a lot with Willy while they were east. "I think you'll find that Willy has changed some of his ideas about how much fighting Cooper should do."

I went from queasy to mad. "This is a puzzle and is of a puzzle's dimensions only. I can work on it, manipulate the pieces, but I can't feel about it."

"You appear to me to be feeling plenty," Stu said.

"My feelings now are about you, and they aren't nice. Besides I'm a technical director and it isn't legal for me to think about the writing."

"Adviser," Stu said, "adviser. And you're going to be a writer again next week so you'd better start warming up."

"I begin to understand," I told Stu, "what they mean when they say a writer prostitutes his art in Hollywood."

"The prostituting you've done will never get you into the union," Stu said.

"I'm not joking. Look, this is the way it is. When I write something I love it. I don't mean my words, but I love the people I write about leading their lives, doing what they do. I love their bright answers and good hearts, and I suffer with their sorrows and failures. Here, this is a better example. It's as if you, as a matchmaker, introduced me to a man. I accept him. I love him. I don't care to look at anyone else. Then, just as I've settled down to the quiet happiness of a real union you snatch this man from me and say, 'Sorry, here is a better specimen. Love him instead.' And another. And another. Finally, love is impossible. Ridiculous to even think about. One may still accept, say, 'I will do my best—as a professional. But don't expect love or devotion. This is a business proposition; I will give it my contractual attention! In other words, I'm a prostitute."

Stu got so upset he ordered another glass of V8. But I had cured myself of my anger by speaking. Though I continued to speak; for I do believe that unless the writer writes from full inner conviction he is no better in the juggling of events for effect than any nonwriter called in off the street to give an opinion. But Stu understands this. We decided after much more V8 and much more talk to give ourselves a vacation for the afternoon by going to the Pickwick Book Shop, which is not far from the Brown Derby. I bought Stu two thirty-nine-cent bargains, Elizabeth Bowen's *Impressions and Comments,* a treasure at thirty-nine dollars, and Lillian Ross's *Picture,* which he had read but didn't own; so he forgave me.

And I forgave him; but his words are still gnawing like mice under my breastbone.

*Wednesday*
*July 9*

Tomorrow I am going to look for another apartment, nearer the studio. Portia and Robert began calling other apartment houses the moment they heard how much the rent is here. They think it's ridiculous, when what I'm paying for is something I don't care about—a "good" address, a "fashionable" location. Stu got the place for me when the studio was paying my expenses, and I've stayed on here sheeplike ever since. And apart from price it is foolish to live way out here, an hour's drive from the studio.

Expensive, inconveniently located, shoebox that it is, I've come to like it; this means that I like what I have felt here. I am subjective about it, as most women are about most things. Do we ever love a man? Or do we love ourselves, in love? Do we love all that openness and gaiety and content, that tenderness at the corners of our mouths, which we feel when we are in love, rather than the loved one? We love the person we become, in love.

*Thursday*

Found new apartment. This is my last night here. I go to Napa tomorrow evening. When I come back Nicky will

197

have moved my belongings to the new apartment. I have postponed packing the living-room stuff until tomorrow so that on this, my last evening, I can have a sentimental time with everything "just as it always was."

I am also celebrating having survived the ride with Robert to find the new apartment. Our progress was a perpetual shivaree. Cars honked at us from every side. Robert quite possibly didn't hear them. He is either a very good driver or he is God's dearest child. The latter, I think. I took the first apartment that was available. It's only ten blocks from the studio. Four rooms furnished like a home with white curtains in the dining room and a coleus in the living room. There, the pool *is* a pond—almost. And all this for two hundred dollars less a month. Ah, but this was my bridal chamber so to speak. Here with yellow roses and I. W. Harper and an Oldsmobile convertible I plighted my truth to the cinema. Moments like that are memorable and not to be thought of in terms of dollars and time.

*Napa*

Now I am really homeless. Wilshire Boulevard behind me. Los Feliz still ahead, and home in Napa a shambles of reconstruction. I agreed, when I was last here, that this would be a good time for the remodeling we have long had in mind; but I didn't know that remodeling meant destruction. There is a toilet in Fred's room; all other plumbing is disconnected. For a bath tonight Max squirted me with a hose on the back terrace.

I spent the day arguing with Max and Don Macky, the architect, about my bathroom, which they want to make as functional as the men's room, I suppose, in Union Station. Shiny tile everywhere. I will not have a bathroom like that. I would rather have a nice whitewashed privy, sweet with lime inside and honeysuckle outside. I am writing this in the kitchen, which I don't like either. It's an open kitchen, and I can't cook *and* talk. Who invented the open kitchen, anyway? No friend of food or women. So I feel really desolate. I cannot envision the new house. I can only mourn the old that is being destroyed.

# VI

*Los Feliz*

Robert has gone to France, partly because of business, partly, I think, because he doesn't want to be around while his brother has *his* say about the script. Anyway, I gave a lunch for him and wrote a document, Quaker style, which we all signed. It was copied after those carried by traveling Quakers to assure others that the bearer was a Friend in good standing, with debts paid and matrimonial alliances in order.

Now the publicity department has seen the document and wants me to write an invitation in a similar style. They plan a cocktail party for the press and others "in the industry" at the "Rolling Lea" ranch to celebrate the beginning of the picture. My document for Robert said, really, "Robert is a good man and we love him"; and since it was an imitation of a statement carried by early Quakers it had to use "thee" and "thy." But a publicity party is something else. "Will thee buzz out in thy Thunderbird? Will thee have a Martini? Thy presence is requested . . . wear thy First Day dress. . . ." No, I don't think I can do this. If this were a Catholic movie, how about invitations printed on replicas of St. Monica's napkin?

Horrible headache last night. My third night here. I have been reading of the day Caesar put 400,000 Germans to the sword. At the height of my nausea this fact, with attendant details suggested by my imagination, took hold of me. Much groaning and retching!

Now I am smiling and weak, broken and happy. "Sweet day so calm, so cool, so bright," a migraine sabbath. My work here is so odd. The white curtains lift in the air just as I thought they would. I will get up carefully, water the coleus, drink more coffee, and read two or three wonderful books, simultaneously.

I love waking in the morning and all morning things: sunlight, coffee, books, birds; night's gentleness receding, day's excitement beginning. I love the morning postponing too. The knowledge of all that I could be doing but which will wait while I say, "In a minute, in a minute."

The apartment house is built on three sides around a cement pond, and the tenants center their lives about this water as residents of a French village center their lives around the village square and its fountain. This is an old, not a new, pattern. Hollywood and its pools! Easterners speak of them as if water were a newfangled, decadent invention. Easterners do not go naked because God didn't send them into the world skirted and breeched—but they hoot at us for supplying by pool the ponds God denied us. "What *we* fabricate," they say, "is fine. What *you* fabricate is spurious."

Thoreau built himself a cabin and a fireplace. Why not build Walden Pond, too, if the climate needs it and nature hasn't supplied it? Thoreau would be the first man to advise it. A poor substitute maybe, as the fireplace is a poor substitute for the sun. But in a sunless season, the fireplace; in a waterless land, the pool. The pond is a pool here. That's aquatically the only difference.

*Friday*

I looked at tests made in New York this afternoon of some actors and actresses being considered for roles in—well—the movie. That "Mr. B goes to B" my pen refuses to write. This was the first time I've heard lines, written by me, spoken on the screen. I had the same feeling of uneasiness I have in seeing a story of mine in print. I tried to forget the lines and watch the people.

*Saturday*

The visit to the house, the old woman gone, probably never to return, the old man living there alone. Furniture that I dusted and lived with for two years long ago. The sofa I bought with money I earned writing society notes for the Yorba Linda *Star*. Terrible little knickknacks, presents of mine which have been kept and valued. The material mementos of a human life, so few, so junky, so meaningless without the day's living wrapped around them. Yet saved, rejoiced in, and life at certain times, I suppose, a disaster without them. This whole house does not contain objects any secondhand man would pay five hundred dollars for. The bride and groom ornament from a daughter's wedding cake, preserved under cellophane. The 1925 program of *No No Nanette,* perhaps the only play this old Quaker woman ever saw. A picture of Rudolph Valentino, with the date of his death written on it. A newspaper clipping about the growing control of venereal disease. That is what is left. So paltry, so superficial, so graceless. And yet I cannot believe the whole of her life was lived on this level, was so arid. The things have disappeared that were her real measure and expression. She really lived out the housekeeping at which I play-act, baked the hot milk sponge cake and the nut bread, made the big dishes of applesauce and the floating island, fried the chicken and the pork sausage, kept the little white house neat as a beehive and far more hospitable. It is as if you judged bees without knowledge of honey from the litter left behind after the life of the hive was over.

Mr. Wyler talked with me again about what I can only call "the shine of love," man for man, man for God, which he hopes will be reflected in this movie. I don't know whether or not it can be managed; but when I talk with him about it I also long for its presence in the picture.

Out to location again today. Dead-beat. I was never cut out to be a technical adviser. First off, Mr. Wyler has had to reverse churches. Mr. Wyler now sees that by using stone for the Quaker meetinghouse and white clapboard for the Methodist church the Quakers appear to be a rich, high-falutin people and the Methodists by contrast a plain simple folk hating all outward show. So today he gave orders to switch churches; to take the steeple from the Methodist church and clap it onto the Quaker stone. This can be done, expensively, I suppose, but money seems not to be the issue around here. The switch upsets all the well-calculated plans for the buggy race, and the pattern for this Mr. Wyler must work out once more.

As technical adviser I think I failed Mr. Wyler, or the picture, or myself on the matter of the churches by not protesting the use of stone for the meetinghouse more vigorously. Though I'm discovering that Mr. Wyler is a man who learns what he does want by seeing what he doesn't want.

Dorothy and I don't see eye to eye just now either. She would like the picture to be visually beautiful; so would I. Every room, building, cornfield, the curve of every sofa, can contribute to the felt meaning of each scene. Since the life led by this Quaker family was characterized by considerable simplicity and beauty, it is suitable that this beauty and simplicity be reflected in house and furnishings. But not at the expense of truth. By truth I don't mean facts. A few facts can fly out the window, in an attempt to get at the truth.

Dorothy has been looking at pictures of Shaker build-

202

ings and furnishings and she has been seeing Japanese movies. I agree with her that it would be possible, using the methods of the Japanese and the backgrounds of the Shakers, to achieve visual compositions so beautiful that it wouldn't matter much what went on in the way of human activity in front of them. And I agree also that the full meaning and import of much that does go on would be made more apparent to the audience if played against a pure, simple background. But I will not yield to anyone in an understanding of the delight to be had from a composition of dock leaves, or of a naked heel on a worn doorsill, or of chicken tracks in summer dust, or of a shawl hung across a ladder-back rocker.

Why do I disagree with Dorothy? Is it in the manner of her presentation? Not completely. The Quakers were not Shakers. They had curtains at their windows, rugs on their floors, peacock feathers on their mantels, and carved olive wood from the Holy Land behind the glass doors of their walnut secretaries. That fact had as well be faced. They were good people but neither aesthetically nor morally perfect. I agree with Dorothy in her desire to see that things don't get too slicked up . . . that a weed be left here and there. On the other hand, Jess Birdwell was a nursery man, and it is impossible to believe that he would have had a flowerless yard.

Delmar Daves, who is Hollywood's most fabulous individual as far as I'm concerned, so unbelievable are his multiple accomplishments and interests, called Dorothy an "enthusiast." This is a word I haven't heard used since the days when I studied English literature, and I've been thinking about its appropriateness as applied to Dorothy. My guess would be that it is a word sometimes used about me. Perhaps I can dish out enthusiasm better than I can take it. Anyway, when I hear Dorothy speak with rapture of visual effects, I want to reply dryly, "Let us make a list of the furnishings, colors, etc., we'll need."

Since Dorothy is so beautiful and gifted a woman I do not like these dry responses in me. The "dry response" may be the explanation of everything. She is a much more committed and related woman than I. The emotional distance between her and her friends is very small. She operates "close." Her caring reaches out to include all of her friends' activities and she will help build their houses, design their coats, plan their journeys. Not I.

## August 1

Eliza has been selected! I think I've heard every actress in Hollywood mentioned for the part: Margaret Sullavan, a former wife of Mr. Wyler's; Ingrid Bergman, if she would have risked a reappearance in the United States; Maureen O'Hara, who had the fire Eliza needs and tested for the part; Mary Martin, too hard to photograph; Vivien Leigh, too English; Eva Marie Saint, too young. So Dorothy McGuire is the final choice.

Living on the water! Living on the water! When I am not in the pond, the pond is in my living room, as it is now, a quiver of reflected light on my ceiling. It is evening, day dying in the west, light both pinking and graying as if warming and darkening simultaneously.

I have just come out of the water. I swim as others drink—less for the taste than the aftereffect. Immersion in cool water intoxicates me. It is reverse inebriation, drunkenness working from the skin inward. Cleansed and cooled, with harmonies of light moving above me, I have now all the happy sot's convictions of timelessness; I sit here as transcendental as Emerson, as blessed as a pilgrim still dripping from the holy Ganges, eating my evening cheese and drinking my evening beer.

I wallow rather than swim, but I *am* Los Feliz's champion floater; I am in the water here much more than on Wilshire. There the swimming was so professional that every time I entered the pool I felt like a housewife trying to break into a Rockette routine with a little waltz step picked up back in Red Wing, Minnesota. The water there was less a pool than a stage, and the people in it less swimmers than performers. Here the water is for getting wet in, and it is not necessary to stay out of it even though you will not remind anyone of Ariadne.

There are three good times for swimming. The first is

at ten o'clock, when the midmorning sun has just burned through the haze and a milky pallor still touches the water; the men are at work, the children at school, the women sleeping, shopping, or dishwashing, and I and three grandmothers (out for sun, not water) have the pond to ourselves. I am alone in the water; the grandmothers consider me agile; the whole experience, because of the hour, has a forbidden quality. I float, listen to vacuum cleaners, and think I have put something over on the world's time clock, I have slipped a monkey wrench into domestic machinery.

The second good time is the moment I get back from the studio or location. Then the pond is filled, and I swim in spite of the crowding because, hot and tired, my body is hungry for the touch of water.

The third good time is a few minutes before the pool closes for the night at nine. Then I float very deliberately, shifting from side to side with a gentle rocking motion which breaks the reflected stars into little pieces, diminishing but also multiplying. Voices came to me over the water, Red so confused, Peepers so put upon, Miss Brooks so persistent, Gracie and Lucy so immemorially silly. I float and sing to myself, "Row, row, row your boat . . . life is but a dream."

Tomorrow I start going to Mr. Wyler's house to talk with him about the script. No sooner do I move out here near the studio than I must begin driving in the opposite direction, back to the neighborhood where I once lived.

Just when I think that I have exhausted the entire supply of good books in the world, the good books come flooding in: Laurie Lee's *A Rose for Winter,* Edwin Muir's autobiography, Morton's life of Belloc, L. E. Jones's *A Victorian Childhood,* Colette's *My Mother's House.*

*August 5*

Since I am not as movie-centered as they are, my meetings with Mr. Wyler haven't seemed as important to me as they have to Stu, Portia, and Robert. My feeling is script-centered rather than Wyler-centered. Can the script be bettered? If so, how?

Portia, the last few days, has often spoken to me of the pleasure I would have "seeing how Mr. Wyler's mind works." The trouble is, I become so absorbed in the workings of my own mind and in the products of the working of Mr. Wyler's, I forget all about the "how" of his.

Robert has a wonderful economizing faculty, which means, in the long run, a dramatizing faculty. Time and again he has showed me where I "gave the show away." It is too soon to judge what William Wyler will do to the script. I remember Robert's warning, "Don't let Willy ruin the story line by improving scenes." Today we worked upstairs in Mr. Wyler's study as usual—and his two smallest children ran in and out. They don't give a whoop how Papa's mind works or that he is thought to be a genius over at the studio. They are handsome, sturdy children—a girl of four or five, a boy of two or three. They gave me impulses to hug, but I refrained, deciding there wasn't time enough to be both a script writer and a hugger. Also, they moved pretty fast for anything as stationary as hugging.

I arrived with several things to say about earlier comments of Mr. Wyler's. He has been afraid that Eliza needed "sweetening," that she is too stern and domineering to be lovable. Comment on this is that if Eliza starts sweet and docile, how does she change? If she is to be mellowed by the events of the picture she must start a little acid.

Second comment: We don't have to account for Josh's friend Caleb's not fighting. He is a Quaker and pacifism is normal for a Quaker. When they do fight, then we must account for it.

Third comment: The characters who remain in our minds longest are those we are still trying to figure out.

I have decided that the script writer's relationship to a producer-director is that of an architect to a client. The client is not going to build until he gets the blueprint he wants, and the architect had as well recognize the fact. The architect can do his best to persuade his client not to add that cupola, exclude this window; and he may succeed. But the architect's only real assurance of being permitted to produce something that is his own is to pick out the right client in the first place—a man who sees eye to eye with him as to what constitutes a good house. So script writer and producer-director had better more or less agree as to what constitutes a good picture. Of course, the chances for that are enhanced when the producer has already elected to make a picture based on the scriptwriter's book.

Stu over for supper. He's a fine man to cook for, willing to call a bottle of beer and a bowl of tuna salad supper. If there happen to be chocolate cake, strawberries, coffee, and brandy afterward he doesn't mind. But the first will do.

Except for Mr. Wyler himself, no one has as many responsibilities in this picture as Stu. He follows every word of the script; he carries around with him ten pages of lines from my first script which were dropped and which he now hounds me to include in the present version. He works, as far as I can gather, half the night and would phone me at midnight with a good idea except that when he does this I hang up. He gazes tirelessly at TV screens, hunting new actors (he found Mark Richman, who will be Gard in the movie, this way); he reads new books and old; and I have no idea how much else he does in connection with the movie, its casting, its publicity, etc. He gets without knowing it, I think, too imperious, too dictatorial, and too demanding at times; and he makes enemies in this way. I never realized this so fully until the other evening. We were leaving the bungalow after dark and had stepped off the sidewalk in front of a car coming out of the studio parking place. Brakes were slammed on and a man's hard mocking voice said, "Oh, did I frighten you? Well, I certainly wouldn't want to do that, because little Stu might be a great big producer someday."

I never heard more hatred in a human voice.

Tonight Stu, who has never ceased to worry himself and me about the ending of the picture, persuaded me, he himself ringing the number, to call Mr. Wyler about a minor change. "I don't want to bother him," I told Stu, but Stu said, "Do you think anything about this picture is a bother

207

to Willy? He eats it and sleeps it now. He has to. If you think what you've just told me about the ending is an improvement, tell him. Tell him now."

I told him, and Mr. Wyler said we could speak of it at length in the morning.

When I hung up, Stu wanted to know at once what had been said. When I told him, he said, "Promise me you won't stop talking to Willy about the ending."

I said, "We're going over the script gradually. We'll take up the ending when we get to it."

"Take it up now," Stu insisted. "Tell Willy at once if you have any new ideas. Promise me?"

I promised him. But I'm pretty content with it as it is.

Sitting here in my parlor, my shell of light, my trap for sunsets, eating my supper and watching the day go dark and the room, as the successive tides of light grow smaller, draw in upon me.

The light of the sun changes in color and intensity from minute to minute. The room inhales the light; it grows pink with respiration; the walls appear to move. The ceiling is aquiver with dapple of light reflected off the water. It is tadpole-colored, tadpole-speckled. I sit with my back to the western windows—and the sun and the water—and watch their effects rather than them.

I, who have a hard time entering into the rituals of others, soon develop my own. Though it may be pretentious to call a two-week practice of swimming, followed by eating the same food, and watching the light, a "ritual." What it may be is only habit. Where is the boundary between habit and rite? Each night I come home, take off my dusty clothes, then roll like a parched log in the water. The real swimmers go by, flailing, and I am in danger of getting a leg or arm mixed up with their machinery. Finally, cleansed and cooled, I come out of the water and drink one glass of beer while I watch the first act of the drama called "Play of the Lights." In the intermission I get my supper, always the same: broiled meat, sliced tomatoes, melon. (Not watermelon—but Cranshaw, honeydew, musk, casaba.) Supper ready, I bring it to my chair by the window and eat as I watch the last of the light play; and to the pleasures of this minute are added yesterday's memories, and so the rite (if it is rite) strengthens, or the practice (if that's all it is) hardens. But at any rate I anticipate the evening; I walk into it as into a place of worship. And if the difference between rite and habit is that habit is an end in itself, while a rite is the celebration of something beyond itself, then this food, this light, and the immersion which preceded them, do constitute a ritual.

But even as ritual they don't leave me tonight anything but a hardheaded, dusty old farmer. I went out to the buggy farm today with Dorothy and Mr. Wyler. The buggy farm is a ranch where there has been collected all the automotive wheeled vehicles in the world from gocarts to hearses, with every intermediate step represented: surreys, sulkies, gigs, broughams, buggies, buckboards, chariots, and jaunting cars. The day was sweltering, the buggy farm dusty, and a dozen vehicular experts were determined to find Mr. Wyler anything he wanted, or could imagine he might want. Mr. Wyler is an imaginative man, and his mind, freewheeling amidst all that was so conducive to that exercise, imagined plenty.

He saw an Irish jaunting car and said, "Jess and Eliza on one side, Mattie and Little Jess on the other? That would be funny, wouldn't it?"

"How would Jess have gotten hold of that rig in Indiana?" I asked.

Mr. Wyler left the jaunting car reluctantly, but almost immediately found a topless buggy with a little two-foot shelf projecting at the rear. The wranglers, the buggy-farm proprietor, the buggy-farm experts, Tommy Carr, who is going to direct the battle sequences, Dorothy, others whose functions are unknown to me, and I watched him examine it.

"Think how funny it would be," he bade me, "to have Mattie and Little Jess crouching there, hanging on for dear life while Jess drives hell for leather in the race." And Mr. Wyler stood there writing that scene in his head and filming it and hearing an audience's laughter as they watched it on the screen. It was then I became the old hardheaded farmer, the fellow with an oat straw in his mouth and doubt in his heart. No, it wouldn't be funny. It would be preposterous and painful. What kind of a man would have a rig in which his young lady daughter crouched like a dog in a basket, exposed to all the dust of a country road? With another hero—not Jess, some sadist . . . but that was another story. For our story this bobtailed buggy would never do.

"Would you take your daughter Cathy to church hanging on to the spare tire?" I asked.

The beam went out of Mr. Wyler's eyes as he stopped filming that scene and took up once more his search for something suitable. To find something "suitable" is dull work. The pleasure is in finding the "apparently" *unsuitable* object, the object which, though wrong in all superficial ways, is in some deeper manner suitable. It was this intrinsic suitability Haworth was looking for but did not find in his fish weather vane.

In a picture, which is a growth fostered by many hands, the danger is that it may be pulled lopsided by someone who begins to feel that an apple-shaped apple, say, is dull. Or has forgotten, even, that apple was the fruit we started to depict. When this happens, someone must shout "apple, apple." This is not a job I like, though I had to do it today. I had to keep saying, "Not for Jess, not for 1860, not for southern Indiana," until I did feel every inch a dusty old farmer amidst imaginative artists.

The excitement and the joy is in finding, not excluding; in hitting upon the right word, or insight or object. And such discoveries are perhaps dangerous as well as joyous for me, for this joy binds me to Hollywood. All agree that it is wrong to be bound to Hollywood; though no one has suspected that the bonds, instead of money or fleshpots or easy work, might be the joys of shared effort. I give something which, though my own, becomes part of something beyond me; and Hollywood's pull for me becomes the pull felt by the member of any order.

And I have never been a member of an order. No lodge, no Young Republicans, no ladies' bridge club, almost no organized church, since one Quaker and God constitute a meeting which Quakers honor. So this experience comes doubly strong and doubly fresh to me, like the marriage of an old maid finally wed after having accepted, though never having been reconciled to, single blessedness. And perhaps this is the only kind of an order to which I could comfortably belong—an order in which all are working to create something. Churches, political parties, P.T.A.'s, they all tell people what they ought to do. I can't bear that—and I don't mean being told what to do, but telling others. All I want is to make an object—a story, a novel, a poem, which says "life." This, a motion picture can do; and the union we enter into for its making is perhaps the only one to which I could ever be faithful.

Mr. Wyler asked me the other day what I thought of movie making by now. He looked startled when I told him I thought movie making might be for the twentieth century what cathedral building was for the Middle Ages. I don't say that *The Bowery Boys* or *The John Philip Sousa Story* are the equal of Burgos and Chartres and Canterbury; but the making of a movie is, as was the building of a cathedral, one activity in which many persons work together to produce a record of the lives of men and women. Miserable and flimsy and superficial as the film record may be, still it is such an attempt and the attempt bewitches me. To share in anything whatever is a great grace for the unrelated and the unattached. To share in what you value most may be dangerous. After that all else may pall.

Though God knows Mr. Wyler, Dorothy, and I were all moving in opposite directions today in our cathedral building out at the buggy farm. Dorothy discovered a big buckboard which she thought exactly right for the Birdwells' churchgoing. Why, I don't know. Perhaps, as with the cows in the basement, she thought it factually right. Perhaps, as with the Shaker interiors, she thought it scenically good. But the buckboard was as wrong as the jaunting car or the bobtailed buggy. No "well-fixed" farmer would think of going to church in a buckboard. He'd have a surrey. I said so, and one of the buggy-farm experts asked me, pointing to Dorothy, "What's she do?" "Costume designer," I said. "What's she doing *here?*" he persisted. "Going to make pretty fly nets for the horses?" He was an outspoken man and, when Dorothy continued to champion the buckboard, he asked Mr. Wyler a question that separated Mr. Wyler from it immediately. "You know what driving that buckboard to church would be like today, Mr. Wyler?" Mr. Wyler said no. "Like driving a two-and-a-half-ton truck to church."

211

This straight thinker and I went to sit on a corral rail, though I was prepared to leap down should Mr. Wyler and his entourage pause overly long in front of anything peculiarly wheeled or topped or shaped. It was now well past midafternoon. The trucks were beginning to be loaded with horses. They would be driven through the night to locations in Arizona and northern California and the San Fernando Valley. Tomorrow these horses would be hearing Rebel yells and Indian war whoops and Texas drawls; Spurning the earth of the staked plains, the pampas, the steppes. They looked well cared for, but I'm glad my Dandy isn't an actor. Though he'd survive, old cynic, who thinks only of Dandy.

## Sunday—Whittier

Alone in the house, in the many-windowed upstairs bedroom of this Swiss chalet, built by an Indiana farmer, and around which the wind off the Pacific is sweeping. I've just written ten pages to Mr. Wyler . . . and my hand still shakes with emotion. But here, with Frankie's be-good bell ringing down the street and the palm trees rustling with their Sahara everlastingness, is the best place to have written what I had to say.

Friday afternoon, talking with Stu about what we call the "ending" of the picture, though it is not the real ending but the battle scenes which precede it, I outlined a simpler action than we now have.

The minute I had done so, Stu called Mr. Wyler and said, "Miss West wants to talk to you." I didn't want to. This change was minor, I would see Mr. Wyler on Monday at his home, and I could talk to him then. But Stu was determined. He walked me over to Mr. Wyler's office and thrust me in the door.

Mr. Wyler listened to my proposed changes. Once, while I was talking, his wrist alarm clock went off. I don't know the purpose of these alarms. They seem to startle Mr. Wyler as much as anyone else—and they always make me feel that I'm keeping him from something important. Perhaps *that* is their purpose. Mr. Wyler stopped his alarm; I made my talk as fast—and convincing—as I could.

When I had finished Mr. Wyler said, "There's something I've been intending to tell you. Tommy Carr is going to direct the battle scenes. And I have asked him to get a Western writer to—put the battle scenes in order for shooting."

"Western writer," I repeated. I tried to keep my voice from shaking, but I think it did. This, since Mr. Kleiner's advent, has been my routine response to the word "writer."

"I didn't even know his name," Mr. Wyler hurried to say. "I left it all up to Tommy. Just somebody accustomed to arranging the details of fighting as you and Robert aren't. 'Crouch behind log.' 'Run two steps to overturned wagon.' 'Stumble over fallen body.' That sort of thing, you know."

"If more details . . . about the fighting are what you want, I can provide them by the million."

"It's not just details," Mr. Wyler admitted. He looked unhappy, wound his watch, then turned to face me. "I take full responsibility for this," he said. "I want you to understand that there is going to be something with a cannon."

"Something with a cannon and Jess?"

Mr. Wyler nodded.

"Jess shoots?" I asked.

Mr. Wyler was happy to reassure me here. "Not a shot. He doesn't fire a shot. There's a Confederate cannon —the horses hitched to it have been killed, and Jess hitches his horse and Sam's horse to this cannon. These two horses, accustomed to racing each other, really outpull themselves hitched together. Jess drives them, and the cannon, between the two remaining Confederate cannons— completely knocking them out. With these out of commission, the Confederates haven't a chance. They retire."

"And Jess wins the war?"

"He doesn't fire a shot."

I didn't say anything. I thought I might cry.

"I don't even know this Western writer's name," Mr. Wyler said once more. "I left it all up to Tommy. This is your battle . . . just put in order a little; Cooper has to— his audience expects it—engage in a little action. They've got to see Cooper as a man of action. That's what they came for."

I left without crying. Stu came out of his and Robert's bungalow as I walked toward it.

"Now you know," he said.

We went up the street to the Los Feliz Brown Derby for supper. "Did you tell Willy what you thought of this plan?"

"No."

"Why not? You don't like it, do you?"

"Of course not. It's terrible. But I was too ashamed, too humiliated to say a word."

"What did you have to be ashamed of?"

"I wasn't ashamed of a thing for myself. I was ashamed for Mr. Wyler. I wanted to find every reason in the world to justify what he'd done. I wanted to hide it with words. I did everything I could to find excuses for him."

"But didn't you tell him he couldn't do this?"

"No. In the first place he *can* do it if he wants to. In the second place I wanted to get away as fast as possible. I couldn't bear it, confronted with all that evidence of un-derhandedness."

The minute I said "underhanded" Stu exploded. He had known about these cannons and this Western writer and this momentous charge of the erstwhile rival horses. He had maneuvered me into Mr. Wyler's office; he wanted me to persuade him that he must not use such a scene. But he would not let me say one word against Willy. He talked to me for an hour. "Never, never mistrust Willy. Never doubt him. Believe in him implicitly. Accept his need of examining all the ways of doing a picture. Trust him with all of your principles."

I can't remember a tenth, a hundredth, of what Stu said. But before he had finished, my impression was that I was listening to an impassioned sermon from a preacher who was in great fear of backsliding from the true faith himself. He berated me for things I'd never said; he adjured me to hang on to feelings I had never departed from. He reminded me of truths that were self-evident. There was no use talking to him because he wasn't talking to me. Nor even to himself. To Willy, I think. He could not very well make to Willy's face this confession of faith . . . but he had to make it, and made it to me, since he had been the instrument by which I had, for a moment, seen that Mr. Wyler was what I had never doubted: a human being beset by many practical difficulties in the making of a record of a human life.

We left the Brown Derby tired out, dead-beat. Stu helped me buy groceries. We went to the Japanese market which I visit at the end of each day with the same pleasure a Parisian writer might visit a café. When I got back to Los Feliz I sat on the couch with my groceries heaped round me. I don't know for how long. That was one day that darkened and died without my observing it.

Then I phoned Stu. I told him I was going back to Napa, that it was useless for me to try to work on the picture any longer—since I did not, in fact, know from day to day what picture I was working on.

Next I called Max. Max had been saying, "Is this script writing to go on forever?" and I thought he would rejoice when he heard me say I was taking the next night's Owl home—to stay. By the time I got Max, my sad stunned silence was over. I was raging with anger, overflowing with words, and all the things I could not say to Mr. Wyler and that Stu would not let me say, I poured into Max's astonished and patient ear. "I am coming home. First of all, I cannot work on a picture which I am kept in the dark about. Even if this cannon-wrecking scene were good, I can't write on something that changes its very nature without my knowing it. But this cannon scene isn't good in itself—and besides, it begs the whole question of the picture. Look! Jess was the only Quaker in the picture who holds out for nonviolence. Josh goes off to war; even Eliza gets into a fight. Somebody in this picture about Quakers had better act like a Quaker. And it had better be Jess. He isn't just *a* Quaker in this picture. He's Quakerdom itself. You know that, Max. If Jess fights, the picture is either tragic or an attack on Quakerism. If a man turns his back on his principles, the reversal is sorrowful, if the principles were any good. The only way to avoid this is to say the principles were bad. As a Quaker I won't be mixed up with a picture that attacks Quakerdom. And as a writer I'm not going to be mixed up with a picture that should be a tragedy—but isn't. I'm coming home. I won't struggle with this any longer. Please meet the Owl Sunday morning."

I thought Max would say, "Hurrah, you've come to your senses." Instead, he said, "You told Mr. Wyler all this?"

"No," I admitted. Though I hated to admit it.

"Why not?"

"I couldn't. He should see it himself. And besides, I was so shocked at what he'd done that I tried to act as if he hadn't done it. To pretend that it had never happened. I even tried to defend him, to help him find reasons why he should have hired this Western writer."

"Well, you lied to him, didn't you?"

"Max, I'm about to die from tiredness. I worked all day. I thought up this new ending. I told it to Mr. Wyler. I found out about this trick cannon stuff. Stu has lectured me for one hour. And now you tell me I'm a liar."

"You are if you don't tell Mr. Wyler what you've just told me."

"Don't you want me to come home?"

"I want you to come home. But not because you don't have enough courage to tell Mr. Wyler what you think."

"Courage!"

"What is it then? Promise me you'll tell Mr. Wyler exactly what you've told me. And stay for one week after you've told him."

So I promised. But I went to bed feeling as if I had been abandoned by everyone.

Next morning bright and early (for him—and for me) Robert Wyler, home from France, came to call. "You must not leave," he said. "You must tell Willy exactly what you think. And you must not believe that because Willy did this behind your back that part of his reason wasn't that he didn't want to hurt you. Just as you don't want to hurt him now. But you must tell Willy for Willy's sake even if he didn't tell you. Willy is a good man. You don't want to hear family history, but he has been a good brother to me. Willy believes in this story. It's not just another picture to him. But behind the scenes are all sorts of pressures you don't know anything about. You must be one of the pressures helping him to resist these others."

"I'm not a pressure, Robert," I said, "I'm a writer. Or trying to be."

"Tell Willy," he said.

"And all those Quakers coming to see me Monday afternoon to ask me about the picture."

"All what Quakers?"

"Two," I admitted. "Two bigwig Quakers. Shall I tell them Josh shoots, Eliza strikes, and Jess wins the war single-handed, putting those cannons out of commission like some super Ben Hur? Shall I?"

Robert went flying about the room, his lips pursed with pleasure. "Tell Willy," he said. "Hold those bigwigs over his head. Help him to do what he wants to do."

Stu phoned. "You still leaving?" he asked.

"No," I said, "I promised Max I'd stay."

"I'm glad at least one of the McPhersons has good sense," Stu said.

I'm alone here. Papa and Mama are in the Gaspé Penninsula by now. That cross-country jaunt by car and trailer for a seventy-six- and a seventy-three-year-old, both broken physically, is about the equal of the Lewis and Clark expedition in the amount of effort and courage required. I've thought about them all day, here in this house which even smells like them. And it isn't the fictional "dry leaves," old folks smell either, but Mama's toilet water and sweet soaps, and Papa's ripening avocados and stacks of magazines, and the fireplace, always half filled with ashes.

Oh, poor flashing, vaunting, loving, hating, and suffering Mama. Never was anyone more exposed in every fiber and tissue to life. So greedy for life and brought up to believe that she must renounce so much. She, who could have been actress and clown, *was* actress and clown, and under this cloud of unknowing still keeps that identity, though she often loses the more particular one of Grace Anne Milhous. Here in this room for two years she, by persisting in her belief that there was nothing else I could do—or wanted to do—persuaded me to continue to live. Every time I renounced the world she presented it to me again. On the day when, finally, I was able, though I had to be carried down the stairs, to go to the doctor's office for an X ray, she bought me a new spring hat. Not through "kindness" to me but because she didn't want a daughter of hers, though far gone in tuberculosis, going to see the doctor, a handsome man and a leading citizen, looking so draggle-tailed and tacky. The idea of trying to spruce me up was as revolting to me as the whitening of any other sepulcher, and when Mama insisted that I wear that beflowered beribboned hat, I suddenly kicked it, with energy I didn't know I had, under the bed. This was supposedly one other rejection of the world Mama ceaselessly offered me. But she outsmarted me here as elsewhere. That kick kicked, was far more significant to her than hat, worn or not worn. (Though she saw that I wore the hat too.) "But I knew from the minute you kicked that hat under the bed that you were going to get well," she told me afterward. "Nobody dying could be that mulish."

Mama would have had her say about these cannon without wasting a weekend in emotional writing of document, she might even have agreed with Mr. Wyler and the Western writer; but for or against, no one would have been in doubt for a minute as to where she stood.

No wonder Mr. Wyler looked startled when I compared movie making and cathedral building. Building the way we were, he going in one direction, I in another, the two halves of our cathedral might never have met.

*Los Feliz—Monday Evening*

I feel tired but glorious; I've suffered through it—the whole morning with Mr. Wyler, the whole afternoon with the Pasadena Quakers. It is always this way, the difficulty of making "the clean breast," and afterward the lovely contentment. Nothing needs to be changed by the stand I take. As I'm not sure now that anything has been changed, except me—I'm changed. It is not a matter of "fighting for what I believe," or of winning that fight. Perhaps it is, as much as anything else, a matter of confess-

218

ing, and the clean-washed feeling is the natural result of having "come clean." All I need do, apparently, is to express my horror, my distaste, my dislike; and having done so I am freed entirely from the burden of these emotions. No one need agree with me; but if he will listen to me say, "I think you were wicked and wrong—and for these reasons," the wickedness and wrongness vanish like smoke.

So it was this morning with Mr. Wyler. I went with my cogent document in hand—and left it with him. I had thought it might have to say everything, that I might be unable to speak. But I kept the tears down. I said, "I will have to disassociate myself from this picture, have my name taken off this script if Jess does any fighting." And I told him all my reasons.

Mr. Wyler listened and listened. He said, "But you yourself had Jess involved in a fist fight."

I said, "To be carried away momentarily in a fist fight . . . and to participate in war, which is organized violence, are two different matters. It's the difference between making love to a girl—which may be wrong—and running a whorehouse. There's a degree of calculation in the second activity which separates it from the first."

Mr. Wyler smiled. He said he had never thought of it that way.

He told me about making *Roman Holiday* in Italy and the Italian fear that he was making Italian policemen "funny." When the picture was finished the Italian government decorated him for his service to the country. "After we have finished this picture," he said, "the Quakers will decorate you and me."

This unlikely idea made me laugh . . . I don't know what the Quakers could decorate us *with* . . . even if they wanted to. "Order of the Bonnet and Shawl?" Then Mr. Wyler said, "Write the battle scenes for me you were telling me about Friday."

I came back to Los Feliz, wrote until four, then sent the manuscript over to Portia to be typed. At that time the Quakers, Sanders, and Peckham came and we talked about the picture. I told them everything—that while the picture certainly would not say, "It is wrong to fight," that it would say, "This is the story of a man who believed it was wrong to fight . . . and of a time in his life when he didn't know whether or not he would be able to hang on to those beliefs."

I read them the meeting scene, and Peckham, listening, had tears in his eyes, and I felt like Eliza herself entertaining a visit of the Ministry and Oversight Committee. Now I'm going to bed, not walking but flying. This has been a happy day.

### Wednesday

Tommy Carr, the "battle director," was over this morning with my typed battle scene in hand. In pocket, the Western writer's cannon scene.

"Willy says to follow your outline," he said.

This was bad news for Carr, who had already begun to align cannon and horses and heroes according to another plan; and bad news, too, probably, that instead of having a male Western writer to work with on his battle scenes he was going to have a female Friend. But he is a philosophical man, has been in the movies a long time, beginning as an actor, and is beyond surprises of this kind. Besides, I think *I* surprised him with my old farmer side; so we sat down like Lee and Jackson to map our wilderness campaign. His old farmer side delighted me; sometimes, when imaginations get to racing around here I feel myself to be insufficiently an artist. South bank, north bank, slight rise of land, all matters of terrain had practical meanings to Mr. Carr, so that I didn't feel stodgy, talking of them to him.

Mr. Carr thinks of the action completely in terms of the camera. He wants down on paper not the action alone but the manner in which the camera sees this action. He visualizes ahead of time. Mr. Wyler improvises, I judge, more than he. We worked all day long making a sentence summary of the entire battle sequence. I feel as if I've been through a long campaign tonight—but if we win the war it doesn't matter. Last entry, I see, I was flying off to bed. Tonight I march. Don't need, but would like, "El Capitan" as played by Mama.

Apartment canaries, pianists, electric razors, coughers and snorters, disposals, white curtains moving in the tinged-with-autumn air. Smoke and summer (which is what this morning is) anticipates autumn. I am so happy. Drinking coffee. Nothing to do until ten, when Tommy Carr comes and we finish our war.

I went to Napa over the week end. Fine time. House as demolished as if bombed. Impossible to think of doing any housekeeping, so I didn't. Only got mad at Max once. He said we had to go to a cocktail party to which we were invited and to which I didn't want to go. I threw the noncocktail skirt which I was putting on when he delivered this ultimatum out the window. Threw it into the sprinkler, as it turned out, and ruined the skirt. Went to the cocktail party and didn't want to come home either—but kept my skirt on when Max said we must leave.

The day that gets too dreamy is liable to go bang; the euphoria bubble that grows too big will burst. Yesterday after all the glory of the "licked ending" it burst. Headache, took all the known pills, blistered my head with hot towels. About six it began, slowly, to recede. As it left me, I, not so much went out for a walk, as began to walk and found myself outside. I hadn't left the apartment all day—it seemed longer than a day—it seemed as if these were my first steps abroad after years in a dungeon. I walked past the bungalows at the hour of homecoming, when lawns are watered, and children run to the corner to get a ride home with father. The air was milky and sweet, scented with the city and with the ocean, with the dripping geraniums and hibiscus. Inside the houses the movements of table setting were going on, less like housework than ballets of mysterious meaning.

Then suddenly and miraculously the bungalows ended and without transitions I was in a small and very busy city, not six blocks from my own apartment, but of whose existence I had never dreamed. I could not believe it. It was like coming upon a fleet moored in a meadow or discovering a mine shaft behind the snapdragons at the bottom of the garden. Stores were open late and families sauntered along the sidewalks like visitors at a county fair. They were taking their time and their ease; their voices were quiet and when they lifted them it was to laugh, or to praise a basket of Santa Rosa plums or a split Klondike with seeds like black ladybugs on red velvet. There was a little—not exactly a bookshop—but a magazine and card shop which carried books, and it was filled with people reading, as if starved for print. Children darted by the slower moving grownups like little flip-tailed fish amidst schools of whale and tunny. But the current on the whole was very slow, as if where we were going would last forever, as if we had eternity in which to get there—and it would be a pity to miss any good thing on the way.

I felt so tender toward these my fellow human beings; last night, washed round with the evening air, they were luminous and vulnerable, and I was a being especially endowed to register that luminosity and pity that vulnerability. I am trying to put into words offhand what would need a week's or maybe a lifetime's thinking about, first to understand, then to record with words. Perhaps I shall think about it for a lifetime—and even then never find the words.

It was like the home-coming of a foreigner, an outsider; the discovery of his own kind by one who had been searching for them for a long time. And it was a discovery which filled him with delight. I am one of these! How miraculous! They have such pleasant voices; they are pleased by such small things; they are trying so hard; they are fond of their children; they dress themselves neatly after a day's work; they like bright colors and sweet flavors and if they bump you they say, "I beg your pardon a thousand times."

I came home and went to bed without turning on the lights and when I woke up this morning I said to myself, "I had a wonderful dream." Then I remembered that it was no dream, but real.

No wonder I can't get any writing done. The phone calls for the day have been:

1. Portia saying she would send for material to type at nine.

2. Harcourt, Brace representative calling to ask would I sign some books and be on a TV program.

3. Portia calling to say William Wyler had returned from Pebble Beach.

4. Carr calling to say he'd be here at 12:30.

5. Portia calling to ask why she hadn't received ms. Told her man hadn't arrived to pick it up yet.

6. Stu to ask could Carr and I promise him all the war scenes by evening.

7. Harcourt, Brace telegraphing thanks for catching typographical error in new book and that they had changed "six months in the can" to "six months in the san." "Agree six months there too long," Denver Lindley said.

8. *Herald-Express*—will I subscribe to their paper?

9. Millar calling to see if ms. was ready.

10. Napa Woman in town. Would I have dinner with her.

11. Carmen calling from Whittier. Papa and Mama home from their trip. Mama has had another small stroke.

*Friday morning*

Clear fall sunlight between the apartment buildings this morning. The three young actors have arrived from New York: Phyllis Love who plays Mattie, Mark Richman who plays Gard, and Tony Perkins who plays Josh. The Richmans and Phyllis Love and her husband Jim McGee are going to stay at Los Feliz. The astounding thing (to me) is that they don't bear the mark of their trade upon them. They don't look like actors (which for me means, I guess, that they don't look like John Barrymore or Greta Garbo). Phyllis Love, in the test scene, was a hearty, firm-muscled, flyaway tomboy; off screen she is thin and quiet with pale clear skin and smooth brown hair. What I saw her doing was acting. Mark Richman in his test was an ingratiating, burly wooer. He, too, is smaller, a thoughtful ex-pharmacist. I go around staring at them, waiting for "actor" to emerge like a Jack-in-the-box from inside these normal covers. None of them have been in the movies before, so they and I alike are the newcomers here in this movie world.

Rehearsals have already begun, and I have had my first demonstration of what an actor can do with lines that are very slight in themselves. Mark Richman, when first he visits the Birdwells, has nothing to say but the usual, "How do you do, Mr. Birdwell," "Hello, Josh," "How are you, Mattie?" But he was able to make those commonplace greetings mirrors in which we saw reflected the character of the people he addressed. That was an extraordinary revelation to me. "How do you do, Mr. Birdwell," and we saw, because of the way in which Mark Richman said those words, that Jess was a man whose approval was worth having . . . and whose approval you could get only by being a good man yourself. If everybody can do that with his lines, the horizons of this story are capable of shooting out beyond mortal eyesight—mine, anyway.

*4:30*

Beauty? Or is it well-being? The eye that sees; or what is seen? What is lovely now? The light, the quality of light. Don't say "quality." Specify, specify.

While I was waiting to specify, the quality has changed. I've spent an hour talking with the Japanese boy who delivers groceries from my grocery-café or grocery-club. He's about twenty, short, stocky, pock-marked. We first became acquainted when he carried groceries to my car and stayed to admire it. This evening we talked about the "trial" which has freed the murderers of Emmett Till. Joe had more reasons than most of us for being caught up into a kind of agonized incredulity over that trial. He's young and it's not easy for the young to be reconciled to the injustice of the world; he's dark-skinned himself and what happens to dark-skinned people is closer to him than to us uncolored ones; and as a person (not a youth, not a Japanese) he has moral imagination. These three combined so that Joe suffered Emmett's death by proxy here this evening.

He shook his head wonderingly in an effort to understand how men and women could have treated Emmett as they did. He rightly concluded that Emmett had been murdered because of the color of his skin. And this could be the result, he supposed, only of a lack of knowledge on the part of the murderers of colored people. He told me about a colored women he knew who supported five children and a paralyzed husband.

"Sometimes I help her," he said. "I don't want to, because I got plenty to do with my own work—but she's working so hard and she's so cheerful that before I know it I've said I'll wash her windows or clean up her back yard. I can understand getting carried away helping. But carried away to murder! That don't do our country any good. Murder."

He is a squat little pock-marked Japanese but his heart is open to the world.

*Friday, Sept. 2*

110° yesterday. Going to be 108° today, the paper says. I bought Edward Thomas's *Poems* yesterday and they make me lonely; poetry requires two readers. They need to be read aloud, to be sung, cried bellowed; they need to be exclaimed over. Prose can be read alone, as one can eat a sandwich alone; but poetry is an intoxicant, and solitary drinking is a vice. I long for a fellow drinker.

I enjoy, more than I had ever dreamed, working with others on the picture. But I don't lose sight, I hope, of the nature of picture making. Here, the emphasis is not on the writer's vision but on the audience's response. Will what is being written make the audience laugh, cry? Will the audience understand? I try to think of an analogy. The audience is thought of as a big baby to be dandled, lullabyed, and fed sugar tits. And if the audience doesn't fuss, if it sits quietly, if, glory of glories, it wants another sugar tit, you're in, you're a professional baby-sitter and a paying member of the Screen Writers' Guild.

110° again today. The apartment-house residents have moved outside. Many slept beside the pool last night. The nine o'clock swimming curfew has been rescinded—swimming goes on all night. Fighting the heat, like fighting a war, has united everyone. Sweat, like blood, is a bond. It is a strange sight, at midnight, to see the poolside chairs and cots filled and residents who, in cooler weather, almost never speak to each other, talking companionably. Hot weather breeds sociability, and should this keep up we would soon doff both clothes and restraints and live around our fountain like any tropical people.

Mark Richman, in his swimming trunks, was called into the office by Maggie, the colored maid, to take a phone call. Maggie, if she were any other color, would be a model; she makes a costume out of whatever she wears and dramatizes her green uniform by outlandish additions so that it becomes funny and you can laugh with her at the silliness of Maggie O'Brien's (that's her name) wearing a *maid's* uniform.

Mark came out of the office pink faced. Maggie had greeted him by saying, "Man, what a torso! What a physique! Man, if you were only black, how I could go for you."

Mark answered, "Maggie, that sounds like discrimination to me."

This reply Maggie topped by saying, "It ain't discrimination, Mr. Richman, just safety first. Wake up in the night and see a white man in my room I'd be scared out of my wits thinking I was being visited by a ghost."

Spent the evening over on the windy, twilit Allied Artists lot watching the trucks being loaded for Chico and the Battle of Finney's Ford. Racks of uniforms, Confederate and Union; guns, sabers, dead horses, and dead men (papier-mâché hardened into the stiff-legged, belly-extended agonies of death). I had the feeling of a real campaign starting and of real battlefields ahead. I was overwhelmed by these symbols of finality; I don't mean of life—but of the script. I have worked on it for so long that, without realizing it, I had come to believe I could work on it forever, always making it a little better. Now its flaws will be embalmed so that anybody with the price of admission can see where we failed. I felt like saying to the truck loaders, "Wait a minute. Not so fast. Don't hurry me. I need a little more time." And if I feel that, what about Mr. Wyler? It takes some resolution to start the men and the millions to rolling.

And suddenly it seemed very odd, standing there in the hot windy twilight, watching the stowing away of crutches, false beards, saddles, and synthetic blood, that all this effort was being made for something so childish and simple as the telling of a story. It did not seem possible that the hunger of people for a story could be strong enough to call into being an entire industry, strong enough to make millionaires, to transform private persons into public stars, to impose ways of dress and of speech and thought upon us all. But let people wake up one morning with no desire to hear a story, and that industry would collapse, those stars fade and these trucks, loading for a Civil War skirmish on the banks of the Sacramento, would have to find more reasonable employment.

To "hear a story" no doubt puts it too simply; complex wants lie back of the joy we all take in storytelling. The chief of these, I think, is to learn, by watching the lives of others, something about ourselves. "Who am I?" "Who am I?" we ask ceaselessly, and we get partial answers at least from every character with whom we feel some kinship. And stories, by multiplying, if not the length of one's life, at least the number of lives one apparently leads, defy mortality by thus extending and intensifying human consciousness. Even remembering all of this it seemed, standing there between the brick buildings in the darkening court, that, like children carried away by a charade we had ourselves enjoyed, we were perhaps staking too much on the chance that our make-believe would be everybody's. But with the fake dead horses loaded, the real horses already on the road, the men hired to fill the empty uniforms and shed the canned blood we had better make our charade everybody's. Just the same it was queer, all that machinery—to tell a story.

If we read stories in part to find out who we are, I suppose we write them for that purpose even more so. I don't know why I postponed writing for so long. Perhaps I feared self-knowledge.

From the age of twelve I kept notebooks filled with "story ideas." Librarians hated me because of my compulsion to trace "J. West" however faintly in every book that passed through my hands—which was, roughly, the entire library.

I remember an afternoon in my middle twenties. I was working at the university for a doctorate in English. I had been studying, happily I thought, for several hours, when suddenly overcome by a wave of desolation I went to a window from where across the tops of eucalyptus trees I could see the blue glitter of San Francisco Bay. There, with my cheek against the glass and with enough tears for a final bereavement, I asked myself (or was asked by some other self), "When are you going to write your stories? When are you going to write your stories?"

I do not understand to this day the reasons that had prevented me from doing so. Fear of failure? A determination not to abandon the plow to which I had already put my hand? I had elected to be wife, mother I hoped, certainly a housekeeper, and a student. Tuberculosis did for me soon what I could not do for myself. It took my hand willy-nilly from the plow I had elected and gave me the pen I longed for but had done everything to avoid.

Why must we come at what we love only by such round-about and painful ways?

One of the saddest sentences I ever heard in my life was spoken by Charles Snow, a Napa writer. Mr. Snow is blind. Until the time of his blinding, in his forties by an accident, he had been a mining engineer. I said to him that it must have been very hard for him to give up that profession, with its travel and its outdoor life. No, Mr. Snow said, this was not true. So much did he love writing that he blessed the hour of his blinding which had alone brought him to it. I have never been able to say that I blessed my bedfast years, the lost ten years of my life, because they brought me to writing. They were too terrible. They deprived me of too many things. And I'm not ready even yet to exchange life for writing. I still want both. And though it may be true that without those years I would never have come to writing, I still will not bless tuberculosis but choose rather to curse myself for what was uncourageous and stupid and undemanding in me.

Why must one, or some of us anyway, be unable to pick up a pen without a feeling of guilt? Why, unwounded, must we court the wound before we can justify the use of the bow? Or is it only a public wound we court, a justifying wound in lieu of the other, the invisible and shameful one? Storytelling is so natural; I don't suppose there is a man or woman alive who hasn't told one. Why, then, were Mr. Snow and I able to come to it only by the road of suffering? Of course we didn't want to *tell* stories only; we wanted to write them, to have them printed; we wanted them to endure.

I'd better leave Mr. Snow out of this and conjecture about myself only. Has anyone ever thought of the assumption which the man who wants to be printed must make? He must assume that he has something to say that people want to hear. And this assumption for persons who have, for one reason or another, renounced their right to speak and be heard is a frightening one. Frightening and separating—and frightening because separating. Few people claim this right. Few people should. The minute one claims it one separates himself from others. It is an assumption so overweeningly smug, so madly egotistical that, timid by nature and conventional by training, one shies away from it as from the devil. Stand up there and shout, "Now hear me"? In school and home we have had twenty years' training in how to avoid such unseemly action. Perhaps for a twig so bent only the direct break, the eyes plucked out or the lungs punctured, will suffice to effect so complete a reversal, produce the courage to shout, "Now hear me. Now hear me."

Also there are those who cannot approach what they love except obliquely. At any party you can spot the inclinations of these perverse hearts by observing those they avoid. Or let them once approach and be hurt, since they are often weak or sensitive or both, and they may never again stake anything on loving.

I had, in my freshman year in college, a beautiful teacher of English, a tall Rossetti-like woman with pale luminous skin and a great billow of red hair. She had every romantic attribute a sixteen-year-old girl admires in a woman: the proud carriage, the flaring nostrils, the coral-colored lips. She had a low soft voice and a laugh which sounded like water flowing from a deep spring. To a country girl, this teacher's dark clothes (she was a city woman) were beautifully severe and sophisticated. When she went for walks in the dry hills back of the college she wore gloves; I could not have been more impressed had she put on a mask for these trips. She was a woman of real learning and of delightful fancies. Shadows by moonlight, she told us, were far more beautiful than those made by the sun, and I believed her and became a moonlight shadow connoisseur.

I had come up to college from high school a confident student. I had edited the school paper; the school constitution had been altered so that I could hold two student-body offices simultaneously. I was on the debating team, represented the school in forensic contests, and had been sent round with my compositions so that underprivileged classes who did not have me as a member could hear me read them aloud. All in all, I had had pleasure in and from my classes and expected this to continue in college. I did not mind that Miss Fisher was exacting. I wanted great demands to be put upon me. I thought I could satisfy them and the honor for me would thus be greater —and Miss Fisher's approval stronger.

In our freshman year we wrote themes three times a week. One day, I watched two separated lovers in the college library bending upon each other ardent glances which, in the golden light of the afternoon sun, appeared to meet and braid and mingle until there was a palpable bond uniting them. I wrote a theme in which I described this phenomenon. I did not know then that Donne had earlier described the same thing; nor evidently did Miss Fisher.

On the day when this composition was to have been returned Miss Fisher asked me to remain after class. I anticipated praise. What I received was—shame. Miss Fisher spoke in tones which indicated that she had been sullied by my account of those braided eyebeams. She made me feel that I had handed her something noisome, a toad broken open or two snakes entwined. She finished speaking by saying very very coldly, "Will you please try, hereafter, Miss West, to curb your imagination."

I didn't have to try. My heart was too heavy to permit any fanciful flights. And God knows there was nothing imaginative in the pedantry of the composition, a routine piece of writing, I should imagine, for a seventeen-year-old, which finally so completely outraged Miss Fisher. It was called "Live Life Deeply," and I have saved it all these years. It could not have been more innocuous; I had no real idea what I was saying, though I believed every word of its passionate declaration of ignorance and innocence. I said one "should live to the heights and depths of one's being." I said college *was* life, all the life we then had, at least; and that we should not treat it as "preparation." Miss Fisher, I believe, credited me with a knowledge I was a good many years shy of having, even as verbalizations —let alone experience.

I walked, on the day that theme was to be returned, into a classroom where I encountered what amounted to my first publication. the whole of "Live Life Deeply" faced me on the blackboard, written in Miss Fisher's distinguished, thin-looped hand. My words faced me from three directions and my response was that of any published author—pride and happiness. And a unique pride and happiness, because the publisher was someone I loved —for I loved Miss Fisher. I may have been published —but the purpose of publication was not my happiness

231

but my correction. The entire hour was spent by Miss Fisher in demonstrating to my delighted classmates that I was incapable of defining "life," let alone what constituted its "height" and "depth"; and that if college was not preparation for life, what it was; J. West knew not; in fact, that if ever there had existed a wild-talking, pretentious, ignoramus of doubtful morals and negligible intellect I was she. And I believed every word she said. Like any brain-washed convert I wished for death so that I might make amends for the pain I had caused Miss Fisher in forcing her to read such tasteless nonsense.

The minute class was over I began to wish for death for my own sake, not Miss Fisher's. I could not put my head out of a door on the campus without having some exuberant classmate shout to me, "Come on, let's live life deeply," or "Let's stop preparing and start living." I suppose there are those who lived on that campus during that week without any knowledge of "Live Life Deeply"; that theorems were solved, translations made, and battle dates memorized as usual; but, egocentric, I appeared to myself to be the shameful center of a universal awareness of my —the word for it seemed almost to be—nastiness.

Finally, I thought I could no longer endure the pain. I planned suicide. I did not actually want to die; but I did long to be unconscious for a month or two. I don't know why I didn't think of running away, of fleeing to another college where, smart enough to keep my mouth shut about living life deeply, I could start life anew. But fleeing never occurred to me and death seemed the only solution. I chose the one way, in southern California, by which death, except in the rainy season, is most difficult to come by. I chose the maiden's classic means—death by drowning; but in southern California, where except in a time of flash floods, there is not always enough water for lawns and baths let alone enough standing water to snuff out the life of a good-sized maiden, death by drowning poses problems.

I arose at dawn, dressed myself in my best white flannel pleated skirt, newly cleaned, and a blue flannel middy—a fine costume it appears in restrospect for a nautical adventure of the kind I had in mind. I left the campus before sunup and began my search for water. I walked

232

through the morning fog and grayness as one who has already said farewell to the earth. This is a place I used to live, I thought, and I felt no sorrow and said no farewells. I knew that there was, back in the hills, a reservoir of the size and depth I needed to defeat what I recognized might be my unwilled determination, once I got in the water, to swim. When I reached the reservoir I found it firmly boarded over and saw that before I could cast myself in I would have to use a crowbar and ax. Access to death by such grubbing means took me out of the class of Ophelia and Harriet Shelly. I was still determined to join them, however meanly and laboriously. I headed back to town for the tools I needed. The sun came up. The fog lifted and the town was filled with the smell of toast and bacon and coffee. My long walk had made me very hungry; my farewell to the world had robbed the world of some of its power to hurt. I decided to postpone suicide until after breakfast. After breakfast I decided to postpone it a little longer. Thus, postponing, I managed to live. But I also, I fear, postponed living life deeply; and I remembered, as urged by Miss Fisher, to curb my imagination. Then tuberculosis pushed me into depths of life of which I had never dreamed at seventeen and by robbing me of so much else made me at last accept my imagination. And finally, it forced me, through deprivation, to the one act which I had been for so long simultaneously avoiding and loving—the writing of a story.

Still, I will not bless tuberculosis, but curse instead whatever in me made me elect such a fearful path.

I bought a first edition of *Farewell to Arms*, which I always associate with Cooper, inscribed with this message, "For Cherry who has been an oasis of joy in this Hollywood desert." I told Stu that I was going to get Cooper to autograph it and add, "My sentiments exactly, Jessamyn." Stu laughed a good deal about the enterprise. I showed the book to Cooper but he seemed loath to sign *anything,* so I never mentioned the cryptic message at all. And never got the autograph at all. Perhaps I didn't make my asking sufficiently straightforward. Cooper is not the man to presume that his autograph is wanted, rush over, and volunteer.

# VII

I came home without a word to anyone in Hollywood. This has been a lovely day in spite of beginning it with a four-brain-shrinker, four-Optalidon headache. Lovely in spite of the fact that I've read no poem, written no poem, told no one I loved him. I've survived though, that's something. I've sunned, sweated, bought two bargain dresses which I needed, one a blue halter sundress, the other a fine blue-and-white striped shirtwasit dress; also a blue-and-white bathing suit which I do not need. Why all this sky-blue and forget-me-not stuff when my colors are red, brown gold? Why? Bargains, infirm character, laziness.

The air this morning was cold. The seasons are changing. I respond with excitement. Something is passing, something is coming. William Carlos Williams wrote, "The descent beckons no less than the ascent," and it is true, it is true. And Thomas Hornsby Ferril said, "Wishing back is how you name the future." And that's true too. Oh the beautiful poets. I remember them even on the days I don't read them. Now I resolve to be awake and to think of

235

my novel. And, in spite of my dying interest in this movie, to make it, as far as in me lies, good.

## 10 P.M.

Tireless Stu, damn him! I wish *he* would start writing poetry or get himself so deeply involved with a girl she would take his mind off this movie. When he sleeps, he dreams *Friendly Persuasion*, I'm sure; and when he's wakeful he counts good gray Quaker sheep. He called to urge? command? implore? I'm not sure which, that I come back tomorrow. Mr. Wyler feels that Dorothy McGuire does not understand Quakers—and, more particularly, Eliza, who is a Quaker minister. My. Wyler has spoken to me of this before and asked me to talk with her. When I asked what he wanted me to do—to explain Quaker doctrine, the position of women in the church, etc.—he snorted. "Just go and be a Quaker," he said. Well, there are Quakers and Quakers—and I'm not Eliza. Dorothy is an intelligent woman and will discover her own Eliza. But I seem to have become Stu's or Wyler's or this picture's Trilby, so I said—reluctantly—that I'd come back.

I was interested in the difference between McGuire and Cooper in their approach to Quaker meeting. Cooper, when he went, became (as far as I could see) a Quaker. He didn't look about at all, but centered down into the silence. Dorothy, after her visit, spoke to me of the various attitudes and responses of the Quakers as she had observed them at the meeting and of those she intended to use in her portrayal of Eliza in the meeting scene. I was surprised at this use of the meeting, and Dorothy was surprised at my surprise.

"What else," she asked, "should I have done? I went to see the various ways in which those people worshipped and to choose for Eliza whatever seemed the most effective way."

Pragmatically, her way may turn out to be better than Cooper's. But I understand Cooper's way better. I must become the character I write about, not put a set of

236

observations on paper. However, there is no necessity for using either method exclusively. One might, as Cooper appeared to do, "become a Quaker," and then demonstrate that "becoming" by using the mannerisms of other Quakers. Cooper's method traditionally is regarded as the feminine one of intuitive identification; Dorothy's as the masculine method of rational observation and selection. Dorothy was a craftsman, Cooper an artist, insofar as their methods were unmixed. But what method ever is?

*Sunday*

Another call from Stu. Proceed not to the meetinghouse, but to the battlefield. In other words, don't go to Hollywood and be a Quaker for Dorothy but go to Chico and be a general with Tommy Carr. A role that I like much better. One thing I didn't like: a hint from Stu that he feels that Josh fires too soon in the battle scene. The purpose of the battle scene is to provide a testing ground for Josh. Battle as battle is not important. The minute we see that Josh is able to do what he thinks he must do, the battle is, dramatically, over. With all this I agree. But my heart bleeds for Carr if he has to align his cannon and cavalry once more.

*Oaks Hotel*
*Chico*

Blazing heat. Max came up with me and is out now inspecting the battlefield. Since Mr. Wyler must have Cooper back in Hollywood as soon as possible, the battle, which is being shot out of sequence in the picture as a whole, must itself be shot out of sequence. Cooper is in the final scenes of the battle only, and these will be shot first so that he can get back to Hollywood. Carr must arrange for overturned wagons, dead horses (they were here when we arrived), and blown-up cannon to be in the places and conditions where in the early stages of the battle we'll see them being overturned, killed, and blown up.

The unit manager said to me, "Thank thee, dear, for sparing us a full-scale war." This is the first theeing I've heard on the set, though I've been told it's becoming common. I smiled to hear it.

Chico has had too many battles fought along the banks of the Sacramento to take this latest invasion very seriously. Though they're serious about Cooper. There's a delegation of high-school girls from a town thirty miles' distant waiting for him now in the lobby. He, very prudently, is sticking to his room. If one thinks of these girls as high-school girls and of Cooper as a man of fifty, such a visitation is very silly. If one thinks instead of Cooper as a god (which is easy) and of these girls as Worshipers (as indeed they are) come to place garlands on his brow, their action is not only suitable but even conventional.

We all ate last night in the dining room here. With Cooper was a very handsome red-haired young woman. I asked Dorothy Jeakins (evidently with too much avidity) who she was. Dorothy laughed and said, "Did you think she was his mistress? She's his hairdresser." I don't suppose the situation is necessarily either-or though. Max, at least, as a camera fan, is delighted to have so photogenic a female here amidst this crew of dusty Johnny Rebs and home guardsmen; while other people are snapping Cooper, he's busy snapping Cooper's hairdresser. It has been my observation that the secretaries and hairdressers in Hollywood dress and look more like the public's idea of a star than the stars themselves. Dorothy McGuire and Phyllis Love could walk down any Main Street unobserved. The only place some of these secretaries could pass unobserved would be on a well-populated burlesque stage. The girl who takes care of Cooper's hair, a very calm dresser herself, spoke to me with disdain of the women here who so overadvertise their sexual attributes and availability. "The breast that wags the bitch," she said.

She is a very skilled worker. Cooper is by no means bald. He only needs his hair thickened a bit on top, and the job she does is nearer that of thatching than simple toupee-anchoring. If she ever runs out of balding stars she can get a job on the roofs of English cottages, for the skill

238

required must be much the same. Besides keeping Cooper's hair thatched, she sprays him with sweat when he needs sweat, disarranges his hair when his activities require it, keeps his eyebrows neat, and arranges for tears when the going gets sorrowful. Cooper's manly chest is covered with a mat of manly hair and this needs no thatching; but there is a scene in which, shirtless, he chops wood, and the hairdresser will no doubt be responsible for dampening, disarranging, etc. As the area of responsibility increases, does the pay, I wonder? She told me she had traveled all over the world keeping George Raft thatched. And to think that there are girls who believe that their best chance of seeing the world is to become an airline stewardess—a job combining, as far as I can see, the worst features of being a railroad conductor and a waitress. I have never been able to understand why this work, which if done on the ground would be so dull, gets glamorous at twenty thousand feet.

Max paid for the drinks at our table last night—Cooper, Carr, Bob Swink, Mr. Wyler's very accomplished cutter, Mr. Wyler. He plunked down his money very happily, saying that what he had was, in the midst of all the expense accounts, "real." And somehow my drink actually seemed more "real" than if, as I might have done, I had used *my* expense account and signed for it.

Mr. Wyler spoke to me last night about a talk he'd had with John Huston. Huston has read the script. He likes it. Others have read it and liked it, but Huston's liking, I could see, was special. "Huston likes the script," Mr. Wyler said, "but he thinks Jess shouldn't touch that gun. He says that when he saw that Jess was going to pick up his gun . . . he had to stop reading. He said it was painful for him to watch Jess, a man whose whole life had been given to nonviolence, waver. John's a very fine director. His feeling about this troubles me."

Mr. Wyler's feeling about Huston's feeling amazed *me*. He is moving inward on this script and these characters, as he must. Jess is becoming Jess, not Cooper, with audience expectations to fill. But those cannon are so recently behind us! Is Chico the road to Damascus and Huston the angel? No, Huston is no angel here. He is dead

239

wrong. In many places I've been unwilling, either through lack of knowledge or conviction, or easygoingness, to stand and fight. Here once again I'll stand and fight, and this time Mr. Wyler and I have seemingy changed places.

"Good," I said, "fine. I'm happy to hear that Huston does not want Jess to take up his gun. If he had wanted him to, the whole telling of the story would have been wrong. We are gambling everything that an audience will feel exactly what Huston does: 'Don't take the gun, Jess. Don't take it!' The audience must feel here what it feels when Othello believes Iago. 'Don't, Othello, don't,' they implore him. The audience must feel what it feels when Lear is being taken in by the flattery of Goneril and Regan, 'Don't believe them, Lear.'

"Jess is a good man, but a man with a flaw. He must be tempted to violence; and we must see him tempted. We have promised the audience that. And he must have the means of killing in his hand at the moment of his temptation. And we must see him decide, in spite of the provocation and in spite of the means, to refrain. Even though the refraining may lose him his life. Otherwise we don't have a drama—we have a chronicle. Otherwise we don't have a hero acting, but someone passive being acted upon. Give the audience what it must want at this juncture—and Huston says he wants—a Jess who does *not* pick up his gun, and the picture is over right there. That's what this story is about. Will Jess fight? You can answer the question in a vacuum here in Jess's bedroom as he looks at his rifle. Or you can answer it in action. where Jess is willing to test it—and would test it. Jess was no rule-follower. He did not refuse to fight because Quakers say it is wrong to fight. That's imitative action, and Quakers despise it. He refused to fight because as a human being he could not bring himself to take a human life. We must see him make that decision as an individual; we must see the individual and the Quaker become one. Who's interested in seeing a man keep rules? Let alone a man like Jess, who is no rule-keeper."

We were talking in the bar, which is dark, but I could see Mr. Wyler smile. "Am I going to get a ten-page document tomorrow?"

"No, you've had it."

"Johnnie is a very sensitive, very bright man," he said.

"Look, he's too mixed up with that whale of his to take on Quakers too."

"Johnnie isn't limited in the number of things he can consider simultaneously."

There was no use arguing about Johnnie's talents. I was an admirer of them myself.

"Maybe he doesn't want any competition for *Moby Dick*."

Mr. Wyler stared at me. He didn't believe me capable of such a black thought any more than he believed Huston capable of double-dealing. Neither did I for that matter. "It's a joke," I said.

"But you promise me to think about it?"

I promised him. And I will. And I'll shake in my boots, too, until this scene is filmed. And screened. It's the hub of the picture.

I've lost track of time. Still at Chico. I wake up in the quiet red of another hot dawn and watch the cars in front of the hotel being loaded with cameramen, technicians, script clerks, wranglers, Carr—God knows who else—all leaving for location.

The scene of the skirmish is ten miles or so from town, on the banks of the Sacramento. I can't decide whether the aspect is that of carnival, picnic, or war. Perhaps war has its picnic-carnival aspects. Trailer dressing rooms for the stars; portable kitchens and dining rooms; tents for dressing the extras, for make-up, for pay clerks; trucks for sound equipment; vans for horses. It would be easier to wage a real war. A real war would, by death and destruction, soon simplify things a bit—though I suppose replacements would constantly bring back the status quo of complexity.

I have always believed that a man was what he did—or possibly what he thought. Here a man is his appearance; they are their uniforms, their beards, their grease paint, their burnsides, their dust, their horses. I am amazed at Tommy Carr's cleverness in picking his extras and the make-up department's skill in making Reb raiders and farmer home guardsmen out of them. These raiders are haggard, saddle-weary, knowledgeable, brutal, and tired to

241

death of war. These farmers are fresh, awkward, determined, pursy, as invincible as the raiders are irresistible. I know that these men are local college boys, storekeepers, amateur actors, and particularly anyone with a horse. But my eye refuses to accept the facts. Perhaps the uniforms, beards, and sabers *do* transform them. Perhaps a Confederate officer was a bearded man who had been given a uniform and a saber. Perhaps in 1860, as now, he was otherwise a storekeeper, a college boy, a farmer. The fancy hangs in my mind that these men, transformed in appearance, may suddenly begin to live, instead of act, their parts. That a fighting war will break out here between these convincing opponents—just as a loving love sometimes breaks out between play-acting lovers.

Coop says pensively, "I think this is the seventh time I've fought the Civil War—and several of those times right here on the old Sacramento."

Coop's double, Slim, is here, a sad man, more granite-faced than Cooper. Any actor is, in a way, a shadow. He is the image, when he is acting, of someone else. How would it be to have been for twenty-five years, as Slim has, the shadow of a shadow? Coop spent a large part of his life being someone non-Coop; and Slim spends his life being a non-Slim being a non-Coop. Slim puts his granite face over a chessboard, and thus looks at real objects as much of the time as possible. I would like to talk to him but to do so I would have to traverse some arid country into which he has retreated. I overheard him say, "Who wants to marry a hungry woman?" and I have new standards for observing a woman. Does she look hungry?

In addition to Slim, Coop has a stunt double. A long shot of Coop in a buggy will be Slim. A shot of Coop rolling up to a log just in time to avoid a cavalry charge will be the stunt double. Coop and Slim are both middle-aged men—but even if they were young, this whole picture and the work of everyone of us here would cease if Coop were injured. Keeping him intact is the one most important job connected with the picture.

The Chico college boys, because Coop is pulled out of the action whenever the going gets rough, call him, with affectionate laughter, "Old Chicken Coop." Coop himself would be the first to relish the joke but there are those who think he should not know it. I am happy to see the hair-thatcher feeding him ice-cream cones and treating him like a hard-working man on a hot day—not a star.

Fred and Nicky came up yesterday armed with cameras and curiosity. Before Fred came to live with us two years ago, Max and I had envisaged ourselves helping quite another kind of boy, a boy as shy as we had been when young, a boy who needed to be encouraged and given confidence. Fred needs, not to be pushed forward—a pleasant action—but to be dragged back out of the elected limelight, which is not a pleasant action. Yesterday he asked me at once to introduce him to Cooper. I refused. The heat, the battle, and Fred were too much to ask of anyone. And Fred is not one to say "howdy do" and leave. He would have elicited, or, failing that, have given, Coop a history of the Civil War, of photography, and the discovery of the Sacramento River. But Fred is not dependent. He will work the angles if he can; if he can't he'll travel a straight course. He had watched the shooting long enough to see Slim and the stunt-double in action. With this information as a springboard Fred bore down upon Cooper and, with the English intonation picked up from hundreds of old English movies on TV, asked Cooper, the one-remove Englishman, "Sir, just how many doubles *do* you have?" Cooper gave Fred a calm look and turned his back, the act of an intelligent man. For Fred would have had Coop in the wrong, fighting for those doubles with his back to the wall.

Poor Fred! His situation here, where he is supposed to do some housework, upsets two cherished beliefs of his: first, that women should do all the housework, and second, that men should provide women with such ideas and information as they have. I struggle to break through both these convictions of his. He has been a *Wunderkind* in too many homes, a polysyllabic source of dicta and information, to benefit by any more bended knees or broken spirits. He makes me weep sometimes, but I never let him see my tears. Power is what the boy has already had too much of.

And inside this domineering show-off is a boy who wants to be loved and who is lovable. He has a perception and sensitivity which is remarkable and an ability to convey it which is enchanting—when he permits himself to step off the professional podium. It is this kernel of sweetness and truth which makes you endure everything, makes you fight and refuse to be done in by the belligerent, complacent outer husk. It hurts him to have that kernel exposed; it hurts me to take hold of that outer wounding rind; but nothing less than man versus automaton is at stake; there is nothing less than a soul struggling to stay alive inside Fred. I wish I could nurture it by open love instead of cold war. But love, Fred takes to be capitulation. I try to demonstrate the love and to show him at the same time that I have not capitulated. That we will eat the food, see the friends, observe the practices of more than twenty-five years. It takes more resolution than I sometimes have. Fred came to us obsessed with two ideas: he would be a leader and he would be consistent. Being consistent meant not departing from convictions already formulated; being a leader meant making other persons accept these convictions. It was a narrow track, and oneway, but a person might travel a considerable distance on it. A number of dicators have. In addition to having a track, Fred kept the rails greased. He was a proficient manipulator of persons and would bone up on the accomplishments and interests of guests before they arrived. He had read Mr. Carnegie, and Fred's two-hundred pounds of concentrated energy influencing people and making friends was as awe-inspiring as a jet take-off.

These were techniques Fred had developed to survive. A weaker or less intelligent boy would have sunk into cheaper and easier ways of leadership. He *had* survived though, and it was time now for him to cast off his survival outfit and put on his outfit for living. He had a fine one, though well hidden.

He came home from school one night and said, "Guess what happened today? A girl gave me a bite out of the apple she was eating." This is the Fred I love, unpretentious, open, eager.

He came in after visiting with some of his cronies and said, "My face is tired from laughing. Or maybe from pretending to laugh." This is the Fred one must fight to preserve.

It's a nerve-racking business, living in the midst of soul making. I talked to Lee Vernon, before he died, of Fred's coming here. "Get him, get him," Lee urged me. "Have some young life in the house." Lee, at sixty-five, was younger than the sixteen-year-old Fred who arrived here. And instead of being tugged out of our middle-aged ruts by adventuresome youth we found ourselves berated by a tyrannical old grandfather for *our* venturesomeness. But Fred gets younger every day. It is our hope to meet him face to face before he leaves us.

Mr. Wyler has been in bed for twenty-four hours with migraine. He had his usual shots but without the usual help. Stu took him some of my brain shrinkers and they are easing the pain, so I feel that I've made an unexpected contribution to the film.

Stu and I worked half the night rearranging the battle scenes so that Josh's determination to fire—after his first failure—will not come so early in the encouter. Just as Jess's story ends when he refuses to fire, so Josh's ends when he does fire. This was Stu's idea—that the present sequence presents the firing too early. He will not present these ideas directly to Mr. Wyler, which perhaps I *would* resent, but neither does he want me to tell Mr. Wyler that the idea originated with him, which makes me uncomfortable. If the idea is good, I want Stu to have the credit; and if bad, perhaps I'd like someone to share the blame. Whether this is because Mr. Wyler has told him, as Robert did, to stay out of the script or whether, as he says himself, "Willy would rather hear it from you." Once in a while I get to feeling like Stu's cat's-paw, though Stu bends over backward in warning me about this. I try hard not to be persuaded by his force and cogency but to keep myself alive, in recesses of my being deeper than that of intellectualizing, to the people of the story. When I am really convinced but might fail, out of easygoingness or inertia to press the issue, Stu is iron for my anemia. And the minute Mr. Wyler recovers from the combination of pain and painkiller I shall talk to him.

Tommy Carr came into Stu's room last night, where I was working with Stu, and I felt like a turncoat to be advocating one more change in a battle order, so easy for us paper-men to dream up and difficult for him to execute in terms of cannon, wagons, horses, men, terrain, and cameras. Stu, on the flood tide of a conviction, tends to engulf minor obstacles like second-unit directors. And Tommy wasn't being engulfed until William Wyler had spoken. And he resented Stu's assumption that the change was an obvious improvement. I like Carr and think that his position is difficult. He told me when we were working on the battle sequences that he had had to give up acting because, "While I became older my face stayed boyish."

And it is true. A gray-haired boy *is* disquieting. There is something anomalous in that combination, and anomalies upset us. Women with mustaches, midgets with wives and children; if these were commonplace their opposites would turn our stomachs. As human beings we are not visually very adaptable; what's new or unknown is nasty. And we never stop to think that we accept and praise organs and appurtenances of human functioning which apart from function cannot be regarded as aesthetically very stirring. White teeth are possibly better than yellow, but teeth at all, those carnivorous chompers suddenly revealed in all their incisiveness inside, so to speak, the head are no prettier and much more threatening than rake prongs. Mouths are rather odd, disguise them as you will with lipstick or mustaches. And I've seen sickening ears, like big faded flabby cabbage leaves. Eyelids fall down white as the bellies of sow bugs. I rather like eyes, but because of what can come in behind the eye rather than for the eye itself. Hair, even if it grew on bushes, would be pretty.

And it's a good thing that the desire to express themselves sexually is strong in most people, for it's as though a cynical nature, setting out to manufacture human beings, had said, "Look, people are going to like this so much we don't have to waste any money on packaging. They'll clamor for this in any shape or form we give it to them." And nature, as always, was right. Of course with cleavages and cod pieces, falsies and suits of light, human beings have tried to enhance nature, or disguise it or amplify it. But finally one must, unless he goes to the trouble of developing a fetish, accept the unaugmented, unvarnished natural object. And one of the virtues of intercourse for the race, if not the individual, is its lack of dignity. A pompous performance in this line is not unimaginable but the chances are always working against it. And an alderman or dictator will, though the pleasures may have been godly, remember that the attitudes were not, and function in office more like plain Zeb Smith and less like Jove Almighty because of it.

What we consider sexually attractive is very fortuitous. When we are young anything which is our opposite sexually puts us in a tizzy of delight, and the adolescent girl can brood for hours on the miracle of whiskers making a scraggly first appearance on the chin of her fifteen-year-old hero. Adam's apples, bobbing up and down above a sweat shirt, are for her beautifully masculine; and big feet, flexing cheek muscles, and an indiscriminate appetite for cheese and onion sandwiches, say "male, male, male." Loveliest word in the language at the minute for her. And no use for Mama to say, "What do you see in him?" *That's* what she sees in him, and if Mama has forgotten, she will be of no help in any case. The most beautiful and talented girl in town was throwing herself away on a scamp, because "he's such a beautiful walker." He was. I've watched him. But instead of fighting this beautiful walker why didn't someone try to find the girl an accomplished walker who could also read? This boy couldn't always be walking, nor the girl watching. Then what? Disenchantment.

But apart from raw masculinity and femininity, which is so intolerably exciting when we are adolescents—and which though it becomes more tolerable remains for so long exciting—there are fashions in the manner of its exposure and garnishing. When I was a girl, the height of femininity was to be short and flat chested. There's no way to make five feet seven short, but stooping helped. The function of the brassière when I was in high school and college was to eliminate the breasts. I can remember standing in front of the mirror at high school and regarding the broken plane of my chest with all the disgusted despair of a businessman sizing up the continued growth of a bay window. That bulge was just sickening, separating me forever from being fashionable or interesting, and I tightened my brassière and stretched my sweater until it disguised more or less my health and buxomness. Then I went home and lived on a vinegar-and-lemon-juice diet for two weeks, a regimen that caused my skin to break out, my ribs and hipbones to protrude like those of a worn-out nag, but left me still curving where I shouldn't have.

I read editorials today about the unhappiness of girls without big breasts—and what to do about it. Remind them of the changing attitudes toward the female figure. When the breast was for suckling its size, if large, was not romantic but rather the reverse: an intimation that one was built for practical purposes. The changed attitude toward the breast is exactly the same as the changed attitude toward the wagon wheel, the coffee grinder, and the fireplace. We romanticize the nonuseful; we are sentimental about whatever we have outgrown as necessity, but about which memories still cluster. The old wagon wheel has become a symbol in the West of the days when, without it, we were stuck. Now we whitewash it or gild it or plant it with geraniums; we make it a gate or a support for lights.

The coffee mill has moved up front out of the kitchen into the living room, and people who once didn't give a thought to the coffee mill as long as the brew was satisfying now remark on it, examine its finish, and give the handle a nostalgic whirl or two.

And the fireplace, once our necessity and about whose decoration we had no more formal interest than about the decoration of the kitchen stove—it *was* the kitchen stove —has become an object to be decorated, garnished, displayed, sentimentalized. And the bigger the better. Modern living rooms have fireplaces you can walk into. The modest grate which threw out heat—since heat is no longer the object—is no longer popular. Conspicuous consumption is the motto here. And to have a big nonuseful object is about as conspicuous as you can get in that line.

And the breast, like fireplace, wagon wheel, and coffee mill is, since it is no longer functionally needed, displayed, augmented, and gilded for the same reasons which cause these comparable objects to be valued. The big breast, since the advent of the infant formula and the baby bottle, has become a kind of antique, and a man enjoys owning one or two and displaying them for the same reason that he enjoys owning a piece of Paul Revere silver or a 1902-model Reo. The man's desire to possess this antique is understandable; the woman's satisfaction in being possessed for these reasons is less so. Women want to be wanted by men and have learned not to examine men's reasons too closely, though they might be very moved by a man who could love them for reasons more uniquely personal to them both.

Men, in their double-breasted coats, their pleated, wide-legged trousers, have taken the veil as far as their bodies are concerned. There is no telling what that drape shape contains in the way of a body. One of the shocks of William Sheldon's fascinating book *Varieties of Human Temperament* is its revelation of the varieties of male physique. One would have to be either a very experienced or very imaginative woman to dream that underneath that rectangle of herringbone, dacron, and flannel so many combinations were possible of the really limited number of elements—legs, arms, torso—which go to make up a man.

Men have forced women to come out in the open with their bodies: if we have bowed legs, thick waists, non-existent shoulders, exposed clavicles, flat chests, big behinds, there they are for all to see. And the best girdle, the sternest uplifter, and the highest heels, will not, for all their agony, disguise our bad points one half as well as wide-legged pants and loose coat, half to the knees, do the job, comfortably, for men. A woman at least always knows that a man's response to her is not one of physical curiosity. What she is physically is plain to see. What he is physically cannot even be guessed—though Mr. Sheldon gives several astonishing hints.

The earlier men, yes even that old monster Henry VIII, chop and change as he would, valued and courted women as we are not valued and courted today. Then, with lace and ribbon, with cod piece and leg padding, men showed their concern for the good opinion of women. Now the shoe is on the other foot—or rather the falsie is on the other frame, and women now court men, entreat them to take a second look, even if that second look is for the most part nostalgic and is in memory of a role for which we were once, but are no longer, necessary.

Perhaps we played that flat-chested part too long. I can imagine men saying, "If we're going to have to put up with what is manly in appearance let's have a few manly virtues to go with it." Though I myself am never sure about this division of sexual virtues, or anything else, along such strictly bipartisan lines. I bought Gerhardi's *Memoirs of a Polyglot* last week because I opened it to these lines: "women with whom I think I could have been lastingly happy. One was Katherine Mansfield." I like to read about Katherine Mansfield—so I closed the book and bought it. When I got home I found him saying next, "Her mind was as genuine as a man's," and at that I could only close the book once more and ask myself what in God's name Gerhardi meant. That makes no more sense to me than if he had said, "Her legs were as genuine as a man's," or, "To my delight I discovered that her toenails were as real as a man's" and that women, the nearer they approach men, the realer they get. At best then we are never going to be really real or genuinely genuine but only in an organ here or an aptitude there reminiscent of the real right thing. The masculine thing.

A man spoke to me the other day admiringly of a woman who was "all woman, full of coquetry at sixty-five." As usual, when I hear something which makes me thoughtful, I carry on with other subjects while I turn this matter over in my mind. So it is only after a day or a week that I am ready to pursue what was the important part of the conversation for me. By that time the person with whom the subject should be discussed is far away and I must be satisfied with an interior conversation. But I suppose that it was the "coquettishness" which was the sign of the "hundred per cent woman" to this man. And it is here I think that he may have been taken in if, as seemed to be the case, he is an admirer of the "all-woman" type. First of all I needed for this conversation in absentia to know what was meant by coquettishness. I've looked it up in the dictionary to be sure I'm not supporting some concept of coquettishness which will sustain me in my side of the argument. (For I admit that I am arguing, and since my luncheon companion doesn't know this, the least I can do, when I present his side, is to give him the best arguments possible.) To coquet, according to Webster's New World Dictionary is "to flirt, to attract attention or admiration, usually said of a woman"; and a coquette is "a woman who tries to get men's attention and admiration."

In looking up this definition, I discovered what I'd forgotten: that the word comes from the French *coqueter*, which means, literally translated, "to strut like a rooster"! One more example of the shoe now being on the other foot. Cocks used to *coqueter;* now the hens, poor drab creatures, so inaptly feathered for the job, are the coquetters. Here Mr. Gerhardi might truly say, "Her coquetry was as genuine as a man's."

By Webster's definition ninety-nine out of every hundred women are coquettes. Though a coquette is not ordinarily thought of in terms so broad; everything a woman does from baking muffins to keeping her neck clean might thus be argued to be part of her efforts to "get men's attention and admiration." Coquetry, to most women, is some other woman's eye-rolling, flattering, fluttering, thigh-patting campaign to engage the attention of a man. And this, by any woman's definition does not mean "all woman" any more than similar tactics on the part of a man mean "all man" to her. It only means a certain kind of woman.

What if I had said to this "coquetry, all-woman" man that I had met a man who was "all man, flirting with me every minute." He would, I am sure, have doubted the equation; unless he, too, were a flirt. And perhaps this is the gist of the matter. Never having been able to master the conventional attitudes and gestures of coquetry, I resented being downgraded as a female because I was not good at furling the fan or lowering the lashes. And also, I suppose, if proof of womanliness were wanted, I've spelled it plainly out here in my personal response to an impersonal remark.

Another misapprehension about the nature of womanliness lies in the common designation of the man who is neat, precise, frugal, timid, dry, unresponsive, and conventional as "feminine"; this is, instead, the old bachelor type, the old maid's opposite number, a man who is completely masculine, so completely masculine that, insofar as women are concerned anyway, he would be improved by considerable additions of femininity. The most appealing men for women are not these "all-man" types. The men who have most enthralled women are those who combine an exterior which is extremely masculine with a psyche which has much femininity. No man without this admixture would be able to be with a woman as much as she wants him to be, or would have the tact, the intuition, the tenderness which, finally, enthrall her beyond all derring-do.

*Sunday*

Home in Hollywood. Strange to unite those words so naturally. Max put me on the train in Sacramento last night.

It is still hot here but the heat wave is over. My neighbors tell me how they weathered the siege. It was almost as warm in Chico, but along the river and under the valley oaks the heat seems easier to deal with because more natural. In the country, heat is only the sun, an old neighbor busy with his known and necessary work.

It is evening. I sit in my white-curtained home and the soft milky air lifts the curtains with a seaside rhythm. A swimmer, silent except for a little languid splashing, makes our pond sound like a fountain. The man who was reading *War and Peace* when I left, is still in his deck chair and still reading. "Look," I would like to say to him, "I have been fighting a war while you read one."

The movement of the curtains: the classic domestic movement. Or is it? Flame in the fireplace? Pendulum in the clock? Light across the floor? Fall of a petal? Steam above a kettle? Leaf shadow on drawn blind? Classic domestic smell: sponge cake in the oven and blackberries stewing. Classic domestic sounds: fire, clock, wind round the corner.

Who could enter . . . not interrupt, but look at the room, the sky, the rocking water, and see what was needed in the way of a human . . . and be that human being. Too much to ask? Of coure. I'm not asking it.

Crossland says Colette has three rules when writing about herself. "1. Do not be self-conscious. 2. Do not be self-pitying. 3. Do not tell the whole truth." I think I break number two more than any other.

I went with Teddy Richman, Mark's wife, for a little scramble up to something so beautifully Hollywood and southern California and human and me, I expect, that I embrace its memory and swear to return many a time. The land upon which this apartment house and a half a dozen others beyond it stand ends in a pie-shaped promontory which faces on to Los Feliz Boulevard and is backed by Griffith Park Boulevard. On this acre or so of earth, which rises at its highest point perhaps a couple of hundred feet above the boulevards below, is the home of something called a "Metaphysical Institute," a flat clay-colored building with oriental motifs, covered loggias, and urns of half-dead flowers. Bulletins announce courses in subjects of an occult nature. The metaphysicians are now all on vacation; weeds grow about the pleasant building; and better even than weeds are the wild tobacco trees of the arroyos of my youth which have never been grubbed out. From this promontory the San Gabriel Valley and the Sierra Madre Mountains are visible. Almost at our feet, it seemed, in the clear dry air of evening, was Forest Lawn Cemetery, a place at which, for all its fame with visiting Englishmen, I was having my first look.

But what was remarkable and moving was not the view; though it was strange to have a five-minute walk produce a mountain range, a river (dry), and a valley which were completely invisible from our apartment. What was remarkable and moving was to find loneliness, and emptiness, dust, and weeds, in the midst of all the traffic, green lawns, swimming pools, and "to let" signs. To find, in fact, a little antioasis: a little sand amidst the palms, a little silence amidst the tire whine, a little spot the caravans avoided. And the charm was augmented by the knowledge that this place, too, was sometimes thronged, thus giving us the pleasures of ruins; or if we cared to remember that the throngs would be returning, the pleasures of usurpers and trespassers. Once or twice we thought we caught sight of a lama in the auditorium; but the lama turned out to be a coat swaying on a hanger, an even more transcendental metaphysician than we had imagined.

What was delightful, apart from the wind and the silence and the dryness, was the secrecy, the thing alone, the solitary possession, the theft. The thing that must be fought, that must be fought, surely? And yet if I could get rid of all the other lamas what joy in living on this barren promontory, a desert father facing, for the rest of my life, Forest Lawn?

\*     \*

Spent the day being a Quaker with Dorothy McGuire; and she spent the day being, I expect, very patient with me. She has moved out of her home, away from husband and two children, and into the Beverly Hills Hotel, the better to concentrate on Eliza, Quakers, Indiana, the plain speech, and whatever else may occupy an actress preparing for a role. Dorothy is prettier on the screen than off, because the camera emphasizes what the naked eye, following color like any bull, misses: that is bone structure. All of Dorothy's face is clean, pure, and spare; though rather with the cleanness of a lean little girl than with the austerity of a face which passion has worn to the bone. She has a face like a raindrop fallen onto an unpainted and somewhat worn rooftree. The raindrop is the little girl who survives; the timber beneath is the woman. I suspect it is the juxtaposition of the pristine and the used which makes her face interesting. Had her girlishness been of the round and dimpling kind, she would have been faced with Tommy Carr's problem. Fortunately for her, her youth is in her bones.

Dorothy no doubt knew why I was visiting her, and under these circumstances we had a pleasant day. We ate, drank, talked Quakers and *Friendly Persuasion*. I believe she thinks of Quakers as I once thought of nuns—a people wooden but very holy. There is a scene in which Eliza does not want Jess to tell the children that she once danced. This troubled Dorothy. "But why?" she asked. "That is so natural and happy a thing to do. How could she possibly object to her children knowing? I don't think I can make that scene convincing."

Intellectually she could accept the fact that Quakers had felt that way, but she could not accept it emotionally.

Nor did I get very far with suggesting that she imagine instead that Jess was going to tell the children she had once been a B-girl or had gotten her start as a strip-teaser. She was all for the unvarnished truth with the children even under these circumstances and rather than say that Quakers were antitruth, I spoke of the times, of Mrs. Grundy, Queen Victoria, and all that.

I never resent the success of other books. The only time I ever wrote a letter protesting a review was when Diana Trilling lambasted Eudora Welty in the *Nation* for faults she did not possess. Why then do I resent the praise of other directors and other pictures? I do not wish Huston well with *Moby Dick*. I think Kazan overpraised for *East of Eden*. Heaven knows William Wyler is in no need of protective feelings from a tyro script writer. But there is a kind of family feeling here among us workers. What created it I don't know. But though I can't account for it, I do react to it. And the only times in my life I've been so angry that I was literally beside myself were times when, not I, but members of my family were attacked. Then I felt all the ferocity attributed to a mother tigress. This is not an infection with the "Willy is a genius" virus; I would still save that word for the Shakespeares and Goethes. No, it's a family feeling, a feeling for something of which I'm a part; but the fact that I am only a part of it permits me to be for it in a more wholehearted way than I can ever be for what I, alone, am making. Am I then more "for" this picture than for my own writing? No. I *am* my own writing—which is a different matter.

Portia asked me a week or so ago why I never talked with Mr. Wyler's secretary when I was over in Mr. Wyler's office. He's a sandy-haired, freckled, bespectacled young man, long Irish upper lip, very pleasant, very busy with all his phones, typewriters, mechanical stenographic devices, to say nothing of Mr. Wyler. I thought he thus had his hands full without chitchat from a script writer. Something Portia said made me think he would like to talk, so up I spoke, and Quirk is his name and quirky is his nature. He's older than he looks—is in his mid-thirties—has had experience in the Near East with the State Department and a story in the *New Yorker*. Having had one there he is satisfied, he says. He wrote it just to see if he could get one in, did so, and has no desire to repeat himself. This is a discouraging thing to say to a writer who would not mind having a story in the *New Yorker* every month; is wrong aesthetically and morally too, as I told him, since it puts the publishing cart in front of the writing horse. One writes not to conquer the *New Yorker* but to conquer the material and one had as well consider love-making a form of athletics as writing a form of magazine conquest. But Russ knows this. He seems to have arrived at a pretty clear understanding of what pleases him, which I admire in anyone; and he seems to be contentedly putting his knowledge into practice, which I also admire. He has a white Cadillac Eldorado convertible and the first time I rode in it, he put in at a service station and asked for one dollar's worth of gas. The service station attendant was at least as amazed as I at this request and seemed for a time to ponder the legality? the sanity? of the request. He finally delivered the dollar's worth of gas while Russ explained to me that by having small amounts in the tank he cut down expenses. "The fear of running out of gas makes me take short trips." (I wish Max could pick up this fear of small amounts of gas. He takes long trips with small amounts and we do run out.)

We set forth with our fresh dollar's worth, and as we went out of the service station there was a considerable clatter. Russ stopped, lifted a pasteboard carton from between the back and front seats and rearranged the bottles, jars, and tins which it held.

"I'm on a health kick," he explained. Vitamins, yeasts, elixirs, laxatives, Lord knows what there was in that carton, enough to stock a drugstore it looked like, but Russ was delighted while the kick was on to keep faith with it. "There's something to be taken almost every hour," he said and took out two pills, of the approximate size and color of buzzards' eggs, and swallowed them smoothly down. So, the car meagerly and Russ plenteously fueled, we took off once again. Portia is a confederate of Russ's in this health kick and they consider me, because of my simple diet, unconsciously one of them; though they urge buttermilk rather than beer. We are going at this health kick from opposite directions however; I am eating what

I love; they are loving what they eat. The difference seems to be that while they stay lean I'm getting fat.

I certainly have the right car for Hollywood. First the back of the front seat collapses with Cooper in it. Then, last night going for my twice-weekly guzzle of print at the Pickwick Book Shop, the right rear door began to smoke. All eyes were on me as I cut across traffic into a service station. An attendant ripped out the door's interior and the automatic window raising-and-lowering apparatus, whose shorting had started the fire. A pity that this car, which has so natural a gift for assuming striking public attitudes, should not be owned by someone who can profit more by being the public eye than I.

I wish I had kept track of the number of times I've said, "This finishes it." And here I have written two new scenes as excitedly as though I had only started on the script. Yesterday Mr. Wyler told me that Dan Taradash, who has read the script, thought that Josh, with all of his soul searching, might seem too namby-pamby, prim and negative. "We know what Josh is against," Mr. Wyler said. "What is he for?" Second, Mr. Wyler, who hates time dissolves and would, I verily believe, have an entire picture consist of a series of consecutive scenes if he could manage it, asked me if I couldn't devise some means by which Sam Jordan's visit to the Birdwells might be shown without a time dissolve.

"What is Josh for?" He is against death, he is for living. He is against destruction, he is for love. How is this to be shown, dramatically and visually? He is a farm boy, he loves animals. Let us see him helping at the birth of a farm animal. When I told Mr. Wyler this, he approved, but accused me, smiling, of a cynicism. "When in doubt, use an animal." I wasn't in doubt, but this is now my favorite scene.

Mr. Wyler's second suggestion, that Sam appear at the Birdwells' without a time lapse, resulted in a scene so funny to write that I have had to draw back from it time and again to smile. In it Sam comes after Eliza has taken up residence in the barn. Jess tries to cover up her absence. Later, after Eliza's return to the house, Sam asks

Jess, "How did you persuade Eliza to come back in?"
"Reasoned with her, just reasoned with her," says Jess.

Mr. Wyler, with his need to see what he doesn't want
before he is sure of what he does want, used to frighten
me. I begin, as I see him discard, to trust him more. This
one-time exponent of cannon becomes more and more a
Quaker. Once when he thought Quakerism needed considerable overt explaining in the picture, he asked me to
write a scene in which Jess and Eliza have a theological
dialogue. This was one of the most difficult pieces of writing to which I ever put my mind. The dialogue occurred
at the conclusion of the scene in which the elders visit
Jess and Eliza and Jess prays to cover up the sound of the
organ being played by Mattie in the attic. I tried to give the
theology a leavening of humor. Mr. Wyler read the scene,
threw out the theology, and kept the leavening. Now he
becomes a Quaker indeed.

There remains only one scene which I cannot stomach,
a scene which Mr. Wyler loves with the unreasoning in-
fatuation of a Titania for Bottom. This is an episode,
which he inherited from the original script, of Jess's visit
at the home of the Widow Hudspeth. The visit occurs in
*The Friendly Persuasion*—but not written as is this, with
Dogpatch exaggeration. The Hudspeth girls fall upon Josh
as if they were cannibals and he were meat. They roll
with him on the floor. They all but unbutton him. There
is a stupid mock raid in which Jess and Josh sit like dolts
while these three Amazons defeat a small army. There is
no humor without humanity, and these girls are inhuman.
Pseudo passion in red drawers and shouting, "I vum."
This does not tickle our funny bones. It dislocates with
one monstrous walloping blow our belief in all the other
characters and scenes. Day by day I soften the corn, move
the scene a few steps out of Dogpatch. No willingness yet
in Mr. Wyler to let these changes stand. Robert who
usually sees eye to eye with me disagrees here. Those
Hudspeth sisters hold the Wyler brothers in thrall. I think
it is because their picture-making sensibilities are delicate
that it pleases them to be responding here to something
so cinematical and vulgar. It suggests to them dimensions
of their personalities they didn't know existed. It is as if a
civilized, an overcivilized man found himself stirred by

the charms of a plowgirl or charwoman. "Gad, what range I have," he says to himself, astonished. God knows *I* don't want—and whatever I may want, am unable here —to shorten any man's range—but these scenes are not funny.

Stu, who doesn't think them funny as they stand, believes Willy can do anything and that this heavy buffoonery will emerge under the magic of his directing, a soufflé of the most delicate wit. "Why penalize Willy?" I ask Stu. "Why not give him some wit to start with?"

"Willy likes to do things the hard way," says Stu.

I am going with Russ to the *première* of *Desperate Hours* tonight. First for him, first for me. "This place is suddenly lousy with virgins," says Stu, whose life has been filled with *premières*. Russ inquired if I would mind going with the top of the convertible down. This is not a part of the health kick, a desire for fresh evening air, but an honest admission that on an occasion when see-and-be-seen is the game, Russ intends to play the game straight. And why not? This is one of my reasons for liking Russ. I, brought up in small communities where one hides so many things, perfectly natural things for which there was no reason for secrecy, rejoice in Russ's openness: one dollar for gas, the pills, the health kick, the pleasure in seeing the stars. And the pleasure in going tonight in a conveyance as spectacular as any that will be there. Top down and, as Mama would say, "head up and tail over the dashboard."

I intended to buy myself a spectacular dress for this outing. Though this would only postpone the disappointment of the spectators when they saw that all the dressmaking had been wasted on an unknown middle-aged woman. But it would've shown Russ that, on my own level, I was trying to keep pace with the Eldorado. But I never got round to buying the dress, and the only thing I could think to do to mark the occasion was to stop at the drugstore on the way home from the studio to buy a bottle of fingernail polish to apply to my toenails. I do have a new pair of shoes—a sole, a heel, and about two straps. So I have for the first time in my life reddened my toenails; in an effort to co-operate from the ground up in this gala occasion.

Stu phones me this morning to drop everything and get out to location, where Mr. Wyler was shooting his first scene. I was deep in the writing of odds and ends—speeches from the barkers, a song for Jess—but Stu, no man ordinarily to countenance laziness on the part of the staff, was shocked to find me so employed. This, he said, was the beginning of the end, the feedback of all we had been making into the camera which would stabilize (more or less) its volatility. "You must be there," he said, "for the first day."

So I put away pen and paper and went out Ventura Boulevard through the worst traffic in the state of California to the "Rolling Lea" ranch. It was a September morning of dazzling freshness. The corn about the Birdwell house is taller than Cooper—which is tall. The fake peaches hang with sunshiny cheeks on the real trees. The Quaker church, which is the Methodist church with its steeple lopped off, couldn't be better. I wished for a gesture, hallowed by centuries of use with which to salute it. Crossing myself would not fill the bill. To kneel in the dust was a little conspicuous. So I stood and looked. I knew the church was a fake. It could be pushed over with a strong hand. What does that matter? It has its language, its cinematic language, as words (which are not the real thing either) have theirs, and it speaks of Frankie's good people.

The rooster weather vane is up on the barn. The wind is from the west. The wash bench stands in front of the kitchen door. The springhouse remains, but Mr. Wyler would not permit the building of smokehouses, carriage houses, woodsheds, the whole literal paraphernalia of a farmyard. "Looks too much like an auto court," he said. A privy is against the moral code. We suppose that there is one but the prudish camera always manages to look the other way. Oleanders have been planted and are blooming. I hope the horticultural purists stay home. The barn is filled with enough artifacts of the 1860's to stock a museum. Jess obviously never thew anything away. Animals of all kinds have been installed—old hens, young chicks, cows, calves, horses, sheep, doves, and with all these a couple to look after their needs, a real farmer and his wife. I notice that their clothes don't fit as well as Coop's and Dorothy's. There's a wash on the line. Monday morning evidently. Dried apricots are spread on a tray on the back porch. In Indiana? I wonder how many people are on "Rolling Lea" today. Crews to do everything. Spray leaves a greener green. Put dust on Cooper's hat. Cook. Care for horses. Man cameras. Man lights. Man reflectors. Teach the kids. Drive cars. Blow whistles. Record takes. Repair clothes. Hoe the corn. Hold up the fake trees. Rehearse actors. Move chairs. I moved my own and saw at once I had done a wrong thing, broken a union law being the least of it.

This is it! Far more than Chico. Now Mr. Wyler exposes the heart of the story and if we have dreamed the wrong dreams, it is too late, to change. Mr. Wyler appears calm. Also Cooper. Stu is slightly incandescent. This is the first picture he has been with from the beginning. He appears as exalted as an altar boy. Is perhaps more so. Willy is both priest and God here. Dorothy McGuire is nervous. She used the wrong lotion yesterday to prevent sunburn and today her face is blistered. I feel quiet—and curious. Not excited, but "fated." The way it is when I know the written word is beyond my recall and being printed.

The first scene is the "barn scene": Jess and Eliza in the barn at night. It is suitable that the first scene shot should be one in which so many of us had a hand. Robert, whose idea it mostly was, is in New Orleans having an operation. I think he chose this date on purpose. Now it is Willy's picture entirely and Robert absents himself.

After watching what happened in today's shooting I have two observations to make: first, that if a modern saint is to emerge in America, he will emerge from the sound stages, the sets, the locations of Hollywood; and second, that Mr. Wyler works like a sculptor, molding script, actors, and locale into a form which strikes him at the moment as being significant.

The scene on which they worked today appeared very simple on paper. Eliza, having refused to stay in the house if Jess keeps the organ, is in the barn seated on a comforter which is spread over straw. Jess brings out additional bedclothes. He sits beside Eliza; they talk. What could be less difficult?

Well, first of all the place was an oven for heat, a Grand Central Station for numbers of people involved, an industrial arts show for amount of equipment, a zoo for animals seen and heard, in addition to being a stage for the playing out of a tender love scene between a man and a woman. Occasionally something went wrong with the way in which Cooper entered, or Eliza responded, or both said their lines. More often something went wrong with something else and occasionally with everything else.

Lights failed continuously. "Rolling Lea" is used for pictures of a pre-electric era because there are no electric wires. Generators supply the power, and the generators lines on the place, and hence no anachronistic poles and when all the other elements were functioning properly went out. When the generators functioned, planes flew over. The most frequently spoken words on the set were the sound man's, "Hold it," as he detected an incoming plane. The kiss, the clasp, the wit, the laugh, ceased while transportation took its toll of time and nerves. The horse, in its stall, must look up as Jess enters the barn. Before the audience sees Jess, it is to see the horse seeing Jess. This horse had no interest in seeing Jess enter the barn. Beside her in the stall was a man who, while keeping out of sight of the cameras himself, must induce an expectant attitude in the mare. Dorothy had to move about on the straw without causing the straw to sound over the microphone like timbers in a tempest. This required something that looked like straw but did not sound like straw. Technically not easy. Cooper, when he turned an oat sack over to make a seat, had to hit a specified spot on the floor: otherwise he would not be in a comfortable position for courting Eliza. Cameras and lights needed aligning and realigning. Whistles had to be blown and reblown permitting and refusing the passage of cars on "Rolling Lea." Dorothy and Coop, for a night scene, shouldn't have beaded brows; Coop's thatcher was concerned about the state of *her* handiwork—for the close-ups.

And all the time Mr. Wyler was searching in the midst of these distractions for the addition or omission to the dialogue, the gesture or intonation which would make the point of the scene more clearly and economically, and hence more movingly and beautifully. And when, finally, no generators failed, planes went over, whistles blew, straws crackled, horses refused to look, sacks fell awkwardly, brows beaded, hairs unthatched, lines came wrong, or faces spoke of strain and nervousness rather than love and humor, then at that exquisite and longed-for moment the sound man said, "What is that damned cu-ca-rooing I keep hearing?"

The damned cu-ca-rooing he kept hearing came from the doves installed for the beauty of wings against the sky; or perhaps to make sense of the bird residences in the gable of the barn; but before drama could continue the doves had to be corraled. How that was accomplished I know not. But like the Duke in Browning's "My Last Duchess," Mr. Wyler gave orders and all cu-ca-rooing ceased.

Finally there was a take, and Mr. Wyler said, "Print that."

"Two minutes of usable film a day," Stu said, "is all we count on."

And this is what we ask of movie actors, this treadmill, this galley work, which pays not the slightest attention to needs of the body or the spirit. We require it of them, we tempt them into it by money, by adulation, by diefication. We make them our gods; and after they have become gods we slay them. First we have the pleasures of lifting up and finally, when they tire us, the pleasure of casting them down. We make them, by so regarding them, wholly bodies, nothing but mouths, breasts, and loins. They are our scapegoats. They lust as we fear to, enjoy as we are incapable, kill and torture as we only dream of doing. They assume for our sake all our sins. Then we must crucify these sinners to ease our consciences. And part of their crucifixion, to my mind, is work like today's. My cheekbones and eyes ache from watching. So I say that if we are to produce a modern saint, look for him in Hollywood. A man or woman who has taken the burden of all our sins upon himself and has been crucified and has miraculously, by that assumption and through that crucifixion, freed us from sinning in our own persons and given us an eternity of living through the lives of the many characters he portrays, is he not doing a saint's work?

I'm going to bed. And thank heaven I don't have to be on the set at six tomorrow morning as Dorothy McGuire does.

### Somewhere in October

I've stepped onto the stars' treadmill now myself though I feel no approach to sainthood. It's dark when I get home from location. The seasons are changing fast. I eat grapes for dinner instead of melons, big blue grapes that burst like balloons as I bite into them. Max has killed his first deer of the season. Merle's children are preparing for ghosts and witches. I talk to Mama every night on the phone. Often I weep, though I swallow my tears silently. Last night she was happy. Papa had just told her that he had loved her since she was a girl, had never loved anyone else or married anyone else. She remembered it all long enough to tell me. To drift without a past to moor to! To moor *to?* We are our pasts. The past is not the mooring but the ship itself. The sun makes this room a storehouse of light. Some memory echoes in my ears as I write that phrase. Am I remembering it? Leaves, put there by autumn and wind, float on the milky pool.

Last night I went directly from location to Mr. Wyler's to look at the dailies. As we walked toward the living room, Melanie, the Wyler four-year-old, ran toward her father calling, "Papa, can we see the dream? Papa, can we see the dream?"

I was walking beside Bob Swink. "What does she mean?" I asked Bob, " 'See the dream.' "

"That," Bob said, "is what her father calls this picture."

I was frightened to hear it. Dreams go very deep. It is serious enough being mixed up with your own—let alone anyone else's.

Tonight I got home while it was still light. I walked again toward the town I "discovered" that night on Vermont. I wanted to see real things, real persons, with no burden of "conveying" attached to them; people and things in the purity of being. Not peaches to say "summer" or scythes to say "farm" or buggies to say "1860" or flat hats to say "Quakers." I was hungry for something in itself, and the street of Vermont is about as free of conscious meaning as you'll find. I went first past the bungalows, the tended flowers, the swept porches, the starched curtains, loving their tenders, sweepers, and starchers. A small girl at the magazine store was pulling at a man's coat, interrupting his reading: "Father! Father! Joe'll be back in a minute." Father looked blank. He'd forgotten Joe.

There was once a mermaid who said, "Better than any jewel I love something human." So did I, walking the city streets tonight.

I first visited a city when I was eighteen. Oh the frightening smells of Indianapolis. The wicked pathos of gas! I came out of a warm, clear barren country into a poor section of what is at best an ugly and dirty city. I was constantly sad and frightened. There was this oppressive smell. A city smells like death, I thought; and it was gas—and I didn't know it.

## Still October

First rain tonight. Oh the smell of first rain falling onto the six months' dry earth. Rain splashes on the window the shape of pepper tree leaves, and sweetest of sweet smells, fallen pepper tree leaves trodden underfoot on the wet pavements. Oh nights of autumn and youth, of rain and youth. Nights with more contradictoriness, more torque than spring and youth. Conjunction of opposites, and each traveling in the direction of the other, youth toward autumn and autumn toward spring. Reading Swinburne in the rain, impossible to tell which was drip of water, which beat of verse. Coming home from the library soaked through; and shot through with intimations of dauntlessness, Captain Courageous himself. Rain across the spring-green hills of Yorba. Linda and Papa looking up

265

from his carpentering to fool us with his false April Fools' Day cry of "Jack rabbits! Jack rabbits!" And four children believing him, who never yet had fooled us, and seeing, at his command, rabbits in the rain, gray arcs flashing in the gray downpour; and had, painstakingly, to be defooled before we could believe again in a rabbitless landscape.

Robert came home from New Orleans today. I was leaving location when I saw him coming down the road on foot in his blown-thistle way. I had the driver stop, got out of the car, and ran to meet him. He looks well since his operation, though thinner. He didn't want to talk of himself but of the picture.

"How is it going?" he asked eagerly. "Are you satisfied? How's Dorothy? How'd the barn scene go?"

We got in the car and went back to watch the shooting, a scene Robert had always opposed, of the arrival of Quigley, the organ salesman. The purpose of the scene was to explain the use by Quakers of "thee" and "thy." Robert couldn't help laughing as he watched the scene.

"You did a good job with that," he said. "It's as good as a useless scene can be. But Willy should've taken a chance here. He should've had more faith in his audience. They would've caught on to the theeing and thying without having it spelled out for them."

A movie is a guess at an echo. We guess at the reverberation of its impact upon an audience. Writing, as opposed to script writing, does not aim at this echo. One writes, when one is "writing, not scripting," to give form to a world, a life, which seems significant; one would like that significance to be apparent to readers. One wants to be read. But a book, whose primary aim is to please, is as wearying as a person with the same determination. The determinedly entertaining movie or book is like the determinedly entertaining person who humbles himself to become a little rib-tickling machine, a little ego-patting machine, a little sentiment-satisfying machine. All receive finally a machine's reward. Switch 'em on, switch 'em off, and the minute a new model comes along put the old one on the junk heap. *It* never was loved; only its effect was loved. It, person or book or movie, was only a means, never an end, never a thing in itself. What we loved was the way we felt; not the way it was. The danger in movie making is even greater than in writing or living (if the last two can be separated) of not being "a thing in itself" but always only a means, a guess at an echo.

So Robert laughed at the scene but wasn't convinced. "When you wrote your book," he asked, "did you have a little prologue explaining to your readers that your characters were going to say 'thee' and 'thy'?"

"No, but the readers had more than a couple of hours to get accustomed to it."

"Pish-tosh," said Robert. "Who's the Quaker and who's the movie-maker here?"

"I sometimes wonder, lately. Your brother, who once advocated cannons, will now not let Coop so much as breathe hard in his scene with the bushwhacker. I feel like an old pugilist talking to him about that scene. I feel like Joan of Arc with the Dauphin. My voices tell me, Jess is not going to die rather than strike a blow. Die rather than kill . . . yes. But Jess is no fool. Two minutes of insensibility on the part of someone else are better than forty years of death for yourself."

Robert I could see was delighted with this verbal violence. "You soak up some pugilism, Willy soaks up some Quakerism! Do you both good."

*Monday*

To Napa over the week end. The improvements are almost finished. I feel about them as Hollywood does about a book. Give me time and I can lick the improvements. In the midst of so many comforts about all one can do is to sit down and endure them.

I came back from Napa sore from the unaccustomed riding. Stu hoots at me, getting up and down gingerly and wondering, at Cock 'n Bull, that outpost of old England, if I couldn't be served the equivalent of a hunt breakfast, something I could eat off a fireplace mantel. I see Stu less than I did. His work now carries him into areas where I go only occasionally. There's an N.B.C. Spectacular being discussed, a documentary about the making of this film. I've met two or three times with Stu and the people working on this, but Stu sees them constantly.

He and I, with Dorothy Jeakins, had the job of choosing extras for the Methodist and Quaker church scenes. Dorothy arrived before Stu and I, and was doing the separating on a sheep and goat basis: extras who appeared to be deep-eyed sinners, Methodists; mild reprobates, Quakers. It is distasteful, almost unbearable to choose among extras—for many reasons. First of all, you are choosing bodies and faces. You are choosing flesh. The camera will look at flesh, flesh which neither speaks nor acts. This is as near to an auction block for slaves as I've ever been and nearer than I ever want to be again. I had a hard time looking those men, women, and children in the face. Choosing among them was made even harder because they told me their hard-luck stories, stories which I believed. They saw that I would. And they saw, too, that I was going to be the final authority when it came to choosing Quakers. So I heard a good deal. "A husband paralyzed." "A daughter to be sent through college." "A minister, myself." "Twenty years in pictures." Etc. Etc. In the early morning light, clear and hard and cruel, the old, middle-aged, tired, ravaged faces had been made up to hide these facts. Painted, curled, trussed-up, pulled-in, buckled down. Glance at an old fellow and he would be standing slack, yawning, weary, utterly weary, after getting up at perhaps five to be here at nine; then he would catch your eye and immediately throw back his head, tighten his belly muscles, become before your eyes, a jolly Methodist, or a saintly Quaker; or each in turn, he being uncertain which category was in greatest need of recruits at the moment. It was sickening work—I swore I would go back to my apartment, wash off all make up, take off all girdles, brassières, comb out all machine-made curls, put the straight hair into a knot skewered by two big bone hairpins, and be what I was—a woman of that age when there is only one appealing way to look: like a mother.

Meanwhile, whatever I should do in the future about my

own appearance, choices had to be made at once of appearances here, and I couldn't bear the way Dorothy was making them: first-class people, Quakers; rejects, Methodists. If this choice showed in the picture, the method of choosing was wrong. This whole picture was saying, Quakers are people. Not "special" people or "better" people. People, some of them trying to do better or special things, yes; but that is true of everyone. So if this choice of good faces for Quakers showed in the picture, it falsified the picture, and, what is more important, life. If it did not show it was also wrong, for what then was the use of paining ourselves (though the extras might never know our reasons) by the assumption of such God-like powers? Stu, never a man to hide an honest opinion, reassembled sheep and goats and we started choosing up sides all over again. This, Dorothy did not like; she had been on time and had done the job as she thought best. She said, "Jessamyn, what you don't understand is that many of these faces which you think good, belong to winos, perverts, rummies—they represent every kind of terrible brutal living. I know these people. I've seen them all before."

I did not and still do not get the meaning of this, and am still mulling it over in my mind. Did it mean that, though the extras she had chosen for Quakers looked spiritual, they were in fact not so? And hence my scruples about having good people for Quakers, bad for Methodists didn't hold? I don't know. I finished with the choosing, miserable for many reasons; for having to regard human beings as "flesh"; for having seen how raddled, broken, and unlovely most human flesh is after fifty or sixty years; and, above all, miserable because once again my mind could not follow Dorothy's. I, who am so often put off by appearances and am, as I ought not to be, the slave of my eyes, can look at Dorothy with pleasure for hours; her life is a celebration of courage; the books on her shelves are mine; her house pleases me as much as my own. If I were going to set up as a kidnaper I'd steal her boys. Yet we misunderstand each other. It is like misunderstanding myself. It bewilders me.

And there are many people here whose lives apparently are so much more unlike mine than Dorothy's and with them I never have misunderstandings. Stu and I, Clarence

Marks and I, the Wylers and I, may disagree, but we always know what we're disagreeing about.

It has just struck me that all these "people" are men. Is it that simple? I hope so. The responsibility is not mine then but God's.


*Tuesday*

Stu and I talked publicity all afternoon. The agency that is handling the account is sending people from New York to plan an advertising campaign. Stu took me into the Allied publicity office one day last week, and there I learned facts—and saw a picture—which startled me. The picture was of Coop as the old two-gun fighter William Hart, Jr., a part he has played for thirty years. As a souvenir of an honorable past the picture has merits but as news concerning the man or this movie it is a lie. If a two-year-old child had been asked to devise a publicity campaign for a Cooper movie, this picture would have been his choice. That doesn't mean it's wrong. In some situations the actions of a two-year-old cannot be bettered. But an adult could better this.

The news conveyed by this photograph (and an ad is "news") was both old and false. I don't know how news can be worse than that. If the news had been true, that is, if this movie had been one (once more) of Coop, the gunfighter, I would simply think we'd made the wrong movie, been repetitious, failed to understand that if violence and biceps are what's wanted, there are fresher biceps and more violent faces around than Coop can provide.

But we haven't been repetitious; this part is "news" for Coop and hence for Coop's fans. Let's advertise it that way. Everyone knows Coop's movie persona—the man of courage, of strength, of action. Wouldn't it be interesting to see what such a man would do in a *new* situation, in a role which promises some conflict inside the man as well as outside, with the guns and against the baddies? I think so. And in any case that's the picture we're making, and when truth, excitement, and come-on all lie in one direction why turn your back on so winning a combination?

Such, anyway, were Stu's and my feelings about Quaker Coop, that old two-gun pacifist—killing, whom? Rustlers? Rebs? Reds(kins)? Stu as usual, both because it is his nature and because as one more experienced in movie making it is his right, was more outspoken than I. Urgent, sharp-tongued, certain, impatient. He was right, I thought; but he was also riling people in that office so that those who had been merely anti any new presentation of Cooper were becoming anti-Stu as well. I suppose time will make him smooth, or smoother. Youth's acid will give way to middle-aged oil. Last week Fred, with one of those insights of his which make his occasional pompousness the more difficult to endure—as if something which could fly elected stilts, instead, to gain altitude—said of an acquaintance of mine, "Even face to face she sounds like she's talking to you over the phone." Stu's exactly the opposite. Even over the phone he sounds face to face; and face to face, he's putting grappling hooks of honesty, tactlessness, energy, and egotism into your vitals. He will learn to be less of himself as he learns to value his causes more; but he can never impunge himself, of himself. He will not supplant himself with method, swap the man for means.

Fred also asked me, when I was home last week, to name for him some people I considered "stodgy." As I was thinking over a numerous list of applicants for this title, he asked, "Do you consider me stodgy?" I thought this over, too, and while I did so he asked, "Which would it be best to be, stodgy or insufferable?"

That was easy. "Insufferable. A man is stodgy by nature but insufferable by his actions. He can mend his actions but he can't his nature. And a stodgy man is often insufferable—also."

Stu (though never to me) may seem to others occasionally insufferable. No one can ever have thought him stodgy.

*Monday*
6:00 P.M.

In spite of all of my resolves, after seeing Escudero dance last night, to lose fifteen pounds and have a taut emphatic old age instead of a soft blowsy one, I have had a bottle of beer—which Escudero could not swallow without having a gusset put in his breeches (he's that narrow and they're that tight).

I came home from location after a rainy day, parked the car on Hillhurst and sat looking at the hills, clear green in the glass-clear air; in the south, clouds were building up like back-East thunderheads and were going from purple to rose as the sun lowered. I sat watching for a long time, then drove home and went up to the Metaphysical Institute for a better look. The summer weeds, now sodden, are still there. I like this Oriental timelessness, these transcendental premises. What are weeds to a man who lives in eternity? (Asked whether his metaphysics constituted a religion or a philosophy, the founder? proprietor? Yogi-in-chief? of the Institute reputedly answered, "Neither. It is a business.")

The weeds, bending in the cold wind above the boulevards, were unbusinesslike by any standards I know, but very beautiful. Walking through them, looking my fill at the Sierra Madres going from purple to blue, and the marble of Forest Lawn remaining bone white, I once again responded to their moving combination of beauty and foolishness, of tragedy and humor. The mountains needed Forest Lawn; the metaphysicians needed weeds, and I appear to need the entire incongruous combination.

*Tuesday*

More than usual seemed to be going on today at location. There were visiting bigwigs of various denominations; there was a scene being shot which I have set in water, out of water, with flowers, without flowers, in a swing, out of a swing; and which in its final shooting is an example of Mr. Wyler's sculpting, his use of the fluid material of locale, action, and principals to form something new.

The scene is the one we call "the love scene"—the occasion of Gard's attempted proposal to Mattie before going off to war. In this scene, Mattie, wherever she has been, hillside, pond, or swing, has always been barefooted. Why? I think I wrote it so at first because it gave, to me, at least, some humor in a scene that otherwise might have been too sweet, too pretty. Though this reasoning, if it can be called reasoning, was unconscious. As the scene was first written Mattie, when Gard arrived, was gathering flowers which she dropped to hide her bare feet.

"Flowers on a hillside," said Mr. Wyler, "is everybody's idea of a director's idea of what is a picturesque setting for young love." But he liked those bare feet. "Sexy," he said. And in a picture with scarcely a bosom to be seen (unless some buxom Methodist lady sports a visible curve— or even two, we have to take our sex where we can find it—even in bare feet revealed for fun, not romance).

A wading in a pond scene followed the picking flowers scene; I can't remember now why Mr. Wyler didn't like the pond; swinging in a swing followed wading. Finally, he settled for wading with a little preliminary swinging; and whatever Mr. Wyler may have felt about sex and bare feet in the beginning was today overshadowed by what he felt about comedy and bare feet.

Phyllis Love, as Mattie, waded into the water, long skirts held up so that from the rear a curve of rump in knee-length, white country drawers could be seen. And that curve, as she spoke her prim words to Gard, front skirts lowered to the water's edge, was funny. This, Mr. Wyler, seeing, directed the cameras also to see. So a scene, by a camera angle, is changed without the alteration of a word of the script. If this addition brought to the story by the camera, contradicts tone or character, interrupts or distorts the story it is bad. I think it did not; yet why will this revelation of panties succeed in the picture (if it does) when it could not have done so in the writing? I cannot think of any sentence about these panties which would be funny in a book. "Unbeknownst to either Mattie or Gard, Mattie's white panties, as she made her protests of modesty were, with a firm curve of buttock filling them, fully visible from the rear." What kind of writing is that? That glimpse of panties could only be used in a book in an old-fashioned and editorializing way by a first-person narrator. "I saw that even as Mattie was protesting maidenly shyness about her bare feet, her panties etc."

Is that what the camera is doing here? Old-fashioned editorializing? A dig in the ribs of the audience to say, "Look what we know and what those kids don't know?" A piece of dramatic irony of the same heavy-handed kind as was provided on the stage in former days by a whisper over the footlights to the audience? Is it the camera who is whispering now?

While this oblique look was being taken by one camera at the lovers, my two Quaker friends from Pasadena were watching the camera which was doing the straight-on shooting, unaware that the scene was also being pantie-angled for laughs. And watching also was Terrence Rattigan, who had flown over from England to talk about his play *The Sleeping Prince* with Mr. Wyler. Rattigan sat with me on the bank of the pond watching the shooting and admiring Phyllis Love's acting.

"How do you like working with Wyler?" he asked.

With that question we were both at once on the same side. We were writers and we, up against directors and producers, had our problems.

"Fine," I said.

"I was somewhat surprised by his first words to me, 'We'll put all preconceived notions of what the movie should be, as based upon a literal reading of your play, out of our minds.'"

Well, if Mr. Rattigan is going to be surprised by that, it's a good thing the surprise came early and he should thank Mr. Wyler for his honesty. My feeling about the book *The Friendly Persuasion* has been that, as written, it was not suited for a film. So I have not suffered any in changing it. I have suffered only when the new form we are making, a *film* called *Friendly Persuasion*, seems not to be good. A film ought not be the "picture of" a novel, a visual

274

record of events related in a printed narrative. I would far rather have a good movie which bore very little relation to the book than a poor movie which faithfully photographed the book. A movie is a thing in itself; it should be good in itself, not as a mirror for another form. If it can be good and faithful, fine; but if it has to choose, fidelity, which is less than goodness (though sometimes a part of it), had better go out the window. I have never been able to understand those writers who are interested only in seeing their books "faithfully" filmed. First of all, a process of literal transfer cannot be as exciting to the writer, if he is working on the film, as the making of a new thing; and second, the criterion should be, if faith is invoked here, not faith to the old medium, the prose narrative, but faith to the form one is now embracing, the cinema. If prose narrative is your one love, stick to it. But don't, while the cinema is in your arms, keep looking back over your shoulder, saying, "This is the way I did it with the novel."

*Nov. 15*
*Tuesday*

The moment of the accident is remembered while what led to it remains hazy. The lunch with the advertising men from New York, who were being entertained by the Allied staff, was running along its pleasant, though, it is true, rather aimless, course. Stu and I were present, Stu by Mr. Wyler's invitation, I, perhaps by Wyler's perhaps by Stu's invitation. We were at the Brown Derby and I was enjoying myself. The men were talking of past campaigns, of the special difficulties involved in this one, and I was making known my feeling that if the purpose of an advertising campaign is to get people into the theater, a campaign which was a misrepresentation of the picture and a boring, repetitious presentation of Cooper, would not do the trick. I was pleased, in an egotistic way, to be upsetting their concepts of me as a Quaker author. If the advertising said, "Hurrah for West and Quakers," in that order, they had believed I would be happy. I wanted advertising, as much as they, which would get people into the theater and not disappoint them after they got there, and it was for this reason and no other that I opposed the campaign I had heard outlined.

The lunch was nearing its end. Stu had been very quiet. While coffee and dessert were being brought, he said—I can't remember his exact words, but something to this effect: All these generalities have been entertaining. Histories of old campaigns, while scarcely news, are pleasant to remember. The purpose of this lunch, however, has been to find out what you people had in mind specifically as a means of publicizing this picture. We know very well what the difficulties are. We don't need to be told those. We need to hear, very concretely, what you plan. If you have any plans.

Stu spoke without anger but rather shortly. As if he felt that our time and theirs was being wasted. But I was entirely unprepared for the response from Johnny Flinn, the head of Allied publicity.

"This," he said, "is the last insulting, presumptuous word from you I'll permit. These men are our guests. They are not here to be grilled by you. I've taken all I can from you and you will please to keep your so and so mouth shut. You so and so and so and so. And so and so."

Johnny Flinn is a handsome man, looks like a black Irishman, and had always up to this moment been quiet and smiling. I would not have been more surprised had the picture of Tom Mix, which hung over our table, begun to curse. The eight or nine men around the table were utterly silent. Johnny Flinn's tones suggested a fury so long pent up it might, if stirred by a single additional word, have an even more explosive expression. Stu remained silent. If Flinn, right or wrong, had spoken to me that way, I'm afraid I would have hit him. I am ashamed of what I did do, so fatuous. I put my hand on Stu's arm and said, "Stu is a very good boy." I thought Stu might hit *me,* but I had to say something which declared, if this were an attack on Stu, that I stood with him. I don't know Johnny Flinn's side of the story, but there are moments when it is inhuman to be reasonable and detached, to wait to hear both sides of the story.

How the meal ended or what was said, I can't recall. Stu

and I drove away and when I said something about Flinn, Stu said. "He's a good man. I like him more than anyone over there."

So the situation remains dense.

## Thursday

Stu phoned to say that he is leaving the picture on December fifteenth. He has resigned, and Mr. Wyler has accepted his resignation. Stu and I have been saying ever since the resolution of the cannon difficulty that we were going to have a big celebration of that event, so this seemed the time for it. We went to Scandia for lunch, went very hungry and sat in a room filled with cold pale sunlight and warm firelight and drank white wine and ate Kalfsfilet Oskar from one until almost five. Wine, firelight, and sunlight seemed aspects of one reality and we (this is an editorial we; I haven't asked Stu about it) felt ourselves to be as is not often in a lifetime the case, there, related, a part of the reality. I had left the picture and had returned to it. That Stu should leave it had never entered my head—and I doubt that it had entered his. Change and parting are as much of life and not necessarily sadder than repetition and meeting. If Stu felt any sadness he didn't speak of it. But something was not the same . . . his idea of himself, his idea of others—and practically, this picture, which was his dream, too, was no longer his to help shape.

"But perhaps I have hurt it," he said.

He took me to the Owl and I went home to Napa for Thanksgiving.

## Napa
## Nov. 27th
## Sunday

Looking back on Thanksgiving. My body did not really want to come home and spend my short days of vacation

277

cooking for Merle's five and my two. Three meals a day for eight people is, for me, hard work. Yet once I had moved inside that work and accepted it, I was refreshed, rested, and happy. The only way to health is the way of acceptance and belief; either withdraw or participate. There is no middle ground. On Thursday evening, battered by TV's constant cannonade I began to play dominoes, serious not childish dominoes, with Michael and Melinda, to relearn the game, to teach it, to engage in it completely. Immediately my tiredness left me, immediately I was charmed and delighted by what Michael and Melinda said and did. Melinda said, and this shows the candor and openness of our relationship within the game, "You look like Long John Silver when you play dominoes"; and she demonstrated how my eyes darted from domino to domino as I plotted evil for my opponents. And we all felt the truth of what she said and the truth of the way she looked—and laughed and sunk ourselves, still more deeply, into the game's refreshment.

I am staying up late, sleepy and dead-beat as I am, for the purpose of enjoying my changed room. I sit here as I would at a play watching its performance. I have a fire in my new Franklin stove and must open the windows wide since the night is warm. But my eyes come first tonight. I will give them what they want to see even though I sweat for it.

Now I begin to love this room and because I disliked and even feared it for so long this liking seems weak to me. I wonder what is the source of this veritable panic I feel at breakup, change, and disorder?

To meditate on: this fear of discarding. I do not fear the new, but I do not want to be shut off from the past. At the moment when the old, the accustomed, the once-loved appears to be on the point of death (by my own hand) and the new is not yet fully born, then I am nauseated, am like a man making a crossing on a high narrow bridge. If I feel this (and I do) about the pruning of a rose bush, how much more so about the pulling down of a known house, though the destruction makes way for a better; or the abandonment of one human being for another? I can incorporate the new; but to repudiate the once loved seems impossible. Now if the old house had blown down or been engulfed by a flood I could accommodate myself with almost no lamentation to the change. I can accept fate. But something more is asked of conscious human beings. They are asked to make their own fate. This is where I panic. This is where the old (how learned? why learned?) stoicism enters, the perverse pride of enduring rather than the healthy pleasure of acting.

*Los Feliz*
*Nov. 30*
*Wed.*

In bed drinking bitter breakfast coffee and reading prime Salinger. Still thinking of my golden sitting room at home and how much I love it and saying to myself, "Late, late. How late I discover what I love. How slow and stupid a learner." Nothing truly exists until you break through the barrier which separates you from it. There is no reality for the outsider, and for a person who refuses to be his own fate, any other position is so difficult. It is as though, wanting to swim, you stood on the shore, waiting for the sea to come up and lap you round with the longed-for water. It might happen. Had I been at Lisbon in 1755 say, it would have happened. But the chances are against it; and on the whole it is better to be able to choose the sea than vice versa. The sea is a rough chooser, and sink or swim is all one to the leveling waters.

*Thursday*

I went with Stu to the Paramount lot this afternoon where we saw a rough cut put together for the edification of our publicity brethren—an event arranged by Stu even though he is disengaging himself from this picture. I cannot rely on my feelings about what I saw, since I know that they reflect less judgments about the quality of the picture than my own queasiness, always present, in having to look at something I've had a hand in making. How

279

some writers can read their own writing to others baffles me. That act smacks to me of regurgitation. I except poetry from this stricture. I can read a poem of mine to others. A poem has a more autonomous existence. It exists (personal as its sources are and must be) farther outside oneself. It, and you reading it, transcend the personal. Poetry provides an intoxication which is as potent as alcohol in exorcising the private and loosening the universal.

Anyway, I can't report on what I "saw"; my report is of me "seeing." And only when the camera lingered for a time on an actor, when I had no sense of myself as narrator or of apparent failures in narration, did I really see. I really saw Coop in the scene where Quigley arrives with what appeared to me to be a lifetime of Jess Birdwell's living in his face; I really saw Tony Perkins as he struggled in the battle scenes to make a soldier of himself, to destroy men, and to destroy what in himself made this destruction hateful to him. It was a beautiful scene. Many persons no doubt could feel what Tony Perkins felt here; somewhat fewer could communicate by use of body and face what these emotions were. One, in how many million, with these abilities for feeling and communicating feeling has also the instrument, the body and face which command our belief and sympathy. Tony has all of these, the feeling, the ability, the instrument. And in that scene I wept.

The minute I got back to the studio I went to see Mr. Wyler. If this is chiefly, and it is, a story of a man's final refusal to kill, then we had better be sure we give Coop a scene as big as Tony's and an opportunity as compelling as Tony's to demonstrate the fact. Coop has a face and a body which are fine instruments for demonstrating feeling. But here is a boy with the same power, and if we make his battle scenes too important, the emphasis of the story will seem to be on the boy's decision to fight, not the father's decision to refrain. The one is an adolescent's necessity of proving himself; Jess is past all that; he knows who he is; his question is: Will I put the weight of my accepted identity on the side of what I believe to be right? Will I be an existentialist? And a Christian? (Though I know some authorities say these two ways are incompatible.) But will Coop—Jess—live where he loves? Will he accept the burden of his dream? And have we provided him with the means of doing so, a means dramatic enough to say, *"This* is the heart of this picture."

Stu and I have often talked of this; in the rough cut I saw it. When I talked with Mr. Wyler he said, "It's a thing I've been afraid of. Go out Friday morning with Coop, Carr, Swink, and the others—to location. Talk with them about it."

I already knew that there was talk of having poor old Sam Jordan, Jess's friend, already dead from a bushwacker's bullet, hit once again—after Jess arrives, this to provide "motivation" for a Jess still operating under the veil of Mr. Huston's reluctance to have him "do something." Bullets, possibly, may strike twice in the same place, even if lightning never does; but a dead body twice riddled like a useful pin cushion is not a sight I care to see—especially when the purpose is that of keeping Jess holier than he need be. Let that bullet strike Jess. Let him resist the bushwacker to save his own skin. "Go out to location Friday morning. The studio car will pick you up at 5:30," Mr. Wyler said.

Get up at 4:30! I will never be a saint because I will flee Hollywood before my purification is complete. But this could be the first step on that pathway.

Shooting the Quaker meeting scene today. Dress (and make-up) do make the man. Gone are the extras whose choosing caused me so much pain. They are now country Quakers, mild, bucolic, and pious. I watched Mr. Wyler, taking little Dickie Eyre's place, leap up and say, "God is love," a dozen times. Perhaps Mr. Wyler is a good director because he can act. He made that leap, said those words again and again, and each time he was eight years old, loved God, and knew, as Little Jess did, that he was showing off. It all came through. I have watched him, too, directing a scene, with exactly that same self-forgetting love and admiration in his face you see in the face of a mother watching her—unequaled—child.

There has been an article in one of those pandering magazines about Coop and an actress. I haven't read it. Why bother? It will be like ten thousand other reports of this kind, machine-made to fill a calculated need in a public which asks the movie stars to live the life it does not dare so that it can have the triple pleasures of satiety, safety, and denunciation. Anyway it was a strange sight to see all the extras, the brethren and sistren, in bonnet, shawl, and broad-brim, collected around the corner drugstore, poring over this far from Quakerish document.

Dec. 3
*Whittier*

10 A.M. Upstairs bedroom. Glittering sunshine, blue sky. Santa Ana sending a cold knife under the door. Lemon and avocado leaves shining after the rain. Eucalyptus trees limber in the wind. Palm leaves with their shifting sandy desert sound. This is my last trip here before I go home to Napa. I drove out in a combination of rain and smog last night. Mama ran to the car, disregarding the rain, her voice like a girl's, to welcome me.

After three days of headache I begin again to be what I imagine is a normal person. Or do all persons have the pains I have and hide them as I do? When I am most miserable and aching I put on the greatest show of health and vitality. If I stop for a minute, the pain, the fatigue, the disease, will be apparent. If one week should go by without a headache—I'd be off for Everest, I'd try for a jet altitude record, or I might do nothing whatever. Sit in the sun and sample felicity. I tend to do that anyway when I finally get rid of a headache. First I can't work because I have a headache. Then I can't work because I'm so absorbed in enjoying the lack of a headache. Thus I am forever excused from making any effort whatsoever.

Dec. 4
*Los Feliz*

I left Whittier at noon. Papa lifted the branches of the guava bushes to show me the big, ripe, red-black, rain-washed guavas. "Pick them, eat them," Mama said, pulling off handfuls. So I drove out with my mouth filled, unable even to say good-by.

*Friday evening*

I've been having a nap—after getting up at 4:30 this morning, I needed it. I rode out to location, sixty miles northeast of here in the hills, with Tommy Carr and Bob Swink. We were all sleepy. The morning was foggy and cold; Carr said he hadn't slept for thinking about the scene. They both knew how important it was; if it didn't come off, nothing came off. Mr. Wyler, though he was now able to tolerate Jess's having a gun, could not abide his striking a blow; or even, except under the greatest provocation, disarming a man. That provocation, I was convinced, should not be a bullet into a dead or dying man, and I talked about alternatives and Tommy and Bob talked about the technical difficulties we would run into with the alternatives. But both had only one thought: how to make that scene as strong and honest and effective as possible, and I was happy to be of their company.

Horses, camera crew, food truck, arrived at about the same time we did. The wrangler began to put Sam Jordan's horse, Black Prince, through the riderless run he would have to make presently. The sun was not yet over the top of the eastern hills against whose base we were working. When Coop arrived, looking like a hunter, not sleepy, he said, "I never have learned to sleep late." The actor who was to play the part of the bushwhacker, the man who kills Sam Jordan, and is in turn spared by Jess, arrived. Here, Stu was still with us, since this man had been chosen by him. And he had chosen well, a man with a good face for the part, eyes which could show pain and, when pain let up, happiness. Bob Middleton, who plays Sam Jordan, arrived and was kidded about making a good breakfast, since it would be his last. We all ate doughnuts and drank hot coffee and warmed our hands on the cups. Tommy

Carr, the cameramen, the wranglers, tramped about hunting the best spot for the scene.

Then I went home. I had said my say and had been listened to, and from here on I would be only an onlooker—which is a role that makes me impatient. If this scene conveyed what it should, the picture would not be "made," but if it failed, the picture could hardly be a success.

## Dec. 15

Tomorrow is my last day in Hollywood. Gray day, rain sometimes. Joe Dobashi, the Japanese boy from the store, made the arrangements for my packing for me. The chief trouble is the increase of books. Besides increasing in number they seem to have increased in size. Nine months in Hollywood, a proper gestation period, though I never dreamed (as proper gestators must) that it would be so long. I am afraid I have come to Hollywood and lived my Napa life. A mistake perhaps. Only if my Napa life is my "real" life, that is what I should have done. If not, I should have been experimenting. In any case I hear trains whistling and I'm excited.

## Dec. 16

Crazy, downy, old homeward-bound Owl. I spent this afternoon at the R.K.O. studios where Mr. Wyler was retaking some of the process shots which have not satisfied him. Close-up of Jess and Eliza in a surrey to which a mechanism gave the flying wheels, the rolling motion of travel, while to one side of them another mechanism projected the photographed scenery of the trip which we had already seen them take. We had all long wanted—and particularly Stu—to find a place for Eliza to say to Jess at the end of the picture, "Thee pleasures me just as thee is." Somehow a place for the scene was never found; but Mr. Wyler was directing Dorothy in the replacing of Coop's big Quaker hat at the jaunty angle which Jess liked, but to which Eliza had always objected before.

I went to him. He alone of the people there knew that I was leaving this evening. "You have found a way to say, 'Thee pleasures me' without saying it, haven't you?" I asked. And he had. And he knew it. And it was a good time to leave, Mr. Wyler looking at his actors with that look of brooding happiness which he has when things go well with them; Dorothy and Coop, blooming in their First Day costumes, and the mechanism tirelessly rolling past them that simulated countryside of southern Indiana.

I look out now at the hills of the Ridge Route as the old Owl labors homeward; and this landscape is for the moment more unreal than that which I am leaving behind me—the landscape of a dream.

# THE BIG BESTSELLERS
# ARE AVON BOOKS!

*The Kingdom*
L. W. Henderson                18978    $1.75

*To Die in California*
Newton Thornburg              18622    $1.50

*The Last of the Southern Girls*
Willie Morris                 18614    $1.50

*The Hungarian Game*
Roy Hayes                     18986    $1.75

*The Wolf and the Dove*
Kathleen E. Woodiwiss         18457    $1.75

*The Golden Soak*
Hammond Innes                 18465    $1.50

*The Priest*
Ralph McInerny                18192    $1.75

*Emerald Station*
Daoma Winston                 18200    $1.50

*Sweet Savage Love*
Rosemary Rogers               17988    $1.75

*How I Found Freedom*
*In An Unfree World*
Harry Browne                  17772    $1.95

*I'm OK—You're OK*
Thomas A. Harris, M.D.        14662    $1.95

*Jonathan Livingston Seagull*
Richard Bach                  14316    $1.50

*Open Marriage*
George and Nena O'Neill       14084    $1.95

---

Where better paperbacks are sold, or directly from the publisher. Include 15¢ per copy for mailing; allow three weeks for delivery.

Avon Books, Mail Order Dept., 250 West 55th Street, New York, N.Y. 10019

# Willie Morris

# The Last of the Southern Girls

**18614**     **$1.50**

In all the glitter of Washington's elite, she shines the brightest . . . she's Carol Hollywell, Washington's Golden Girl. The President's favorite dancing partner, the Senator's confidante . . . the rising young Congressman's lover. And in a town used to dirty politics, she brings another kind of scandal.

## OVER 350,000 COPIES IN PRINT!

# THE KINGDOM
## L. W. HENDERSON

### AN EXOTIC,
### SPELLBINDING SAGA
### OF ROMANCE AND ADVENTURE

He came to a Holy Land stained with the blood of warring Christians and Moslems, a bold knight with a sharp sword and a firm faith. Both would be tested in this sunscorched land, as would his passionate love for two beautiful, mysterious women.
**18978 $1.75**

---

Where better paperbacks are sold, or directly from the publisher. Include 15¢ per copy for mailing; allow three weeks for delivery.

Avon Books, Mail Order Dept.
250 West 55th Street, New York, N. Y. 10019